Grant me, O Heav'n! Good Humour, Still to please
My Wife, so long as She consults my Ease;
But, give me courage, if She proves a Shrew,
To Scorn what none could ever yet subdue.

EDWARD WARD

From an engraving by Vandergutch

NED WARD OF GRUBSTREET

LONDON: HUMPHREY MILFORD

OXFORD UNIVERSITY PRESS

NED WARD
OF GRUBSTREET

A Study of Sub-Literary London in the
Eighteenth Century

BY

HOWARD WILLIAM TROYER

HARVARD UNIVERSITY PRESS
Cambridge, Massachusetts
1946

To the Mother
of
Philip, John, and Michael

Preface

I HAVE NO APOLOGY to offer for Ned Ward. What can be said in defense of the Grubstreet wit whose name has outlived his own generation by two centuries, the following pages make some attempt to reveal. As for my own interest in Ward, it has, to be sure, extended over too many years and the preparation of the manuscript has been carried forward only by "fits and starts," as Ward once wrote about his own *Parish Guttlers.*

Certainly one of the most pleasant aspects of the work has been the kindness and helpfulness of those to whom I have become indebted. Unfortunately for the student of Ward, only five of his many publications have been reprinted in the last century and a half, and the others are available, if at all, only in the rare bookrooms of the more specialized libraries or in private collections.

It is a privilege, therefore, to express my appreciation to the directors, librarians, and personnel of the Boston Athenæum Library, the Boston Public Library, the British Museum, the Columbia University Library, the Guildhall Library of London, the Harvard University Library, the Library of Congress, the Massachusetts Historical Society, the Newberry Library, the New York Public Library, the University of Texas Library, and the Yale University Library for their generous permission to work with rare volumes and for the kind and courteous service extended. In this connection I wish especially to thank Miss Fannie Ratchford of the Wrenn Library of the University of Texas, Mr. C. K. Edmonds and Mr. Lyle H. Wright of the Henry E. Huntington Library and Art Gallery at San Marino, Mr. H. W. Morris of The Institute of Jamaica at Kingston, Mr. Allyn B. Forbes of the Massachusetts Historical Society, and Mr.

Frederic W. Cook, secretary of the Commonwealth of Massachusetts, for patient replies to numerous inquiries by letter.

To Dr. R. J. Allen, to Mr. Frank Fischer, and to Dr. Benjamin Boyce I am grateful for numerous suggestions and pertinent information. To Dr. R. H. Griffith of the University of Texas I owe my notes on the Hills' piracies, to Mr. William McCarthy, then of the University of Texas Library staff, some helpful suggestions on the bibliography of Ward's writings. To Dr. Ernest Hunter Wright and to Dr. Ricardo Quintana and Dr. Ruth Wallerstein I should like to express my gratitude for valuable help and guidance in the initial stages of the work, and to Dr. George Sherburn my deep appreciation for a careful reading of the manuscript and many useful suggestions.

One of the aims of the present study has been to identify, and to record the location of, Ward's writings. The results are presented in Appendix A, a bibliography of Ward's writings and their various editions, and in Appendix B, an addendum of doubtful attributions. Title-pages have been transcribed in full, except for a few cases where later editions are identical with preceding ones—and signatures, pagination, and format indicated. In the transcriptions of title-pages, as well as in the quotations from Ward's writings in the text itself, it has seemed advisable to adhere to the original spelling, punctuation, and initial capitalization. In neither case has any attempt been made to preserve a record of type peculiarities or of the use of italics.

H. W. T.

Lawrence College
October, 1945

Contents

Contents

Illustrations

NED WARD OF GRUBSTREET

The fifth and last of our company, was I, quoth the Dog, a poor harmless honest Fellow, almost craz'd with playing the Fool, because I would not play the Knave, half starved in a Calm, yet always a loser when I fish in troubl'd Waters; One that hates Scribling as he does Poverty, yet like a Dutchman in the Rasp-House, is forced to Pump or Drown.

The Amorous Bugbears (1725)

I

The Scandalous Profession

The condition of an Author, is much like that of a Strumpet, . . . and if the Reason be requir'd, Why we betake our selves to so Scandalous a Profession as Whoring or Pamphleteering, the same excusive Answer will serve us both, viz. That the unhappy circumstances of a Narrow Fortune, hath forc'd us to do that for our Subsistance, which we are much asham'd of.

A Trip to Jamaica (1698)

NED WARD's name has long been a familiar one to social and literary historians, who from Macaulay's day to our own have drawn upon his writings for a knowledge of eighteenth-century London. To the biographers and editors of the eighteenth-century men of letters Ward has been one of the host of Grubstreet wits whose writings have frequently furnished interesting contemporary biographical information or whose names and activities have served to give meaning to an otherwise obscure reference or poetic bon mot. More recently the students of early eighteenth-century journalism have come to realize the significance of Ward's role in the development of periodical literature, and for them Ward's life and activities, and especially the identification of his writings, constitute a definite problem. In spite of this, however, Ned Ward has remained chiefly a name indigenous to indices and footnotes, and our only information about him, aside from a few essential facts, is a not inconsiderable amount of half-truth and myth.

Among the few facts about Ward invariably provided in the numerous footnotes to which his name has given origin are the full name Edward and the years of his birth and death, 1667–1731. Beyond that the information usually supplied tells us that he was "of low extraction and irregular education"; that he was both "publican and poet" (the association seems to please the editors) and that after 1699 he operated the King's Head Tavern in Fulwood's Rents, next door to Gray's Inn. If more is to be said, we are reminded of the fact that he is the subject of one of Pope's derisive couplets in the *Dunciad,*

> Or sail with Ward to ape-and-monkey climes
> Where vile Mundungus trucks for viler rhimes

and then, perhaps by way of compliment, that after all he seems to have managed his tavern in "a genteel way."

The statement that Ward was "of low extraction and irregular education" need concern us only momentarily. Ward may well have been "of low extraction," but all later writers are indebted for the information in its original form to the account by Theophilus Cibber in *The Lives of the Poets,* written in 1753, twenty-two years after Ward's death.[1] In the only contemporary account of Ward which concerns itself with factual information, that of Giles Jacob in *The Poetical Register,* no mention is made of Ward's parentage or his education.[2] Ward himself states that his ancestors came from Leicestershire and were men of some means and property.[3] Unfortunately there is no reference in Ward's writings to any member of his immediate family, and the name of Ward being a common one in Leicestershire, as throughout England, it seems impossible even were it desirable, to establish his family connections with certainty. Cibber's phrase, whether accurate or not, may have been properly derogatory in 1753 without carrying any particular significance in 1945. Too often among modern editors the phrase "of low extraction" presents itself as the inherent explanation of Ward's low tastes or on the other hand of his proclivity for depicting the manners of low life, of which more needs to be said presently.

As for the second half of Cibber's remark, that Ward possessed only an "irregular education," it is probably accurate enough if we take it to mean that he was not university trained. Undoubtedly he must have had access to one of the numerous grammar schools in Oxfordshire, where he grew up, and in 1708 took an occasion to express his "indissoluble Obligations" to a certain noble family "for the best and greatest share" of his youthful education.[4] Ward, at any rate, appears to have had a fair knowledge of Latin and French (and perhaps Spanish) as well as a speaking acquaintance with the earlier literature of his own tongue. He was not the equal in languages of his early associates in London, Tom Brown or William King. On the other hand there is no reason to assume he was less well trained for his later career than, let us say, John Dunton or Daniel Defoe.

It is true, too, that Ward was both publican and poet, though he was rarely engaged in both activities at the same time. He did not, however, as we shall see later, set up as the keeper of a public house until late in the year 1712.[5] He did not own or operate the King's Head Tavern in Fulwood's Rents, next door to Gray's Inn, an assertion based upon no more than the ingenious speculation of an anonymous writer in *The Gentleman's Magazine* in 1857.[6] During his early days in London Ward resided in Gray's Inn and no doubt frequented the King's Head, but when after fifteen years as a writer, he relinquished his career for the security of trade, he became in turn an alehouse keeper, a taverner, and later a coffee-house proprietor.

As for Ward's relation to Pope, that is material for a later chapter.[7] It must suffice at the moment to say that the famous couplet is not the full story of his association with Pope, and is certainly among the less derisive remarks made by Pope about Ward after the furor of the former's quarrel with the dunces descended upon the city. So, too, the "genteel way" of a literary host may await its proper turn. For this detail we are at least indebted to the earliest account of Ward, and Giles Jacob, though meager in his information, presents a factual and unprejudiced record. Indeed, since all later writers are indebted to Jacob, it may be well to quote the account in its entirety. "Mr. Edward Ward," writes Jacob,

a very voluminous Poet, and an Imitator of the famous *Butler*. Of late Years he has kept a public House in the City (but in a genteel way) and with his Wit, Humour, and good Liquor has afforded his Guests a pleasurable Entertainment: especially the High-Church Party, which is compos'd of Men of his Principles, and to whom he is very much oblig'd for their constant Resort.

Cibber in turn quoted Jacob, and added, in addition to the remarks about his extraction and education, only the misinformation that Ward objected to Jacob's statement that he kept a public house in the city. To Oldys we owe the statement that Ward's ancestors came from Leicestershire, and the correct assignment of Ward's successive residences in London as Gray's Inn, Clerkenwell, Moorfields, and Fuller's Rents, a sequence too frequently overlooked by later writers.[8] Baker in *Biographia Dramatica* added to the list of Ward's writings, without providing any additional information,[9] and Thomas Campbell's account in *British Poets* merely repeated Cibber's.[10] There the case of Ned Ward versus the editors seems to have rested, save for the suggestion about the King's Head Tavern, until George Aitken provided his rather admirable, though somewhat inaccurate, summary of Ward's life and writings for the *Dictionary of National Biography,* to which all more recent editors are indebted.

But if Ward's biographers tell us little about him, his own writings tell us a great deal. To read all that an author has written is to be granted not only some knowledge of the man himself, but also a certain insight into his world. In Ward's case, despite its less edifying episodes, the story is one rich in humanity and pathos, and brings, too, an awareness of the forces that controlled and evolved much of the periodic literature of the day. We know the history of eighteenth-century periodical literature largely in terms of the writings of its major figures; it is equally conducive to an understanding of the period to grasp the point of view and to understand the problems of the minor writer.

As a penny-catching poet, pamphleteer, and story teller, Ward was one of the host of hack writers, journalists, and literary innovators who from the days of Elizabethan England onward began to depend for their livelihood less and less upon patronage and more and more upon the originality and profligacy of their pens.[11] The freedom from patronage brought its own problems. Out of the dependence upon individual talent, out of the constant concern with the marketability of the product, resulting, as it frequently did, in the profits themselves actually determining the purpose and design of the writings, a new literature gradually emerged. By circumstance of birth, training, and talent Ned Ward was to play a considerable role in that development.

By the closing years of the seventeenth century, when Ward arrived in London, religious and political issues had come to be the dominating factor in popular literature. Parties and political factions had themselves given origin to newspapers and periodicals, and the vicious influence of political and religious intolerance and bigotry had come to pervade almost the entire output of the press. No longer was there any glossing over the frailties of man or his political and social inadequacies and downright knavery. The mode of the literary journalist, the pamphleteer, news writer, and party scribe was abusive and vitriolic. Out of or at least in the very moment of its subjection, journalistic literature came to make extensive mechanical progress. Following hard upon the advent of the newspaper in the eighties, and the recurrent failure of parliament to support a Licensing Act in the nineties, had come the *Athenian Mercury* and the beginnings of periodical literature. No longer was the writer restrained by an official censor or limited to the intermittent publication of the single poem or pamphlet. Recurrently, weekly and even daily, new copy littered the bookstalls and coffee-house tables. To fill four or eight or sixteen folio pages became the daily or weekly stint of the writer; to cater to the whims and prejudices of his readers, to keep them supplied with the current political gossip, or to divert them with the novel and salacious became his opportunity, if not indeed—as many a writer felt—his obligation. Readers in turn became partisans and adherents, and by their response assured the writer of continued opportunity and a steady livelihood from his pen. And it was, one needs to add, out of this constant interchange between author and reader, out of the sensitivity of one to the personality of the other, that the influence for good which periodical literature wielded in the opening decades of the eighteenth century was to come.

To acquire direction and purpose it was necessary to enlist the services of first-rate minds. To do so, periodical literature had to establish itself as an effective, recognized medium. Its history at the turn of the seventeenth century is an endless story of innovation and adaptation, consciously and unconsciously seeking for the effectiveness and permanence of the later *Examiner, Tatler,* and *Spectator.*

For something well over a decade Ward was certainly among the leaders of the new movement. Even in his own day, however, his talent was occasionally eclipsed by that of a number of his fellows and contemporaries. Defoe was a more prolific journalist and a more submissive party scribe. Tom Brown, relatively independent of political party, was a better scholar, facile in translation and adaptation. John Dunton was a greater innovator, an indefatigable worker, completely unscrupulous in exploiting his own or another's talent. Thomas D'Urfey was a more facile satirist in verse, more competent in the ballad and lyric. Ward was in no sense a scholar. He was not really familiar—as was Tom Brown, for instance—with the ancients. He was probably less well read in foreign languages or even the older literature of England. He could not therefore be primarily an imitator or given to the adaptation of other men's ideas. Limited in his capacities and talent, he turned to the only available source of material—his own contemporary world. He could write down only what he could observe and hear —the city of London and its environs, the activities and behavior of the men and women who walked the city streets or loitered in its taverns and coffee-houses, the political hearsay and rumor, the diverting tales told over the punch bowl, the small talk and malicious gossip of the idle. No writing in the period reflects more vividly the struggles of an independent talent or portrays more effectively the picturesque qualities of the contemporary and local world than those of the man whom George Augustus Sala once so aptly characterized as "jovial, brutal, vulgar, graphic Ned Ward." [12]

In terms of his own account, then, the story opens for us on a certain night in the year 1691 when an impudent young man arrived at an inn in Leicestershire, en route from the city of London to his ancestral home.[13] Enjoying a supper of cold meats and ale, he sat some hours conversing with his host and then, indicating his desire to turn in, was shown to a "small common room." This he rejected with great indignation and insisted upon a room "fit for quality."

The next morning the young man continued his journey. To the consternation of the host his guest had been unable to pay for his "quality" accommodations. At the moment, the young man had announced, he was on his way to collect a patrimony left to him upon the death of his grandmother; the debt would be amply repaid in time. It is doubtful, however, if the host was ever reimbursed for the night's lodging. When Edward Ward arrived that day at his attorney's, he was dismayed to find that the grandmother had willed her possessions to her own daughter, residing in the house with her, and that she "had not left poor Ned a Louse." "In the Care of Providence," Ward wrote later, the young man turned back to London.

Of Ward's life before that night in Leicestershire he tells us little. To a reference concerning his own age in the preface to *A Collection of Historical and State Poems, Satyrs, Songs and Epigrams* we owe our knowledge that he was born in the year 1667; it is in the dedicatory epistle to *Nuptial Dialogues and Debates* that he tells us his ancestors in Leicestershire had been men of considerable means and property. There is reason to believe, too, that early in Ward's youth his father had removed with the family to Oxfordshire,[14] and we know that some time before 1691, presumably upon reaching his majority, Ward had left his father's house to seek his fortune in London.

The young man had relatives as well as friends residing in the city;[15] it was one of the latter, he tells us later, who undertook to show him the town. In the days following his arrival, Ward became familiar with the life of the coffeehouses and taverns, took in the sights of the city, enjoyed its theaters and fairs. Convivial by nature, he apparently found it an easy matter to fall into the leisurely life of the gentleman wits and tavern habitués. There were plenty of young men about town who lived gaily on their own means or who in lieu of such resources occasionally earned an honest shilling with their pens. The composition of pasquinade and satire, pamphleteering, and hack writing generally were prevalent, and more than one man whom he met was leading an existence—often precarious—dependent wholly upon his talent as a writer.

There is no indication that Ward had any thought at first of imitating his associates except in the license of their living. His own training, one is led to believe, had not been particularly conducive to the profession of letters. Most of the young wits with whom he associated were university men or students at the Inns of Court, and, though there is plenty of evidence that Ward considered himself a gentleman born, and though he later acknowledges the obligations he was under for his education, he had never been entered at either university. Day after day of that early sojourn in London was apparently spent in good eating, hard drinking, and the pursuit of amorous adventure. Towards the end his funds had begun to run low, but there was always the anticipation of his patrimony. He had a feeling of gratitude, he tells us, for the messenger who climbed the steps of his garret to announce the death of his grandmother.

Whether or not it had occurred earlier to Ward to imitate his associates in the exercise of a literary talent, it is obvious that foremost in his own mind as he returned from his unprofitable journey into Leicestershire must have been the realization that, unless he somehow exerted himself, his agreeable and leisurely London existence must come to an end. No longer would it be possible to stave off an irate innkeeper with the prospect of a patrimony. The debts he had already acquired would somehow have to be paid. When his fortune became generally known there would be no tavern keeper in all London willing to extend further credit.

At any rate his first poetical venture apparently followed shortly after his return to the city. The poem itself was a humorous account of the recent journey into Leicestershire, entitled *The Poet's Ramble after Riches, or a Night's Transactions upon the Road Burlesqu'd*. Written in Hudibrastic couplets, the poem is an imitation of Butler's famous satire, and marks the early influence upon Ward of the current vogue. Beyond that and its meager biographical reference, however, the poem possesses little interest today.

To the title poem Ward appended nine stanzas of doggerel entitled "The Author's Lamentation in the Time of Adversity." The text of the latter poem indicates that it may have been written before the actual journey into Leicestershire. It is a lament to his poverty and though written in the spirit of burlesque it is probably not an inaccurate account of his condition.

> A Shirt I have on, little better than none,
>   In Colour much like to a Cinder,
> So Thin and so Fine, it is my design,
>   To present it the Muses for Tinder . . .
>
> O had you but seen the sad State I was in,
>   You'd not find such a Poet in Twenty,
> I'd nothing that's full, by my Shirt and my Scull,
>   For my Guts and my Pockets were empty.
>
> As true as I Live, I have but one Sleeve,
>   Which I wear in the room of a Cravat,
> In this plight I wait, to get an Estate,
>   But the Devil knows when I shall have it.

When Ward published the poems he already knew there would be no estate from the source he had anticipated. Unfortunately he was shortly to learn that little was to be expected from the exercise of his poetic talent. *The Poet's Ramble after Riches* was not a success.[16] How the young man, cut off without patrimony and unsuccessful as a poet, managed to exist during the interim of seven years, between 1691 and 1698, when he emerges as a successful writer, remains one of the unsolved problems of the biographer. The one item which can be assigned to his pen with assurance during that seven-year period, before his mounting debts forced him to flee the country, is not an original composition but a piece of publisher's hack work. It may itself, of course, point the way to a solution of the problem.

Female Policy Detected, or the Arts of a Designing Woman Laid Open (1695) was obviously written to meet the current market demand for books on the subject of women. For well over a century printers and booksellers had been making capital out of the controversy over woman's role in society and her characteristic virtues and vices. The victims in the controversy had themselves been addressed in print, and that in turn had added a new group of readers whom the printers and booksellers were only too happy to supply with copy.[17] Two years earlier, for instance, the enterprising John Dunton, after having sedulously cultivated the female readers of *The Athenian Mercury,* had launched a woman's magazine, *The Ladies Mercury.*[18] A year later, in 1694, he had published *The Ladies Dictionary; being a General Entertainment for the Fair-Sex,* organized as a compendium of all useful knowledge from Abigal to Zenobia.

Dunton had favored his women readers and flattered them. In direct contrast Ward and his publisher, adhering to an older point of view, addressed themselves to male readers. *Female Policy Detected* was designed, we are told, as a "pocket piece" for all young men to defend themselves against the cunning and slyness of the female sex. Book I treats of the "false allurements of women," and in a traditional vein condemns her vanity, pride, jealousy, and ingratitude, though with an emphasis upon such practical and pert advice as not to pick up a woman on the street, not to accept a hand-embroidered cravat, and to make sure of her portion "even tho' you take her virtue upon credit." Book II is entitled "A Pleasant and Profitable Defense of Married Men, against Peevish, Fretful, Scolding Wives; with several Notable Examples of the Mischief and Miseries which have attended their Lust and Pride"; the latter borrowed without acknowledgment from *Alphabet de L'Imperfection et Malice Des Femmes* of Jacob Olivier (Rouen, 1666). Book III, "A Good Wife is God's Gift, or a Character of a Wife Indeed," we are told is "an innocent and profitable Discourse of use to both Sexes . . . deliver'd at a Wedding some time since," and is probably what Ward and his publisher represented it to be. To the latter is appended a "poetical Description of a Maid, Wife, and Widow," the one item in the volume bearing an unmistakable resemblance to Ward's later efforts.

If this piece of literary hack work deserves mention it is because it is the only item that can authentically be assigned to him throughout this period.[19] Undoubtedly there were others, but Ward was as yet an insignificant writer whose name carried no weight on the title-page. Neither was it an age when the ethics of the publisher demanded an identification of his writers or any acknowledgment of their thefts. In the morass of pamphlet literature, adaptations, and hack work belonging to the years 1691 to 1698, still unassigned by students of the period, it is possible there are a number of items owing in whole or in part to the hand of Ward, but which the kindness of fortune makes it impossible at this date to identify. It is essential to recognize that when the heyday came and Ward's name did carry weight, there was nothing from this earlier period that he chose to have reprinted save *The Poet's Ramble after Riches*. No other material than this poem found its way into the collected writings.[20]

But the literary hack work allotted to Ward by the publishers, even if some remains unidentified, was undoubtedly meager. His money ran out; his debts continued to mount. With inevitable imprisonment facing debtors, life became more and more a precarious existence. In his first successful production in 1698, *A Trip to Jamaica,* he sketches for us his earlier condition. Possessed of "an unhappy propensity" for the conversation of those "unlucky kind of Fortune-Hunters" who depended upon the quill and the booksellers, he writes, he, who "had no more Wit to boast of than another Man, . . . shar'd the Fate of those that had" and was "like to have been stuck fast in a Thicket of Brambles." To clear himself he "bustled like a Fox in a Gin, or a Hare in a Patridge Net." He was willing to accept the world of trade, but when he began to look about for an opening that would forestall the inevitable end of the penurious, he found "Tradesmen Grumbling at the Taxes, Merchants at their

Losses, most Men complaining for want of Business, and all
Men in Business, for want of Money; Every Man upon
Change looking with as peevish a Countenance, as if he had
unluckily stumbled upon his Wifes Failings, and unhappily
become a Witness to his own Cuckoldome."

Apparently unable to find an opening in London, Ward
became desperate. In a moment of remorse, his wits "Wooll-
gathering" after two or three gallons of derby-ale, he decided
to travel. Accordingly towards the latter end of January 1697
he took passage in the *Andalucia,* a "Vessel of 400 Tuns, 28
Guns, and about 50 Men," for Jamaica. To leave the country
of his birth on an uncertain quest in a strange land was
something of an experience. His mood at the moment he
records in some lines of verse later injected into an account
of the voyage.

> Farewell my Country, and my Friends,
>   My Mistress, and my Muse;
> In distant Regions, diff'rent Ends
>   My Genius now pursues. . . .
>
> Despair of Fortune makes me bold,
>   I can in Tempests Sleep,
> And fearless of my Fate, behold
>   The Dangers of the Deep. . . .
>
> Something there is, which touches near,
>   I scarce can bid Adieu;
> 'Tis all my Hope, my Care, my Fear,
>   And all that I pursue:
> 'Tis what I Love, yet what I Fly;
>   But what I dare not, must not Name;
> Angels Protect the Sacred Frame,
>   Till I to England shall Return, or Die.

After a journey of about a month, enlivened by the fear
of pirates and a tropical storm, he arrived at Port Royal.
How long he remained in Jamaica he does not tell us, but
that he found conditions little better than those he had left,
he leaves no doubt. Before November of the same year he was
back in London.

Without realizing it at the moment he had brought back

the solution to his problem. The trip had been a disappointing one. Ward felt bitter toward the agents of the ship company whose overpersuasion was responsible for his journey. Shortly after his return he published anonymously a little sixteen-page prose pamphlet entitled *A Trip to Jamaica,* in which he sketched the details of the voyage and heaped vituperation upon the island. He had described his earlier journey into Leicestershire without success, but there he had relied chiefly upon the Hudibrastic burlesque. This was in essence a vindictive attack. At any rate the popularity of *A Trip to Jamaica* was instantaneous.

In less than a year it had gone through six editions and Ward's financial outlook was more favorable. A few months later he wrote a similar account of Boston and the Massachusetts colony, entitled *A Trip to New-England, With a Character of the Country and People, both English and Indians.* Suddenly his name began to carry weight on the title-page. In the next year and a half he insured the sale of pamphlet after pamphlet with the caption—"By the Author of the Trip to Jamaica." Under this inducement he once more offered the public *The Poet's Ramble after Riches,* and it sold three editions within two years. In the preface prepared for the 1698 edition, he exults in his new success:

I have already Experienc'd what operation my Papers have upon the Publick; some they Please, some they Vex, some Praise 'em, some Damn 'em, some Treat me, some Thank me, Others Threaten me; thus have I made in a Month or two, as much Noise in the Town, as if this Seven Years I had scribled Drolls to Bartholomew-Fair, and had been the Renown'd Author of Whittington-Cat or Bateman.

II

Bishops, Bailiffs, and Bastards

> Bishops, Bailiffs, and Bastards, were the three Terrible Persecutions
> which chiefly drove our unhappy Brethren to seek their Fortunes in
> our Forreign Colonies.
>
> *A Trip to New-England* (1699)

IN THE SUMMER of 1698 *A Trip to Jamaica* made its first
appearance on the bookstalls.[1] The companion piece, *A
Trip to New-England, With a Character of the Country
and People, both English and Indians* came out in March of
1699. Today both of them are of interest as early accounts of
colonial life in America; and it may be well for that reason,
as well as for the fact that they gave rise to a new journalistic vogue, to pause for a moment to examine them at
somewhat closer range.

There are, to be sure, many earlier records of voyages and
explorations, as well as treatises on the flora and fauna of the
colonial possessions. But few earlier travelers in the new
world had returned to the old to chat informally on man
and manners and so present their readers with intimate
glimpses of the daily life and milieu of the colonists. It is
essential therefore to see how much found worthy of comment by Ward in his depreciatory account was based upon
firsthand observation of our forebears. Obviously, if the experiences recorded in the two trips are not those of an
actual traveler, the accounts are in this respect of little interest or significance.

Ward tells us quite unequivocally that in 1697 he visited
the island of Jamaica. The statement has been the subject
of doubt.[2] Unfortunately shipping records sufficient to prove
its accuracy no longer exist.[3] There is, however, sufficient

plausibility in the account itself to warrant the acceptance of Ward's statement.

The device of borrowing from earlier writers and presenting the material to the readers as one's own was, of course, not unknown to Ward and his contemporaries. Dr. C. N. Greenough has substantiated John Dunton's claim that the latter was in New England in 1687, but he has also proved that much of the material in *Letters from New England*, which Dunton represented as an account of his New England friends, was lifted bodily from the characters of Overbury and Hall.[4] Ward, too, borrowed from the accounts of the earlier writers. It is the nature of his borrowing and the character of his unborrowed material that lend weight to the plausibility of Ward's statement in so far at least as it applies to his trip to Jamaica.

In *A Trip to Jamaica* Ward devotes fully two-thirds of the time to casual details concerning the departure and the voyage. It was towards the latter end of January 1697, "upon the dissolution of the hard Frost," he tells us, that he "passed, with many others, by the Night Tide, in a Wherry to Gravesend," where the ship *Andalucia* lay waiting. An easterly wind was blowing, the Thames was rough, and the passengers, crowded in the small wherry "like Essex Calves in a Rumford Waggon," were drenched with the spray. Upon their arrival at two in the morning they were treated by the mate to a supper of cheese and biscuit washed down "with a Magnificent Can of Soveraign Flip," and shown to their cabins. In the morning Ward looked over the ship, contemplated for a time his adverse fortune, and wrote the verses of his *Farewell to England*.[5] The captain and pilot came aboard late that afternoon, the anchor was weighed, and with a good deal of furor and shouting the ship got under way. Passing the Downs they anchored again at Deal for three or four days waiting for a wind.

When it finally arrived it was a violent gale and in the morning as they left, Ward tells us, he saw the salvage boats at work on a vessel driven "upon the Goodwin" during the night. In a little time they had moved out into the ocean and the voyage began.

Ward gives us some account of the passengers, and, with due allowance for his facetious phrasing, they are real enough. One was an Irishman "going over a servant," whom Ward supposed kidnapped. Three of them were women, one an "Unfortunate Lady" in pursuit of a husband who, having tired of waiting for her, had married a "Lacker-Fac'd Creolean"; another was a maid, and the third a widow. Among the others were

> two Parsons, who had lost their Livings; three Broken Tradesmen, who had lost their Credit; and several, like me, that had lost their Wits; a Creolean Captain, a Superannuated Mariner, an Independant Merchant, an Irish Kidnapper, and a Monmothean Sythes-Man, all going with one Design, to patch up their Decay'd Fortunes.

After the first two weeks, when the climate was decidedly warmer, the voyage began to take on a more pleasant aspect. In the long afternoons they sang "Antiquated Sonnets" and psalms under the direction of the two parsons. Or in lieu of that they played "Hob, Spie the Market, Shove the Slipper, Dilly-Dally, and Back-gammon." With Ward backgammon was a favorite and he often made his "Days Labour worth Two Shillings, or Half a Crown, at Two Pence or a Groat a Bout." His chief opponent, he tells us, was one of the parsons who always interrupted the game punctually, however, to step into the great cabin and give "his Sinful Congregation a Dram of Evangelical Comfort."

One night they suffered a severe tropical storm, an event to which Ward refers later in *The War of the Elements, or the Description of a Sea Storm* (1708). With great rapidity the small black cloud on the western horizon spread eastward until the entire sky was overcast. Lightning played from cloud to cloud. The wind came in puffs and starts, then steadied into a terrific blow. Hurriedly the sails were lowered and all was made fast. "Then fell such an excessive Rain, that as we had one Sea under us, we fear'd another had been tumbling upon our Heads": [6]

> Huge liquid Islands broke upon our Bow,
> And did with rapid Force our Decks o'erflow:
> Run fore and aft, as if designed our Graves,
> And rowl'd from Stem to Stern in curling Waves,

Clean wash'd the Deck, and then by slow degrees,
Stole thro' our Skuppers and rejoin'd their Seas.

The rain was followed by hail. The bowsprit was wrenched from the vessel's head. Masts and yardarms crashed on the deck. "Unrig'd and unmast'd" the *Andalucia* rode out the night.

In the morning there were more fears when near the coast of Sully another vessel hove into sight. For an hour it was "down Chests, up Hammocks! Knock down the bulkhead and cabins! Clear the deck Fore and Aft, for every Man to have free access to his Business!" But the vessel proved to be an English one bound from Guinea and the alarm gave way to the punch bowl and a thanksgiving service led by the parsons.

When Ward progresses as far as the tropics in his account, he furnishes the reader with a list of tropical birds and fish and a description of cloud formations. In a few days they made the Leeward Islands—Desirade, Montserrat, Antigua, Nevis, St. Christopher's—then Hispaniola, and within twenty-four hours with a fresh gale, they were within sight of Jamaica.

So far, the casual details of the voyage suggest an actual experience; the formal account of the island of Jamaica, however, does not. Ward had written in the preface,

I do not therein present you with a formal Journal of my Voyage, or Geographical Description of the Island of Jamaica, for that has been already done by Persons better qualifi'd for such a Task.

Two "Persons better qualifi'd for such a Task" were Captain Hickeringill, later secretary to the Earl of Windsor, who had written an account of the island at the request of Charles II as early as 1661, and Richard Blome, who published in 1672 *A Description of the Island of Jamaica, with the other Isles and Territories in America, to which the English are Related,* also dedicated to the king. It was from the latter that Ward borrowed the formal details of his account. Blome gave the island's situation and extent, its climate and commodities, its government and laws. Ward was interested

chiefly in the commodities which he presented under the
title, "Of their Provisions," carefully disguising his borrowing under cover of the burlesque phrasing and greater informality of manner, and in a few matters of climate and
geography which he included in his account "Of Port-
Royal." [7]

To Blome's account, however, Ward added something of
his own, of greater interest at the moment. Blome was recom-
mending the permanent retention of the island by the English. To Ward it was all one whether the island was given
back to the Spanish or allowed during the next tropical
storm to sink back into the sea. The voyage had been ill-
advised, enforced by straitened circumstances. It had brought
him nothing. He had a grudge to settle with the agent of
the shipping company at the Jamaica Coffee-House. Under
the title "Of the People" he gives way to his ire. As for the
men, most of them ex-soldiers, they look "as if they had just
knock'd off their Fetters,"

They regard nothing but Money, and value not how they get it; . . .
They are very Civil to Strangers who bring over considerable Effects; and
will try a great many ways to Kill him fairly, for the Lucre of his
Cargo: . . .

A Broken Apothecary will make there a Topping Physician; a Bar-
bers Prentice, a good Surgeon; a Bailiffs Follower, a passable Lawyer; and
an English Knave, a very Honest Fellow.

And as for the women—well, "A little Reputation among
the Women, goes a great way,"

An Impudent Air, being the only Charms of their Countenance, and a
Lewd Carriage, the Study'd Grace of their Deportment. They are such
who have been Scandalous in England to the utmost degree, either
Transported by the State, or led by their Vicious Inclinations; where they
may be Wicked without Shame, and Whore on without Punishment.

To the island itself he devotes a paragraph worth quoting
in its entirety.

The Dunghill of the Universe, the Refuse of the whole Creation, the
Clippings of the Elements, a shapeless Pile of Rubbish confus'dly jumbl'd
into an Emblem of the Chaos, neglected by Omnipotence when he form'd
the World into its admirable Order. The Nursery of Heavens Judgments, where the Malignant Seeds of all Pestilence were first gather'd

THE ADAM AND EVE COFFEE-HOUSE

From an engraving by Wise

and scatter'd thro' the Regions of the Earth, to Punish Mankind for their Offences. The Place where Pandora fill'd her Box, where Vulcan Forg'd Joves Thunder-bolts, and that Phaeton, by his rash misguidance of the Sun, scorched into a Cinder. The Receptacle of Vagabonds, the Sanctuary of Bankrupts, and a Close-stool for the Purges of our Prisons. As Sickly as an Hospital, as Dangerous as the Plague, as Hot as Hell, and as Wicked as the Devil. Subject to Turnadoes, Hurricanes and Earthquakes, as if the Island, like the People, were troubled with the Dry Belly-Ach.

No wonder Ward felt the denizens of the Jamaica Coffee-House would be angry; nor did his exaggerated rhetoric wholly falsify the general picture. The history of the island in the hands of its English conquerors, though brief, had been turbulent.[8] Port Royal, itself the earlier scene of conquest and pillage, had in later years become a haven for buccaneers, a refuge for debtors and rogues, the home of pestilence and earthquake. Almost completely destroyed by the latter in 1692 the city had not been rebuilt in its earlier splendor, and Ward characterizes the houses as "low, little, and irregular." Sanitary methods were of the crudest and the stench in case of a landward breeze almost intolerable. Prices were high. The greater part of the population was made up of disbanded soldiers and sailors, tradesmen, and adventurers. The two entities in demand were money and titles. As for the general wickedness of the city and the disreputable character of its women, they, too, are amply supported by contemporary records.

In the case of the second travelogue, *A Trip to New-England,* the evidence is against Ward. This is no casual account of a voyage. In none of his other writings does he refer to having been in New England as he does in the case of Jamaica. Neither is there anything in the description of Boston—outside of the material he borrowed from earlier accounts—which Ward might not have known or picked up in any tavern about London without ever setting foot in New England.

He tells us he came over on the *Prudent Sarah,* a ship which records show plied between London and Boston at the time,[9] but he gives no date or any details of the voyage. The omission of facts he justifies by saying,

To entertain this Merry Town, with an exact Journal in Tarpaulin Ara-
bick, is like reading the Revelations to an establish'd Atheist, or repeating
a Welsh Comedy to a Highlander. I shall therefore omit all such ac-
customary Fustian, and divert you with some Thoughts of my own in
the time of my Passage.

The ruse is obvious. In preference to giving an account of a
voyage he has never taken he is willing to beguile his readers with his own whimsies and conceits.

When I first came on Board, I fancy'd a Ship to be like a Country Village with two or three May-poles in't; and the Fellows running about
Deck in Red and White-wastcoats, to be the Young Men of the Town
engaged in a match at Foot-ball.

Sometimes I consider'd them as a Pack of Hounds, and the Pilot to be the
Huntsman: For, like Dogs upon a Scent, they keep a heavy Yelping at
their Business; but in every interval, were as silent as a Beagle at a Loss.

By far the greater portion of *A Trip to New-England* is
given over to a description of the land and its inhabitants
both Indian and English. For his material Ward dipped
freely into John Josselyn's earlier account of two voyages he
himself had made to New England. In the account of his
first voyage Josselyn had written of the geography and extent, the climate and commodities, the government and
laws, the habits and daily life of the people.[10] In the second,
New England's Rarities Discovered (London: G. Widdowes,
1672), he had written on the flora and fauna. From the two
accounts Ward borrowed all of his factual information, re-
arranging it as he pleased, turning Josselyn's matter of fact
style into a jocular one supplemented by metaphor and il-
lustration. Josselyn, for instance, had mentioned four
churches. Ward writes:

To the Glory of Religion, and the Credit of the Town, there are four
Churches, Built with Clap-boards and Shingles, after the Fashion of our
Meeting-houses; which are supply'd by four Ministers, to whom some,
very justly, have apply'd these Epithites, one a Scholar, the Second a
Gentleman, the Third a Dunce, and the Fourth a Clown.

Josselyn had said that the women were excessive smok-
ers. Ward writes:

They Smoke in Bed, Smoke as they Nead their Bread, Smoke whilst
they'r Cooking their Victuals, Smoke at Prayers, Work, and Exoneration,

that their Mouths stink as bad as the Bowl of a Sailers Pipe, which he has funk'd in, without Burning, a whole Voyage to the Indias.

To Josselyn's remark that kissing a woman in the street was punishable by a fine or whipping Ward appends a few bawdy comments and then adds a couple of stories, probably current in London at the time. One is the story of the returning ship's captain who was fined ten shillings for kissing his wife in the street, the other of an inhabitant who kissed his wife in the garden, refused to pay his fine, and upon being given twenty lashes at the gun, swore never to kiss his wife again either in public or private. All of which will serve to show the nature of Ward's own contribution to his trip.

The evidence seems quite clear. Ward did make a trip to Jamaica. Because his account of that journey was eminently successful, he conceived of a parallel attack on New England. In Josselyn and in the coffee-house gossip of London the material lay ready at hand. Life in early New England, no doubt, had its sorry side—hence the hearsay which he appropriated. It is unnecessary, however, on Ward's account to apologize further for the behavior of our ancestors.[11]

As a journalistic feat the success of *A Trip to Jamaica* lay in the immediacy and concreteness of its attack and its facile exploitation of billingsgate. On the day *A Trip to Jamaica* appeared on the bookstalls the Jamaica Coffee-House, a center for the activities of the shipping companies plying to Jamaica, was doing a thriving business. It is not strange that the pamphlet caused considerable stir and hullabaloo; or that, as Ward himself tells us, its author was threatened. Its unique pattern lay in the recounting of the casual and trivial with a primary emphasis, and in the incorporation of the unusual and picturesque into a jocular prose embellished with indecent metaphor and bawdy comment. Granted that the voyage was a disappointing one and that the shipping masters of the Jamaica Coffee-House were liars and knaves, it is still true that Ward neither looked, nor cared to look, beneath the surface. He did not interest himself in the history of the island or its population; nor did he give any thought to its geography and climate other than that exercised in appropriating materials from Blome. He neither loved nor mingled with its people. He was interested only in what was apparent to the most casual observation and in sketching that in lines sharply accented to bring out the grotesque and unusual. All this, one may add, was to remain part and parcel of the fundamental pattern of the later writings of Ward.

If to the modern reader both trips are needlessly scurrilous, it is well to remember that they reflect the taste and attitude of Ward's generation. The average Englishman in the eighteenth century was singularly insular, and London was at all times ready to welcome a scandalous attack on the dependencies and colonies. Neither was the idea of launching a satiric attack upon a country one had visited and disliked, nor the method of doing so, entirely original with Ward. Still rankling in the minds of Englishmen in Ward's own day was the account of Sorbière in his *Relation d'un voyage en Angleterre* published in Cologne in 1664.

Sorbière had, among other things, criticized the English for their sloth, their partiality for the tavern, their food, their rude impertinence to strangers, their smug superiority to the rest of the world, and after that it mattered little that he had also written of his unqualified admiration for the English countryside, the parks, the public buildings, the Royal Society, and Thomas Hobbes. Thomas Sprat in his *Observations on Monsieur Sorbière's Voyage to England* (1665), which the English reader knew better than he did the original, charged Sorbière with having been both trivial in the selection of his material and defamatory in intent. Having called to mind, he says, the ancient examples of Pythagoras, Solon, Thales, and Plato he had expected to find "a grave Philosopher going forth with the Intent to survey all Civil States." "You may think how much I was surprized," he continues, "when I saw the first Fruits of his Travels were an Account of the pleasant Company he had on the Way, of certain Polacks, that spoke Latin, that could play on the Violin, and that gave him a Dance Twice a Day."

It was this same emphasis upon the trivial that had become

the source of William King's greatest derision in his attack on Viscount Molesworth's *An Account of Denmark, as it was in the year 1692*. Molesworth left his post as English ambassador at the court of Frederick III in disgrace. His defense was not only an attack on the country, but a political treatise on the evils of monarchy and a state church. To demonstrate the miserable conditions of the people under a tyrannic ruler he had resorted to an account of the peasantry, their affliction of flies, their propensity for "Apoplexies and Falling-Sickness," their food, their mean-spiritedness and superstition. In connection with the latter he had told the story of how he had secured some green geese from a peasant woman who had at first refused to sell them to him, though he offered her double the price, until at last she came offering him four, for neither she nor her geese had thriven since the refusal and eight of her flock had been devoured by kites. In his reply, *Animadversions on a Pretended Account of Denmark* (1694), King, a good friend of Ward's, made a special point of the general triviality of the account, with particular reference to the green geese. Twitting Molesworth for having published his account anonymously, he writes:

Monsieur Sorbiere put his Name to a scandalous Description of England, tho' he relates several Passages, altogether as inconsiderable and ridiculous, as that the Description of Danmark tells us, p. 95. That being a great Lover of Green Geese, he could get none of the Country People; till a superstitious old Woman told him, she had four at his service, imagining that otherwise the Kite would have them; or rather, otherwise being an old Woman full of Bowels, (as Hostesses usually are) being afraid that the Gentleman should lose his Longing.

It is not necessary to assume that Ward meant to imitate either Sorbière or Viscount Molesworth. The prominence of both men and the general furor produced by their writings, however, undoubtedly gave impetus to the satiric account of foreign travel and to a degree provided the method of dwelling upon the trivial and nonessential, of heaping odium and opprobium upon a people by depicting them in their peculiarities and outlandish behavior. To that Ward added his own jocular manner, the impertinent image or startling metaphor drawn from a world of gross appetites, ill-mannered conduct, and bodily excretions. Even for that there had been a precedent, though it is not at all certain that Ward was as familiar with Owen Feltham as he was with the accounts ridiculed by his friend William King.

Nevertheless, fifty years before Ward wrote *A Trip to Jamaica,* Owen Feltham had published an account of a three weeks' ramble through the low countries under the title *A Brief Character of the Low-Countries under the States, being Three Weeks Observations of the Vices and Virtues of the Inhabitants.* Though the printer tells us that the author wrote it with no "spleen to the Nation" but only to amuse himself and companions in travel, it is essentially as satiric as the accounts by Ward. The similarity of Ward's style to Feltham's is immediately obvious; its dissimilarity is open only to an eye familiar with Ward's greater facility in pornographic metaphor and comment. So close, indeed, is the parallel that immediately after the unusual success of *A Trip to Jamaica* an unidentified writer in London republished Feltham's account as *A Trip to Holland* (London, 1699) in obvious imitation of Ward. Two quotations will illustrate. Feltham, in speaking of the food of the Hollanders, had written:

In their Houses, Roots and Stockfish are Staple Commodities. If they make a Feast, and add Flesh, they have the Art to keep it hot more days than a Pigs-Head in Pye-corner. Salt meats and sower Cream they hold him a Fool that loves not, only the last they correct with Sugar; and are not half so well pleased with having it sweet at first, as with letting it sower, that they may sweeten it again; as if a Woman were not half so pleasing being easily won, as after a Scolding fit she comes by a man to be calmed again.

Of the provisions of Jamaica Ward writes:

They greatly abound in a Beautiful Fruit, call'd, a Cussue, not unlike an Apple, but longer; its soft and very Juicy, but so great an Acid, and of a Nature so Restringent, that by Eating of one, it drew up my mouth like a Hens Fundament, and made my Palate as Rough, and Tongue as Sore, as if I had been Gargling it with Allom-Water: From whence I conjecture, they are a much fitter Fruit to recover Lost Maiden-heads, properly apply'd, than to be Eaten.

To a degree, then, Ward's journalistic scoop was the result of adaptation and innovation, and the success of *A Trip to*

Jamaica lay in its timeliness and in what, in Ward's own day, would have been called its diverting nature.

Of its immediate and continuing popularity there can be no doubt. If the seven editions which followed each other to the bookstalls were not alone sufficient evidence, the host of imitations it produced would substantiate the fact. Ward, as we have seen, attempted to repeat his success in *A Trip to New-England*. Early in 1699 the anonymous writer already referred to borrowed his account from Feltham, remarking in his preface that "Certainly a Trip to Holland may be as grateful as one to Jamaica." In the same year appeared *A Journey to Scotland, Giving a Character of that Country, the People and their Manners,* written "by an English Gentleman." Before the year was out John Dunton, who had earlier taken refuge from his creditors in Dublin, wrote, or more accurately borrowed from an earlier account enough details for *A Trip to Ireland.*[12] In his preface he says:

Since Observations of the same Nature with those which follow, have prevail'd of late for a general Approbation; and it has been more acceptable to the Reader to make Enquiries into the Imperfections of the People which have given Being to the Papers under his Perusal, than to search after their Excellencies and survey their Beauties; I could not but think it adviseable to gratify his Palate, and consult my own Interest, in presenting him the following Remarks.

In 1701 R. B., a barrister at the Temple, published *A Trip to North-Wales, being a Description of that Country and People.* "You have been," he writes,[13] "even cloy'd with London-Spies, Trips to Jamaica, the Bath, and the Jubilee: Perhaps, a Trip to Wales, may, for its Novelty, prove a little acceptable. . . ."

And so the deluge continued. The year 1703 saw *A Trip to St. Helena, With a Description of the Island and its Inhabitants;* 1705, *A Trip to Spain, or a true Description of the Comical Humours, Ridiculous Customs, and Foolish Laws, of the Lazy Improvident People the Spaniards;* 1708, *The Sot-Weed Factor, or a Voyage to Maryland, a Satyr,* by Ebenezer Cook[14] describing the "Laws, Government, Courts, and Constitution of the Country; and also the Buildings,

Feasts, Frolicks, Entertainments and drunken Humours of the Inhabitants of that part of America."

Though many of the trips have apparently been lost, the titles indicate the nature of their imitation. Of the ones still in existence most of them have at one time or another been assigned to Ward.[15] Ward, however, never laid claim to any of them. They were not reprinted in his collected works. All of them carry internal evidence disproving his authorship. In addition to the two trips already discussed as Ward's, there was apparently only one other relating to travel beyond the confines of England that owed its existence to his pen. In 1705 he published *A Trip to Germany, or the Poet turn'd Carbineer*, "a relation of several comical Intrigues and diverting Adventures, with an impartial Character of the Country," now apparently lost.

For ten years *A Trip to Jamaica* and its imitations continued to supply a ready market. Long before that Ward had applied the idea of the trip to an even more popular innovation.

III

Wearing the Bays

If he would have worn as much Bays as the common vogue of the
People had given him a Title to, his Head wou'd have appear'd
as fine as a Country Casement in the midst of the Christmas Holidays.

The London Spy, Part 1 (1698)

THE SUCCESS of *A Trip to Jamaica* having provided Ward
with both method and style he turned in the first flush
of achievement from Port Royal to London. If a satiric
account of the island and inhabitants of Jamaica could
amuse the coffee-house loiterers, why should they not be
equally amused by a satiric portrayal of the city and inhabitants of London. The account could be cast in the form
of a trip, as the earlier one had been. The emphasis, as there,
might be on the casual and commonplace. He could trust
his earlier method of exaggerated characterization embellished with abundant metaphor and bawdy comment to
tantalize and divert his readers. Moreover, with the abundance of material at hand it would not need to be one trip
but many—or better yet under the design of a continuous
trip issued in parts at monthly intervals, he could regale the
town with whatever characterizations and descriptions of
the city he chose.

With apparently something of the whole scheme in mind
Ward issued part one of *The London Spy* in November of
the year 1698.[1] Carefully modeled after the earlier trip it, too,
was in the form of a sixteen-page folio pamphlet. The title-
page bore the caption "By the Author of the Trip to Jamaica." For the title Ward had taken a cue from the popular
*L'Espion du Grand Seigneur dans les Cours des Princes
Chretiens,*[2] currently on the English bookstalls as *The Turk-*

ish Spy. The motif of a country man being shown the town by his more sophisticated cousin or schoolfellow was already a popular one,[3] as well as germane to his own experience.

The popularity of *The London Spy* was as instantaneous as that of *A Trip to Jamaica*. In December he issued part two. Sure now of his public, he wrote a preface indicating his design:[4]

The first part of this undertaking I pop'd into the cautious World, as a Skilful Angler does a new Bait among wary Fish, who have oft been prick'd in their Nibbling; and finding the Publick Snapping at it with as much Greediness as a News-monger at a Gazett, or a City Politician at a new Proclamation, makes me purpose to continue it Monthy, as long as we shall find Encouragement.

Well-launched, *The London Spy* continued to appear at monthly intervals for over a year and a half. The eighteenth and concluding part was issued late in May of 1700. Long before that it had sufficiently over-shadowed his former production to stand on its own feet. Beginning with the thirteenth part issued in November 1699 "by the Author of the Trip to Jamaica" was omitted from the title-page. And so extraordinarily successful was the new venture that henceforth for over a decade all of his writings were to be advertised and sold under the new caption "by the Author of the London Spy."

Largely because of their subsequent reproduction in volume form[5] it has been customary among the students of Ward to treat the eighteen numbers of *The London Spy* as if they had been a single publication, conceived by Ward as a guide to the sights of the city. The essential nature of *The London Spy,* however, is that of a periodical. For the first nine numbers, to be sure, the trip about town remains the basic pattern. Even here, however, Ward does not confine himself to the narration of a trip or a formal account of the sights of the city. From the very beginning the progress of the journey is interrupted by numerous characterizations of taverns and coffee-houses, tobacco shops, and bagnios along the way. Even more significant of the periodical nature of

The London Spy are the occasional verses and songs, presented under the pretext of having been scribbled en route, and the characters of personages presumably encountered with which Ward padded his sixteen folio pages. More important from the point of view of its periodical publication is the fact that as early as the sixth part the trip or characterization of place, gave way to relation of event, and that thereafter Ward more and more frequently turned to the description of current affairs. The seventh part, for instance, issued in May, he devoted to a description of May Fair. In the eighth and ninth parts he returned to the journey motif, but by the time he was at work on the tenth part it was September, and the greater share of that issue, as well as all of the next, he gave over to an account of another immediate event—Bartholomew Fair. So too, the twelfth part, issued in November, he devoted to an account of the opening of the King's Head Tavern on October 27 and the lord mayor's day parade on November 9.

Though Ward later returned to the journey in parts thirteen and fourteen, he was by that time quite ready to abandon his original design. Recognizing a need for further alteration of his earlier pattern, he devoted the fifteenth part entirely to characters, adding at the end a few paragraphs under the title of "Comical Accidents and Occurrences." The modification not being particularly fruitful, he returned in the last three parts to the recounting of events— a Quaker dinner in the city, the christening of a cousin, the funeral of Dryden, and a libel suit between two astrologers.

Even such a cursory glance at the organization and material of *The London Spy* indicates its manifold nature as well as something of its appeal. To the man in the street it was an account of the sights of the city in which he lived. From month to month he could follow the progress of the journey from landmark to landmark. The informality of the treatment, however, and the curious incursion of the out-of-the-way and unfamiliar, plus the large amount of anecdote gave to its pages more nearly the character of a personal journal, almost, one may add, the character of a novel, with its setting strangely enough in the very world in which the reader himself lived. On the other hand the emphasis upon contemporary occurrence with its curious reportorial concern for the casual and picturesque event left untouched by the more formal news-sheets, gave it an immediacy and freshness possible only to the periodical or newspaper. From almost every point of view *The London Spy* was a unique venture and to some degree at least deserved its attendant success.

The first problem for the periodical publication at the turn of the seventeenth century was the one of securing some form of continuity. To attract readers to the first issue of a pamphlet or periodical—itself no easy task—the writer relied heavily upon an eye-catching title, a flaunting title-page, or a lurid preface, inevitably promising more in the way of divertissement, satiric attack, or exposé than he produced. To secure readers was one thing; to hold them another. Innumerable are the publications which failed after one or two or three issues. Rare, indeed, are those which like *The London Spy,* or the later *Tatler* and *Spectator,* continued to hold their readers week after week or month after month.

To entice the casual reader into prolonging his interest, editors and writers alike resorted to numerous devices. Foremost among them was the method of *The Athenian Mercury,* based upon readers' queries answered by the editors in succeeding issues. Not only did this in a sense make the reader a participant, but it also conveniently provided a pretext for the inclusion of the trivial and nonessential or the more outrightly ludicrous and smutty. The important role the latter played in the retention of readers is demonstrated throughout the period, even by the more formal journals like Defoe's *Review,* which found it necessary to subscribe to the readers' taste for the informal and chatty. A second device frequently resorted to, though without notable success, was the solicitation of outright contributions from the readers, or the publication of the writer's own doggerel under the guise of being a reader's attempt at poetry. A third device was the club of writers, each perhaps with his own followers, banding together to fill the pages of the periodical, presumably with the hope that the mystification of the author's identity might be an added inducement. A more simple device was to pretend the existence of such a club and to report solemnly upon its goings and comings.

None of these devices, with the exception of the first, can be said to have been eminently successful before the days of the *Tatler* and *Spectator*. The success of *The London Spy* as a periodical ten years earlier lay in Ward's ability to avoid use of them by the creation of a basic pattern for successive numbers of his magazine with a continuity of interest for his readers. Through the popularity of *A Trip to Jamaica* Ward had hit upon the plan of a continuous narrative. *The London Spy* is basically a trip about town, consuming the rather prodigious time of thirteen months by virtue of numerous interruptions, tangential excursions, and concern for trivia. There is, for instance, an obvious topographical progression from the first to the thirteenth number. The journey begins at Aldgate and proceeds at a leisurely pace to the district of Billingsgate, the Customs House, and the wharves. From there the travelers turn up into the city and, after an inspection of the Monument, arrive at Gresham College, Bedlam, and the Royal Exchange. From the Royal Exchange, they proceed to the Guildhall, to St. Paul's Cathedral, to Ludgate, and from there in later numbers the reader may follow along to Old-Bailey, the College of Physicians, Newgate, Smithfield Rounds, Fleetbridge, Bridewell, and the Temple. By the eighth number the spy and his friend have arrived at St. James's Park and Westminster, and thence in successive numbers up to the thirteenth, they recross the city, via White Hall, the New Exchange, and Charing Cross, to the Tower.

Though the journey moves along leisurely, there is actually very little break in the narrative and almost none between successive issues of the periodical. The concluding paragraph of part one, for instance, anticipates "the Night-Accidents, the Whims and Frolicks of Staggering Bravadoes and Strolling Strumpets" which will be the subject of part two. In parts three to eight the incidents of the journey begin at precisely the point where they had been dropped in the closing paragraphs of the preceding parts issued a month earlier. Part ten concludes with a note to the reader assuring him "That this is but a small part of what's intended on the [Bartholomew's] Fair. And whatever is deficient here, shall be supply'd in the next."

Nor was Ward adverse to using another device, readily practiced by later journalists, that of interrupting his narrative at strategic moments. Only occasionally is the entire account or description of one of the more important sights of the city contained within the pages of a single monthly issue. More often Ward was astute enough to break off the account in the middle and so carry forward the reader's interest. Well on in part two, for instance, on the evening of the first day's journey, the travelers arrive at the district of Billingsgate. Here they stop for the night in a huge sailors' tavern, one of the numerous "Dark Houses" of the locality. Ward includes a rather full description. Coarse fisherwomen are sitting about the fire, their baskets "hanging upon their Heads," each with a "Nipperkin of warm Ale and Brandy." Brawny watermen are eating "Broil'd Red Herring" or bread and cheese and onions. Seamen come bolting in, "short Pipes in their Mouths, Oaken Truncheons in their Hands, Thrum Caps upon their Heads and Canvas Trunks upon their Arses." The fisherwomen engage the travelers in unseemly jests; the seamen boisterously exchange impossible yarns and brutally play an unsavory trick upon a diminutive fiddler. Ready to retire, Ward and his friend are shown to a small upper room stinking of pitch and tallow. It is at this moment that Ward interrupts the narrative. Part three begins with next morning's breakfast of "a Penny-worth of burnt Bread soften'd in a Mug of Porters Guzzle, improved with a slice of Cheshire," and a further exploration of the waterside. So, too, the description of the churchyard and the Cathedral of St. Paul's is neatly divided between parts five and six, and in a similar manner part ten breaks off in the middle of a description of Bartholomew Fair.

In the later parts when Ward turned more and more frequently from the description of place to the recounting of events, the basic pattern of the trip became submerged and finally disappeared. By that time, of course, the reputation of *The London Spy* as a diverting periodical was established and the writer needed less and less to rely upon the readers' interest in any actual journey. Moreover, the nature of the material and the timeliness of the reporting was in itself a sufficient warrant for his readers.

If the pattern of the trip and the description of the successive sights of the city provide a certain continuity of interest for the reader, they are by no means the sole factor in the success of *The London Spy*. Mention has already been made of the London readers' avid taste for the informal and chatty. They were, one may assume—as readers always are—interested in their own city; what they were obviously more interested in, in the case of *The London Spy,* was the direct personal experience of the narrator, and to a degree the personality of the author himself. The uniqueness of Ward's method lay in turning the ordinary world, already familiar to his readers, into the extraordinary and the unusual. Readers of *The London Spy* toured their city in the company of a facile and loquacious pedestrian, concerned equally with the trivial or imposing, one whose sharp eyes were always set for the amusing or idiosyncratic. What they had not seen before, and were now intrigued with, were the comic possibilities in subjecting their every day world to the caricature and burlesque of Ward's impudent and racy prose.

It is impossible to convey Ward's singularity of approach in this respect without somewhat extensive quotation and summary. If the immediately succeeding pages seem to reproduce the contents of *The London Spy, ad nauseam,* it is because only by some such method—where the texts themselves are no longer generally available—can one understand the eighteenth-century readers' interest in the periodical or the nature of Ward's contribution to the journalistic literature concerning the city of London.

The element of direct personal experience has already been noted in Ward's account of the night spent in one of the "Dark Houses" of the Billingsgate district. Ward uses the same personal approach in his description of any one of the

more formal sights of the city. The account of Bedlam (part
III) begins, for instance, with the description of the travelers' arrival at the huge iron gates. He recounts in detail how,
once inside, he and his friend mingled freely with the inmates and fellow-sightseers, conversing for some time with
a former scholar of St. John's, Cambridge, who has been
confined for melancholia. For the reader he recreates the
"rattling of Chains, drumming of Doors," the steady "Rant-
ing, Hollowing, Singing, and Rattling." There are many
visitors and the journalist becomes sharp in his derogatory
comment. Some of the visitors peek through the bars at the
more violent cases. Others entertain themselves by engaging
the inmates in flirtation and in intrigue with feminine fellow-
sightseers. Mistresses of all ranks, he writes, are available
from the "Velvet Scarf to the Scotch-Plaid Petticoat." Every
newcomer is soon engaged in an amour. Though visitors
enter singly, they always go out in pairs. "Tis an Alms-House
for Madmen," he concludes, "a Showing Room for Whores,
a sure Market for Leachers, a dry Walk for Loiterers."

Quite in the same manner, the readers are given their description of St. Paul's (part v). The travelers enter the area
from Cheapside, and are impressed with the immensity of
the structure. In the churchyard itself bookstalls and booksellers are as thick as "Pedlars at a Fair." Beyond them is a
"Picture-sellers Shop," whose "Smutty Prints" stare the
church in the face. Still farther along are the music shops
where the apprentices are "Fiddling and Piping of Bories
and Minuets" with large crowds at the doors. At the west
end of the yard, among the apples, nuts, and gingerbread, a
blind ballad singer is moving his audience to tears with melancholy psalms. Just within the west gate the sawyers and
stone cutters are at work. The cathedral is slow a-building,
and Ward comments, as the modern traveler might, on the
leisurely workmen, the huge pile of stone, the enormous
pillars sustaining the covering of the porch. Inside the travelers are moved by the spaciousness of the building, the "Art"
and "Grandeur" of the choir. They attend afternoon prayers,
and then return to the main body of the church, where,
mingling with fellow-loiterers, they gaze aloft at the turn

of the cupola upon which the three-hundred foot spire is still to be erected.

If these two instances, reduced to barest detail, will suffice to show Ward's method in the description of the more formal sights of the city, an additional example or two will show the degree of adaptability with which he could shift the tone of his account. The prevailing mood of *The London Spy* is one of light-hearted amusement and supercilious contempt. When in the sixth part the journey arrives at Bridewell and Ward presents his readers with a glimpse of the London penal system, he becomes serious, and though he even here lingers over trifles merely to be amusing, the emphasis of the account is strongly denunciatory.

Ward's first comment is an ironic one on the building itself. At first sight, he writes, one would imagine the stately edifice "rather a Princes Palace, than a House of Correction." Inside, the travelers see "a parcel of Ill-looking Mortals Strip'd to their Shirts like Hay-makers" beating hemp on wooden anvils. As at Bedlam, visitors mingle freely with the inmates, and if there is less danger to life and limb, the assault on the ears is equally great. Some beg for drink; others hardened by their experience exchange quips about the halters they are fashioning. On the common side, behind the iron grate, a "Ghastly Skeleton" stands weeping. "I could not speak to him," Ward writes,

without dread of danger, lest, when his Lips open'd to give me an answer, he should Poison the Air with his Contagious Breath, and Communicate to me the same Pestilence which had brought his Infected Body to such a dismal Anatomy: Yet mov'd with Pity towards so Languishing an Object, I began to enquire into the Causes of his sad appearance, who, after a Penitential Look, that call'd for Mercy and Compassion, with much difficulty he rais'd his Feeble Voice a degree above Silence, and told me he had been Sick six Weeks under that Miserable Confinement, and had nothing to Comfort him but Bread and Water, with now and then the Refreshment of a little Small-Beer. I ask'd him further, what Offence he had committed that brought him under this Unhappiness? To which he answer'd, he had been a great while discharg'd of all that was Charg'd against him, and was detain'd only for his Fees; which, for want of Friends, being a Stranger in the Town, he was totally unable to raise. I ask'd him what his Fees amounted to? Who told me five Groats. Bless me! Thought I, what Rigorous Uncharitable thing is this, that so

Noble a Gift, intended, when first given, to so good an End, should be thus perverted! And what was design'd to prevent Peoples falling into Misery, thro' Laziness or Ill-Courses, should now be so corrupted by such Unchristian Confinement as to Starve a Poor Wretch, because he wants Money to satisfie the demands of a Mercenary Cerberus, when discharg'd of the Prison by the Court! Such Severe, nay Barbarous Usage, is a Shame to our Laws, an Unhappiness to our Nation, and a Scandal to Christianity.

Across the court they peer through another grate into the women's apartment. Here old and young alike are toiling at the hemp under the supervision of an overseer, whip in hand. The spirit of the women, however, is undaunted—if Ward may be believed—and they are as apt at their bawdy quips as the men. Back in the first quadrangle, Ward and his friend proceed upstairs to the "Spacious Chamber" where the court is in session. In the next room, seen through the open doorway, is a woman under the lash in full view of the court and spectators. When the judge's hammer falls, the lashes cease. But new cases are even now on the docket. Once more Ward breaks into comment. This is no way to correct the childish errors of a girl of thirteen. Moreover, he continues,

I think it a Shameful Indency for a Woman to expose her Naked Body to the sight of Men and Boys, as if it was design'd rather to feast the Eyes of the Spectators, or stir up the Beastly Appetites of Lascivious Persons, than to Correct Vice, or Reform Manners.

If the world of Bridewell moves Ward to criticism, the more polite world of St. James's Park (part VIII) moves him to admiration. It is evening when the travelers arrive at the park. Lovely ladies are strolling along the mall. Ward is moved to extravagance in praise of their beauty and grace, though he has less to say for their cringing and fawning escorts and for the penurious gallants strolling under the limes of the neighboring Duke Humphrey's Walk. From the parade Ward and his friend proceed to the canal. Ducks are "frisking about the Water, and standing upon their Heads; showing as many Tricks in their Liquor as a Bartholomew-Fair Tumbler." All is peace and silence. Under the neighboring limes,

Pensive Lovers [were] whispering their Affections to their Mistresses, and Breathing out Dispairing Sighs of their desired Happiness. Here also were the Tender Offspring of the Nobility Handed by their fresh-look'd Nurses to Strengthen and Refresh their Feeble Joints, with air and Exercise, suitable to their Childish Weakness; and some having started more forward in their Infancy, were Accompanied with their Tutors, showing such Manliness in their Presence, and such Promises of Vertue in their Propitious Looks at Ten or a Dozen Years of Age, that they seem'd already Fortified with Grace, Learning and Wisdom against the Worlds Corruptions.

More significant in an estimation of Ward's talent than an account of the sights is his ability to recreate for his readers the pulsating life of the city. To follow the account in terms of sights, in the manner just suggested, is to divest *The London Spy* of much of the original material which delighted and amused his readers. It is, save for the bawdy comment and an occasional suggestive reference, the persistent dawdling over the apparently trivial and the innumerable metaphors and similes which vivify the material.

As in *A Trip to Jamaica* it is Ward's concern with the trivial and the unimportant, with street scenes, multifarious personages, and adventures in coffee-houses and taverns, which lends distinctive character to his writings. To read *The London Spy* is less to make a formal tour of the city than it is to become aware of the incessant traffic of its streets, the tatterdemalion crowd, the billingsgate of the watermen and sailors, the obscene jesting in the taverns. Here it is difficult to illustrate the matter by any quotation from the text, for the effect is cumulative rather than dependent upon individual passages. In reading the pages of *The London Spy* one feels even today that he is seeing London as it really was—as it must have appeared to the man who walked the streets or rode in the badly-slung hackney coaches over the rough cobblestones and open gutters. Once again houses and shops jut out into the street, their angular projections, creaking signs, and overhanging balconies obstacles to traffic. Narrow, treacherous lanes, impenetrably dark at night, lead off right and left to an open courtyard or up a pair of stairs, steep as a "Tilers Ladder," to some coffee-house or tavern. Beggars slink from post to post. Vagabonds move along in droves. Bullies quarrel. Fisherwomen trundle along with their baskets. Small merchants, pastry-cooks, and pippin mongers hawk their wares. Whores sit in the hair-dressing shops. Fine ladies are driven by in their coaches on the way to Covent Garden Market or church. Linkboys loiter outside the coffee-houses. Coaches rattle by. When two of them meet in the narrow confines of the street, altercations follow.[6] The coachmen curse each other. Horses become frightened. Wheels interlock. Poles are rammed into the coaches immediately ahead or shatter a window. The women occupants scream for a gentleman to come to their rescue. On the busier thoroughfares the coaches jeopardize the life of the pedestrian as well. When Ward and his friend have an occasion to cross Fleet Street to visit the shop of a famous tobacconist (part VII), the question his friend puts to him is whether he "dare run the hazard of crossing the Kennel." "You may well Stile it a hazard," Ward replies; "for when ever I have occasion to go on the wrong side the Post, I find my self in as much dread of having my Bones broke . . . as an unlucky Prentice . . . is of a sound beating after a Stolen Holiday."

River traffic is equally hazardous. In part seven Ward and his friend, having alighted at White Chapel Bars, make their way down to the Thames, where they board a wherry at the Old-Swan for Salisbury Court. Before they have proceeded "above the length of a West-Country Barge," a "Crew of Lambeth Gardiners" in an approaching boat assault their ears with a volley of indecent language to which their own pilot replies in kind. The gardeners are followed by a boatload of shopkeepers and another of women, equally capable in the exchange of a river vernacular impossible on the streets without precipitating a brawl. "An Academy of ill Language," writes Ward. "I observe 'tis as great a Pennance for a Modest Man to go a Mile upon the River as 'tis for him to run the Gauntlet thro' an Alley where the Good House Wives are picking Okum."

In the second number of *The London Spy* it is evening. Bells toll the hour of nine. Weary apprentices draw the folded shutters across the front of the shops. There is no moon, so the streets are lighted with flickering lamps.[7] Coaches rumble over the cobblestones. Loaded wains lumber on their way to the Salt-Peter House. The melancholy cries of "Hot-Bak'd Wardens and Pippins" echo along the half-deserted streets. Ward and his friend are on their way to Billingsgate. Bolting suddenly into their path from a side street come the "City Waits," in "long Frize Rugs and Blankets, hoop'd round with Leather Girdles," serenading the winter street. Down another narrow lane the travelers are confronted by a drove of "Diminutive Vagabonds," children of "Gipsies and Country Beggars," who "beg about in the Day-time, and at Night sleep at Doors, and in Holes and Corners about the Streets."

Lord bless you Masters [they cry], give us a Penny or a Half-penny amongst us, and you shall hear any of us (if you please) say the Lords-Prayer backwards, Swear the Compass round; give a new Curse to every step in the Monument, call a Whore as many proper Names as a Peer has Titles.

When Ward gratifies their demand, they troop away "with a Thousand God bless ye's, as Ragged as old Stockin' Mops; . . . as Hungry as so many Cat-ta-Mountains." Still reflecting upon the miserable wretches, Ward and his friend are suddenly confronted by a "Midnight King of Clubs," who, bidding "his Guard de Corp hault" and clapping his scepter to the ground, commands them to stand and come before the constable. With uncovered heads they comply, protesting their innocence.

A shilling convinces "Mr. Surlycuff" and the travelers are allowed to pass on. On another night (part IV) Mr. Surlycuff is not convinced, and the incident supplies one of the most graphic episodes in *The London Spy*. The journey has temporarily halted at the Sign of the Angel in Fenchurch Street, where amid "as pretty a Tippling-Society as ever were drawn into a Circumference, round the Noble Center of a Punch-Bowl" Ward and his friends while away the evening in songs and catches. It is midnight 'ere they are aware. While they are pleading with the "Drowsie Master" for still another quart, the watchman enters with his crew, stamps his oaken scepter on the floor, and reminds them in no uncertain terms of the unseasonableness of the hour. When

Ward and one of his acquaintances prove impudent, the entire party is hustled off to the compter. Behind the iron gates there is little to do—since the turnkey's offer of beds is at "unconscionable" rates—save to walk up and down the paved yard and contemplate their misfortune. Finally, for the sake of diversion they request the turnkey to be admitted to the "Common-side" or King's Ward, where, after having paid their garnish of two shillings, they are admitted to all the rights and privileges of the ragged, louse-infected inhabitants. It is not necessary to believe Ward's account of the scenes that follow—though one may remark in passing that the unsavory conduct of the prisoners is probably far more realistic than that presented in *The Beggars' Opera*—but the actual description of the yard at night is undoubtedly an accurate one.

I observ'd Men lay pil'd in Cabins one upon another, like Coffins in a Burying-Vault, possessing only the same allowance above Ground, as the Dead have under, their Breadth and Length, that's all. Other poor Curs, that wanted the conveniency of Kennels (being Supernumerary to the Sleeping-Huts) were lain some upon Benches, as if they had been bred up Courtiers Footmen: Others coil'd underneath, like Dogs, and slept as sound as Low-Country Soldiers; Some lay round the Fire, almost cover'd with Ashes, like Potatoes Roasting, with their Noses in Conjunction with one anothers A—s, like Hogs on a Dunghill: . . . Another was crept into a corner, and had whelm'd over his Head the Ashes-Tub, and so made a Night-Cap of an Ale-Firkin, to defend his Head from the Coldness of the Weather.

But life was not wholly unpleasant to Ward's readers and he was journalist enough to apportion his scenes between public house and compter. The "distance between a Church and an Ale-House" Ward wrote frequently, and for his readers, too, the phrase was a common unit of measure. The trip recorded in the pages of *The London Spy* begins in a tavern at Aldgate, where Ward's physician friend has taken him for his initial introduction to the "Bows" and "Cringes" of the city. Behind the bar is a creature "all Ribbons, Lace and Feathers," whose bell summons from aloft "two or three Nimble-Heel'd Fellows" who "shot themselves down Stairs . . . every one charged with a Mouthful of Coming, Coming." Shown upstairs, Ward and his friend join their acquaintances, and the dinner progresses through calves-head, roast goose, and a "stately Chesire Cheese" to a final bumper in honor of the queen and the church established. The very next house of call is a coffee-house,[8]

where a parcel of Mudling Muck-Worms were as busie as so many Rats in an Old Cheese-Loft; some Going, some Coming, some Scribbling, some Talking, some Drinking, others Jangling, and the whole Room stinking of Tobacco, like a Dutch-Scoot, or a Boatswains-Cabbin.

Here the walls are hung with gilt frames containing advertisements for "Nectar and Ambrosia, May-Dew, Golden-Elixers, Popular Pills, Liquid-Snuff, Beautifying-Waters, Dentifrices, Drops, Lozenges, all as infallible as the Pope."

Each tavern has its own character and strangers do not always choose wisely. Knowing of an excellent Quaker tavern in Finch-Lane, Ward and his friend take their way thither (part IV). Among the black-hatted fraternity "all things were as silent as the Mourning Attendance at a Rich Mans Funeral; no Ringing of Bar-bell, Bawling of Drawers, or Ratling of Potlids!" In the kitchen, which the travelers had requested for warmth, they find a crowd of "Father Ramseys slouching Disciples," each with his half pint. Ward and his friend, however, order a quart, "as if we drank rather to wash away our Sins than our Sorrows," and when the "Noble Juice" has sufficiently enlivened his friend so that he must "needs be so Frolicksome to Tune his Pipes, and entertain us with a Song," they are requested to leave.

Few of the houses Ward describes must have been more interesting to his readers than Man's Coffee-House and Will's. It is in the ninth part that Ward and his friend arrive at the former. In the dark entryway the link-boys "Arm'd with Flamboys against the approaching Night" are playing "their Unlucky Tricks, and Damning each other in their Masters Dialect." An the end of the entry they ascend a steep pair of steps and are ushered into

an Old Fashion'd Room, of a Cathedral Tenement, where a very Gaudy Crowd of Odoriferous Tom-Essences were Walking backwards and forwards with their Hats in their Hands, not daring to convert 'em to their intended use, lest it should put the Foretops of their Wigs into some disorder . . . their whole Exercise being to Charge and Discharge their Nostrils; and keep the Curls of their Periwigs in their proper Order.

Ward and his friend crowd through the "Fluttering Assembly" to a table. After a moment's observation of the "Tom-Dandies" they call for a pipe and tobacco, as if they had been "in the company of so many Carmen." When the materials are brought to them—the attendants do it rather unwillingly—they proceed to smoke out the beaux, who draw "their Faces into . . . Peevish Wrinkles" and crowd to a great window next the street, where there is "such Snifting and Snuffing, that the rest of the Company could scarce keep their Countenances."

At Will's (part x) they find "much Company, and but little Talk." Finally, however, they shuffle through the "Crowd of Philosophical Mutes, to the other end of the Room, where three or four Wits of the Upper Classes, were Rendezvouz'd at a Table" and engaged in subjecting "our Modern Poets to stand the Test of their All-Judging Opinions."

One was a Man of great Judgment, Learning and Fancy, but of no Principle. Another was one that had Writ well, and could Write well, but would not Write. A Third never Writ but One Good Thing in his Life, and that he Recanted. A Fourth had a Poetical Talent, but it was hid under a Philosophical Bushel. A Fifth was a good Latin Poet, but had Sacrific'd his Muse to Bacchus, instead of Dedicating her to Apollo. A Sixth had got a great deal of Credit by Writing of Plays; but lost it all by Defending the Stage. A Seventh had got some Reputation by turning of Old Ditties into New Songs; but lost it all by turning a Spanish Romance into an English Stage-Play. An Eighth had got Honour by a Dull Poem, which his Brother Medicus Envy'd and Vow'd he'd out-do him in Verse, as he hop'd also to be Knighted.[9]

At another table are the young men—second-rate beaux and wits—"who were Conceited, if they had but once the Honour to dip a Finger and Thumb into Mr. D[ryden]'s Snush-Box." They are entertaining each other by a recital of their latest efforts, including, as Ward presents them, "a Panegarick upon Orange-flower Water," "a Satyr against Dirty-Weather," and "a cleanly Lampoon upon Nasty Tobacco-Smokers."

It is in the convivial activity of taverns and coffee-houses
that Ward and his readers believed life was really at its best.
Over and over he presents to them the same picture:

After a Friendly Salutation, free from all Foppish Ceremony, down we
sat; and when a Glass or two round had given fresh Motion to our
Drousie Spirits, and abandon'd all those careful Thoughts which makes
Man's Life uneasie, Wit begot Wit, and Wine a Thirsty Appetite to each
Succeeding Glass; Then open were our Hearts, and Unconfin'd our Fancies; . . . Songs and Catches Crown'd the Night, and each Man in his
turn Elevated his Voice to fill our Harmony with the more Variety.

II

So far in examination of the pages of *The London Spy* it
has been essential to regard it as a trip or a characterization
of place. When Ward, engaged in writing part six of *The
London Spy,* however, undertook to present his readers with
an account of the festival at Mob's Hole, he began an interesting and far-reaching innovation. He himself recognized
the description as "something of a Digression, or rather a
Deviation from the Title," since the subject took him beyond
the confines of the city. More important in reality, however,
was the fact that in including the account the basic pattern of
the trip was forced to give way to that of event. In following
the crowd to Madame Butterfield's and in the subsequent
account of the excursion, because he believed that news of
this "unusual Feast might be Welcome to the Publick,"
Ward became for all practical purposes a sort of free-lance
roving reporter. How fundamental this shift in emphasis
and method became in later numbers of *The London Spy*
we shall see presently. The innovation, of course, is only another manifestation of the search for the novel and interesting on the part of the writer. Ward's account of his intention
to attend the festival as well as to draw upon it for material
is itself an interesting revelation of the journalist's method.

According to his account it was when he and his friend
left Bridewell and were sitting over a pipe of tobacco in a
"Neighbouring Coffee-House," (part vi) that they chanced
upon the rather curious invitation in *The Flying Post.* Ward
did not need to quote the advertisement for his readers, many

of them had likely seen it themselves, but it is interesting to-day to see the item to which he referred and to recognize the general veracity of his narrative. Madame Butterfield had written as follows: [10]

These may certifie all my Loving Masters and Ladies, that on Wednes-day being the 26th of this instant April 1699 at Dame Butterfields at Mobbs-Hole in the Parish of Wanstead, in Essex, within a Mile of Green-man, will be a House-Warming, where all my Loving Friends shall be kindly entertained with Calf, Roasted Whole, and a Flitch of Bacon, Roasted whole, and other Varieties; with Musick: And also, being an old Hunter, I shall Accommodate you with Six Brass Horns, sounding the Delightful Harmony of Hunting. So hoping my Loving Masters and Ladies, Friends and acquaintance, will be pleased to honour me with their Good Company, at the Time and Place afore-said: And, as I am in Duty bound, shall ever return you thanks, and remain yours, obliged to serve you, Susana Butterfield.

It was eleven o'clock on the morning of April 26 that they left the coffee-house. He depicts the crowds moving along Cheapside. The beaux are in boots black as jet, with "Bag-gonet or short Scymitar" hanging from their belted waists; the ladies are "ty'd up in Safe-guards . . . be-Knotted with Two-penny Taffaty." "Pads, Hackneys and Hunters . . . Coaches, Carts, Waggons, and Tumblers, fill'd the Roads, as if the whole Town had been going to Encamp." At Mile-End Ward and his friend stopped at the Globe for "a Sir-Loin of Roast-Beef" and "a Flask of rare Claret." Arrived at Dame Butterfield's, Ward describes the huge crowd milling over the grounds, "Tag, Rag, and Bob-Tail, . . . Promiscu-ously jumbled amongst City Quality from Beau to Booby, and the Merchants Lady to the Thumb-Ring'd Ale-Wife." Some are dancing to bagpipes, others are sitting on the grass or on the "Horse-block," still others climb into the trees. All of them are cramming down veal and bacon. Then he turns to the kitchen "Built up of Fuzzes, in the open Air . . . where the Major part of the Calf was Roasting upon a Wooden Spit" and to the upper room in a neighboring "Out-House" where a fiddler was scraping out "Now Ponder well you Parents Dear," the country people crying and dancing to the tune.

In the succeeding numbers this liberation from the pattern of the trip brought new life to *The London Spy* and undoubtedly prolonged its popularity. The weakness of the trip was after all the weakness of any extended characterization of place. No matter how ingenious the author, there was bound to be a certain amount of repetition and sameness. The character of Man's Coffee-House was not unlike Will's and the account of Bridewell, to a degree at least, repeated the account of Bedlam. Moreover, the coffee-houses and taverns, Gresham College, and the Tower were much the same day after day, irrespective of external events. In this sense the description of events was at once more vital and immediate than the description of place. It was obviously of greater amusement to the reader to pick up the April number of *The London Spy* and read the humorous account of Madame Butterfield's house-warming than it had been in earlier numbers to follow the trip from Gresham College to Bridewell. Following hard upon the event itself, the account of the ramble to Mob's Hole caught an immediate, if momentary, interest.

In an examination of the later numbers it is evident that Ward himself realized the importance of the innovation. A large portion of part six, issued in May, he gave over to a description of May Fair. Parts ten and eleven, issued in September and October, he devoted almost entirely to a description of the annual fair beginning on the eve of St. Bartholomew's. In part twelve, issued in November, he presented an account of the opening of the King's Head Tavern at Chancery-Lane End on October 27. We may pause over the latter for a moment, since few portions of *The London Spy* present a more lively and graphic picture. Indeed the fullness of the description, as well as Ward's avowed admiration for the vintner, has at times led to the misconception among his biographers that Ward was in reality giving an account of his own tavern. There is, however, nothing in the description to warrant the assumption. Ward and his friend are in a coffee-house in Aldersgate Street when they first hear of an unusual sight to be had at the King's Head, where even at the moment a dozen cooks and "Jack-winders" are engaged

in spitting "the whole length of a Huge, Large, Long, Lincolnshire Ox," of such size that "there were no Scales at
the Customs-house, big enough to weigh it." Ward and his
friend hurry over, but the crowd witnessing the event is already overflowing into the paved yard and the street beyond.
After a struggle of some minutes they succeed in squeezing
their way into the kitchen, where the "Jack-winders" in
"Night-Caps and White Aprons" are at work. Spitting the
carcass is a task and the cooks are about to despair, when a
carpenter arrives with his mallet and with a resounding
thwack or two drives the spit through from the right buttock
to the left shoulder—the head cook strutting about "Arms
on Kimbo" crying loudly, " 'Tis Done! The mighty Deed is
done!"

It takes two days to roast the meat, however, and it is not
until Thursday morning that the opening is to be celebrated.
This time Ward and his friend arrive early, but again the
crowd is already overflowing into the yard. Drawers are
dashing about, serving the hungry guests. Bells are ringing.
The kitchen is as hot as "Guinea at Noon-day." The turning
spit is discolored with ashes and soot, "as if one Devil was
Roasting of another." The beef is excellent however—"Rich,
Fat, Young, Well-fed, Delicious." The wine, too, is extraordinarily good. From his seat in the kitchen Ward scribbles
on the wall in chalk his tribute to

> my Honest Friend Ned,
> The best of all Vintners that ever God made.[11]

In the same number (part XII) Ward gives us an excellent picture of still another contemporary event—this time
the lord mayor's day parade on November 9. Accoutered in
"Ancient Drabdeberries" against the unmannerly tricks of
the mob, Ward and his friend take their place among the
spectators at the corner of Cheapside and Blow-Bladder-
Street. The crowd is as numerous as the very "Stones of the
Street." In Cheapside, along which the parade will pass, the
balconies are hung "with Old Tapestry, and Turkey-work
Table-Cloths, for the cleanly Leaning of Ladies." Whenever
the ladies appear, however, the restless mob below pelts

them with kennel dirt until they are forced repeatedly to retreat into the rooms within, "fretting at their Dawb'd Scarfs like a Godly Old Woman that had drop'd her Bible in the Dirt." Finally the first pageant arrives. The crowd presses in. Women and children cry out for room, and Ward himself is squeezed as flat as a "Napkin in a Press."

For the pageants themselves, Ward has nothing but disdain, and though he gives a brief burlesque description of them, with plenty of diatribes at the expense of the tradesmen and city fathers, his chief interest is in the behavior of the spectators. While waiting for the successive pageants, the crowd seeks other diversion. Seizing a dead cat from the kennel, they toss it about among the spectators, crying out, "No Squibs, no Squibs." Next some ingenious tricksters, having tied a leather apron full of kennel filth and pricked it full of holes with a bodkin, toss it about, the excrement spewing out through the eyelet holes. Others take a heavy cloth a yard or more square, and dipping it into the kennel, toss it aloft, allowing it to come down over two or three heads at once, each one trapped pulling a different way to remove it. Bullocks' horns filled with kennel water circulate among the crowd, the contents poured into the pockets or down the necks of unsuspecting victims. One can see where the "Ancient Drabdeberries" may have stood Ward and his friend in good stead.

Acting as a sort of reporter at large and a commentator on local news, Ward found many other subjects ready for his facile and graphic pen. More personal and so less interesting to the modern reader, at least, is the account in part sixteen of his entertainment at dinner with two country parsons and a sharp-witted Quaker and the description of the christening ceremonies for a relative's child in part seventeen. The eighteenth and final number Ward divided between an account of the death and funeral of Dryden and a public trial between the astrologers, Partridge and Parker.

In his concern with contemporary events, as in the parts devoted to the sights, Ward illustrates the journalist's desire to interest and please. Here too, he demonstrates the dependence of the journalist for material upon the world immediately about him. Ward was, of course, far freer in the selection of his material than the writer of the contemporary periodical and newspaper. The news-writer for *The Gazette* or *The Post Boy* was held in the weekly or biweekly issue to a summary statement of events. In the partisan journals, like *The Observator* or *The Review,* the writer devoted himself to an exposition of a political view. For Ward there were no limitations other than his own interest and the entertainment of his readers. He could in a sense create, or at least uncover, as well as record the newsworthy.

From another point of view Ward was less a reporter of news than a commentator. He selected his material. He colored his presentation as he chose. The festival at Mob's Hole amused him, and the account emphasizes the color and gaiety of the occasion. The spitting and roasting of the ox at the King's Head and the free steak and excellent wine afforded the guests delighted him and he was in no sense averse to giving the vintner advantageous publicity. On the other hand, he was a genuine admirer of Dryden and the account of the latter's death is at once news and panegyric. Ward gives the details of the poet's final illness—the lameness in one of his feet from the flesh growing over one of the toenails, the mortification of the whole limb, Dryden's refusal to have the leg amputated. This he does "as a means to put the World in mind of what slender Accidents are sufficient to change the State of Man, and hurry him into the Darksome where of Eternity." Most of the account, however, is panegyrical. Even his enemies, Ward writes, "give him this Character, that he was one of the greatest Scholars, the most Correct Dramatick Poet, and the best Writer of Heroic Verse, that any Age has produced in England." The more lamentable it is, he continues, that though his merit entitled him to a most

magnificent and Solemn Interment, the Benificence of the greatest Spirits could have bestow'd on him; yet 'tis Credibly Reported the Ingratitude of the Age is such that they had like to have let him pass in private to his Grave, without those Funeral Obsequies suitable to his Greatness, had it not been for that true Brittish Worthy, [Lord Jefferies] who meeting with the Venerable Remains of the neglected Bard passing silently in a Coach unregarded to his last Home, order'd the Corps, by the Consent of his few Friends that attended him, to be Respited from so Obscure an Internment; and most Generously undertook at his own Expence to revive his Worth in the Minds of a forgetful People, by bestowing on his Peaceful Dust a Solemn Funeral answerable to his Merit.

Dryden's death had occurred on Wednesday morning, May 1. According to Malone it was on Friday that the private funeral was suspended at the request of Lord Jefferies and the Earl of Dorset, and the body removed to the College of Physicians.[12] The public ceremonies took place on the afternoon of Monday the thirteenth.

Ward gives a rather full account of the funeral. Most of the members of the nobility and gentry in town were in attendance. Solemn music preceded the famous Latin oration by Dr. Garth. The hearse drawn by "Six Stately Flanders-Horses" was adorned with "Plumes of Black Feathers, and the sides hung round with the Escutcheon of his Ancestors, mixed with that of his Lady's." Two beadles of the college "in Mourning Cloaks and Hatbands, with the Heads of their Staffs wrapt in Black Crape Scarfs," and a "Consort of Hoitboys," led the solemn procession to Westminster Abbey. Following the hearse came a long line of "quality" coaches, each drawn by six horses.

In this order the Nobility and Gentry, attended the Hearse to Westminster-Abby, where the Quire, assisted with the best Masters in England, Sung an Epicedium; and the last Funeral Rites being perform'd by one of the Prebends, he was as Honourably Inter'd between Chaucer and Cowley: Where, according to Report, will be Erected a very Stately Monument, at the Expense of some of the Nobility, in order to Recommend his Worth, and Preserve his Memory, to all succeeding Ages.

If the solemnity of the occasion in the case of Dryden's death demanded more than Ward's usual restraint, the trial between the two rival astrologers and almanac writers, with which he closed the number (part XVIII), gave him ample range for burlesque and derision. For Ward it was something of a huge joke that two astrologers who had long assured the world of their own infallibility in reading the stars should in the end have recourse to the law and moreover be doubtful of the outcome. Why had not the plaintiff consulted the heavens and known beforehand that the damages to be awarded him would be inadequate to placate his ire? And why had the defendant not known he would be adjudged guilty of libel?

As a matter of fact the antics of John Partridge and his arch rival, George Parker, had long amused London. Annually for some five years now each had called names in his ephemeris.[13] To Parker the "silly and ill-bred Buffoon John Partridge," bred to the trade of a shoemaker, was both a charlatan in his science and a traitorous dissenter. To Partridge, Parker was an ill-bred cutler who turned Quaker to secure a wife and her dowry, afterwards beat her and locked her up in a garret, and finally poisoned her with a mess of water gruel, and so turned papist again. Ward himself had a year earlier made capital of the quarrel, when in the spring of 1699 he had published *The World Bewitched, a Dialogue between two Astrologers and the Author*. Now, however, Partridge was suing Parker for damages "for the Loss," as Ward puts it, "of a Good Name which he never Enjoyed."

That the entire quarrel had contributed greatly to the amusement of the public is indicated by the notice of the trial appearing in *The Post Boy*,[14] Ward's own warrant for attending:

This Week commences a Tryal at Guild-Hall, between Partridge the Almanack-maker, and Parker, the Astrologer; the first is the Plaintiff: He brings Action for 1000 £. against the other, for Printing in his Ephemeris this Year, That He's a Rebel in his Principles; an Enemy to Monarchy; Ungrateful to his Friend; a Scoundrel in his Conversation; a Malignant in his Writings; a Lyer in his Almanack; and a Fool of an Astrologer. Tho' they are great Men in the way of Predictions, they can't tell how the Cause will go. We hear the polite Gipsies, alias Judicial Fortune-tellers, lay great Wagers on both sides.

Ward's account of the trial at the King's Bench Bar is lively and graphic. All of the "Fortune-Telling Wise-Acres" in town from all "the By-Allies in More-Fields, White-Chappel, Salisbury-Court, Water-Lane, Fleet-Street, and Westminster" were in attendance. The learned "Councel were Conning over the Almanacks," themselves amused by the vituperative powers of their clients. Well-wishers and amuse-

PRISON SCENE

From an engraving by Hogarth

ment seekers were there in abundance anticipating unusual diversion. Unfortunately before the trial was actually called, the two opponents, "thro' the Prudence of some Friend or other, who was willing to prevent their being farther expos'd" agreed to "terms of Accommodation" and temporarily, at least, the fun was spoiled.

Partridge and Parker, however, failing to agree "for want of an Umpire, which the Plaintiff would not admit of," the trial was called for the next sitting, and Ward once more took himself to the Guildhall. It was eleven at night when the case was called "with the Moon and Stars . . . in their greatest Glory." The situation permitted some of Ward's more admirable fooling:

The plaintiff Erecting a Scheme a little before Tryal, found by the Position of the Heavens, the Judge would be the Lord Ascendant in the matter, and that the Jury were the Twelve Signs, towards which, the Planets of the Law, the Councel, were to direct their Influence, and accordingly took care to secure, by the Interests of Sol, the very Mars and Mercury of the Laws, to give his Cause their Assistance, whilst the Defendant had engag'd none but Saturn on his part to bid Defiance to his Adversary.

After all this preliminary build-up the trial itself was a disappointment, since the lateness of the night and the weariness of the counsel precluded much of the diversion expected. In half an hour's time, Ward says, from the beginning of the debate, the business was brought to a conclusion, mutually disappointing to both clients, for alas, Partridge was actually awarded five pounds "for the great Abuses he had Honestly deserved by a just Provocation."

As a reporter and commentator upon public events Ward's chief asset was his ability to amuse. His account of events, as his characterization of place, for the most part emphasized the ludicrous and the droll, presenting in his colloquial and racy language an animated and lively picture. He made no attempt, as the later literary essayists did, to give direction to the ideas and tastes of his readers. He did not, as did Addison and Steele, turn his periodical into an instrument for the edification or improvement of the social group. In so far, however, as the emphasis in the later numbers shifted from place to event *The London Spy* became less and less a treatise on the city and more and more a monthly literary journal, and it is in this respect that its pages are a forerunner of the *Tatler* and *Spectator*.

In still another way the eighteen numbers of *The London Spy* point toward the later periodical journal. From the earliest number, Ward had frequently resorted to the composition of doggerel and the writing of characters as padding. Had either of these been allowed to assume a primary role or been held less rigidly subject to the basic material of the trip or the event, *The London Spy* itself might have assumed more nearly the nature of a poetical miscellany or a later periodical journal devoted to character writing. As it was, the very heterogeneity of the material may perhaps have helped to pave the way for the greater flexibility in content and matter of the literary journal.

The verse itself demands little consideration and remains essentially extraneous. The characters, on the other hand, add color and life to the pages and are on the whole integral to the subject material. They divide rather easily into two groups. To the first belong the comparatively brief and casual portraits of the men and women with whom Ward must actually have rubbed elbows in the coffee-houses and taverns as he went about gathering his material. To the second belong the full-length delineations of character types, which he occasionally inserted in the earlier numbers and to which he devoted part fifteen in its entirety.

Of the two groups the first was, of course, more apropos both to Ward's method and his material. As an example of his ability to characterize the behavior and costume of the individual with whom he came in contact we may take his account in part one of the guests at the dinner to which his friend invited him upon his arrival in town. There was, for instance, "the Gentleman in a Blew Coat, Red Stockins, Silver-hilted Sword, and Edg'd Hat," who sat at the upper end of the table. A "Sword-Hilt-Maker" by trade, he had by his ingenious use of tools become an engraver of medals and stamps, now able to keep his "Brace of Geldings," and to live at the rate of "a Thousand Pounds a Year." Next to him sat a young fellow, formerly apprenticed to a wine-cooper, who owing to the favors of the employer's wife could now wear "a Wheel-Barrow full of Periwig" and "stunk as strong of Orange-Flower-Water as a Spaniard does of Garlick." A third guest, "a Demure Spark, in a Diminutive Cravat, and Fox-colour'd Wig, with a Hat as broad as an Umbrella," was a "Cadator," an "Incomparable Herauld" who could not only give you an "exact Genealogy of most good Families in England" but who has the "Art of making himself a Kin, when he sees it convenient." Still another of the party was a highwayman with "a great Scar across his Forehead, a twisted Wig, and lac'd Hat " who, pretending he was a disbanded soldier, railed mightily at the injustice of being turned off without consideration and so earned for himself the sobriquet of captain among his associates.

More common in *The London Spy* than the individual portraits, however, are the characterizations of types and professions. Many of them, indeed, are not full-length characters, as a complete adherence to the genre would have required, but mere cursory remarks appropriately woven into the general account. In the seventh number, for instance, when the journey has arrived at the Temple, Ward briefly describes the gamesters who set themselves up with "False Dice, and a Pack of Mark'd Cards"; the "Mask'd Ladies, with rumpled Hoods and Scarfs, their hands charg'd with Papers, Band-Boxes, and Rowls of Parchment" who slip in and out of the stairways; the solicitors, "a kind of Hangers-on, upon the Warden of the Fleet" willing to witness in any case whatsoever for a consideration. In the eighth number, with the journey at Westminster, it is the pettifoggers who are the subject of attack, those who set people together by the ears and at the same time solicit the law to make an end of the difference, who call "every Body Fool that pays a Debt till he has forc'd the Creditor to prove it" in court, who call the "Tricks and Quirks" the cunning part of the law. In the same number he continues with a character of the foot soldier "who for the sake of wearing a Sword, and the Honour of being term'd a Gentleman, is Coax'd from a Handicraft Trade, whereby he might Live Comfortably, to bear Arms, for his King and Country, whereby he has the hopes of nothing but to live Starvingly." In the fourteenth number he describes the sailors in Wapping, "so Mercurial in their Actions, and Rude in their Behaviour" that no woman can pass them on the street without being seized and kissed, and quarreling among themselves as to who should be first.

Every Post they came next was in danger of having its Head broke; for every one as he pass'd by, would give the Senseless Block a Bang with his Cudgel, as if they wish'd every Post they met to be either the Purser or the Boatswain. The very Dogs in the Street, I observ'd, shun'd 'em with as much Fear as a Loitering Vagabond wou'd a Gang of Press-Masters.

Among the few full-length characters Ward inserts in the early numbers of *The London Spy* is that of the "Horse-Mountebank" in part six. Even here he makes an effort to introduce the character dramatically by having him ride his halting Pegasus into the midst of a crowd gathered among the movable shops of Fleet Bridge to witness a scuffle between two angry and embattled gossips. The reader cannot but feel, however, that the presentation is an intrusion into the main account, though the character itself is not uninteresting in Ward's burlesque imitation of the mountebank's harangue. "In the first place, Gentlemen," the mounted apothecary cries,

I here present you with a little inconsiderable Pill to look at, you see not much bigger than a Corn of Pepper, . . . yet . . . of such Excellent Vertues, that if you have Twenty Distempers lurking in the Mass of Blood, it shall give you just Twenty Stools, and every time it Operates it carries off a Distemper; but if your Blood's Wholesome, and your Body Sound, it will Work with you no more than the same quantity of Ginger-Bread. . . . In the next place, Gentlemen, I present you with an excellent outward Application, call'd a Plaister; good against all Green Wounds, Old Fistula's and Ulcers, Pains and Achs, in either Head, Limbs, or Bowels, Contusions, Tumours, or Queens-Evil, Sprains, Fractures, or Dislocations, or any Hurts whatsoever, receiv'd either by Sword, Cane, or Gun-shot, Knife, Saw, or Hatchet, Hammer, Nail or Tenter-hook, Fire, Blast, or Gunpowder.

And so on and on, for in this case Ward allows the character to do his own portrait, adding only at the conclusion of the scene,

Is it not a Shame to our English Physicians to suffer such a parcel of Ignorant, Illiterate, and Impudent Vagabonds to Cozen Poor Innocent Wretches out of their Money Publickly in the Streets, who want it themselves to purchase Bread and Necessaries?

It was a shame, of course, and still is—though the modern mountebank rides a less halting Pegasus.

It is in the fifteenth part that Ward, having apparently run short of journey material, turns to the full-length character for an entire number. Hereafter, he writes, he will "Treat more upon Men and Manners; opening the Frauds and Deceits practicable in many Trades." In view of the fact that earlier editors have always associated Ward with the King's Head Tavern, it is interesting to note that the first trade held up to scorn is that of the victualers. Most of them, Ward would have us believe, were in the beginning no more than broken tradesmen whom the parish or precinct allowed to set up as alehouse keepers in order to avoid the necessity of granting them charity. Once established as an alehouse keeper, the tradesman soon becomes known to the community as Captain Rusty, Doctor Grunt, or Alderman Snarl, and his wife perhaps as Mother Huff, Goody Blowze, or Gammer Tattle. That is distinctly a sign of their rise in the world. A third advancement is marked by the victualer's election to a petty office in the parish, from which he gradually rises to the position of church-warden and is entitled to pass the money box in church, then to the title of mister. With his new dignities he becomes too proud for his own ware, now drinks at a tavern himself, lolls at the door of his house, and swings his "Bunch of little Keys half a dozen times round his Finger, before he will answer a poor Neighbour a Civil Question." "There are three sorts of Victualers," Ward continues,

all differing very much from each other, according to the several parts of the Town wherein they are Situated. At Wapping, and that way, they Lord it over the People like a Boatswain over a Ships Company; . . . In the City he is Hail Fellow well met with any of his Customers on this side a Common Council-man; but to all above, he is forced to pay a difference, and bow as low to the Deputy of a Ward, as a Country Inn-Keeper does to the Sheriff of a County. And at Charing-Cross, you may find 'em so very humble and obliging for every two-pence they

take, that a Gentleman Foot Soldier, or a Lords Footman, shall have as
many Bows and Cringes from the Master and his Family over the Drinking of a Pot, as a French Dancing Master shall give the Mistress of a
Boarding-School, when she gives him half a piece for his Days Teaching.

Through with the victualers, Ward turns to the reforming
constable and to the astrologers and wisewomen, whom he
heartily hates and about whom he relates several stories
which he asserts he can vouch for as truth, since they came
from persons of his own acquaintance.

Though the devotion of the entire number to characters
was not successful and Ward returns to the journey and contemporary event in the following numbers, he continues to
use the inserted character to the end. In part sixteen he includes the characters of a "Master of a Vessel," the "Stock-
Jobbers at Jonathans," an Irishman, a "Modish Lady," and
a banker. In the seventeenth part, having attended a christening, he concludes with the character of a gossip. Into the
eighteenth he inserts those of a prize-fighter and an astrologer.

Of the important factors in *The London Spy* the verses
and characters are the least satisfactory and significant. The
former are never more than padding; the latter, as they tend
towards portraiture or as they supplement the characterization of place, become an integral part of the narrative, but
the full-length characters, except in part fifteen where they
dominate the entire number, detract from the whole.

In one respect, however, the characters in *The London Spy*
exhibit an interesting method of presentation, widely exploited later on by Ward and other journalists. As we shall
presently see, the great concern of the journalist was to liber-
ate the form from the necessity of being presented in a
formal series of delineations devoid of setting or dialogue. In
the pages of *The London Spy* Ward had found a method of
vitalizing the character by means of a dramatic introduction
and accompanying narrative, by the provision of appropriate
scene and an adequate colloquy. Ward himself later, as well
as men like Addison and Steele, was to turn the experience
to account.

III

Of first importance in any final consideration of *The London Spy* is the emphasis upon locale. Indeed, it is not too much to say that Ward discovered the city of London for the journalist. Other writers, Elizabethan and later, satirists, authors of topical verse, and writers of characters, particularly as the latter began to include institutions as well as men, had frequently selected for treatment certain features of the life of the city. On the more formal side, too, there had been recurring "histories," and "annuals," and surveys, in the enumerative and statistical manner of Stow. Never before, however, had the sights of the city, the milieu and its inhabitants, been the subject of a similar study. The periodical literature of the day had concerned itself primarily with the news or with current political and religious issues. The travel literature up to the moment had focused its attention upon the unusual and the far away place. Suddenly here the traveler was at home, seeing his own city. He could himself recognize the description, or by an afternoon's excursion verify the account. He saw the names of the places he knew and the streets he walked, in print. Mirrored in the pages of *The London Spy* he saw certain aspects of his own life to which he had hitherto been oblivious. If the experience was not entirely an estimable one it still served the purpose of focusing his attention upon his own environment and of preparing the way for a literature dealing with the realities of his own world. Certainly in Ward's emphasis upon the local scene and his essential concern with the activities of the ordinary man he pointed the way, not only for the later journalists, but for the novelists as well.

On the other hand, one can readily see that Ward could not have continued *The London Spy* indefinitely. Its weakness lay in its essentially indeterminate character. The project began as a trip, though the interlarding of verse, personal anecdote, and character almost from the first served to obscure its basic pattern. Even had the trip remained its dominant feature, however, the life of the periodical would have been limited. The sights of the city are not innumerable, and its taverns and streets from end to end are strangely similar. As a periodical concerned with the events of the day, playing an intermediary role between the more formal accounts in *The Flying Post* or *The Post Boy* and the intimate informal commentary of the *Tatler* and *Spectator,* the pages of *The London Spy* lack essential purpose and direction. It is enough for the journalist merely to amuse his readers; the difficulty is that the appetite fed on amusement alone is soon satiated.

At the moment, of course, Ward had no thought of writing for posterity, but by one of those curious quirks of time the pages of *The London Spy,* properly ephemeral in their own day, have become for later generations an interesting, if not invaluable, record. To know a city in its earlier era is to know more than its institutions, its buildings, and its environs; it is to know the conduct, the attitudes, and the life of its citizenry. For a measure of the former, annals, surveys, and maps are invaluable, but the latter is more apt to be found in the informal chronicle, where men walk the streets or loiter in the coffee-houses. It is true that Ward's account is needlessly vulgar. It is equally true that the flippancy of his style and the constant search for the amusing conceit led to occasional distortion. But for the most part Ward wrote down what he saw, and if at times he did not see too deeply into the life either of institutions or men, he could still characterize their exterior with an unerring pencil. *"The London Spy* is, undoubtedly Ward's masterpiece," writes Charles Whibley, "After two centuries, it still keeps the fresh stamp of truth." [15]

IV

Debtors' Prison and Holiday

What Ways, thought I, do humane Race Devise,
To gratify their Ease and Avarice!
The Field Spy (1714)

B Y 1700 Ward himself must frequently have been surprised by the abundance of his own material. Under the impetus of his successful trips and the growing popularity of the monthly parts of *The London Spy* he continued to utilize the burlesque characterization of place. Steadily, month after month, he brought out new pamphlets and broadsides. Not all of them—as we shall see later—were cast in the pattern of *A Trip to Jamaica,* though it continued to be by far his most successful medium. Many of them, too, were ephemeral enough, meant to catch but a momentary interest, and they remain today of questionable value. Sometimes, as in the case of *The Rambling Rakes, or the London Libertines* (1700) and *Three Nights' Adventures, or Accidental Intrigues* (1701), they are no more than a salacious account of amorous adventure, stories suggestive of late hours over the tavern punch bowl. To accept them at face value would have been for his readers to assume that London was populated only with libertines and strumpets. They represent Ward's most slavish attempts at catering to the baser tastes of his public. At other times, however, as in the case of *The Dancing School, with the Adventures of the Easter Holydays* (1700), the salacity is mitigated by the portrayal of an early eighteenth-century institution universally patronized and approved; and the account of Beveridge's contributes definitely to our understanding of London life. So, in a fuller measure, do those items where the interest centers on an institution of historical note, as in the case of *The Meta-morphos'd Beau, or the Intrigues of Ludgate* (1700), a trip in which Ward presented his readers with an intimate glimpse of the interior of the famous prison.

"What we have not seen," writes Sir Walter Besant after he has presented the reader with his account of the buildings of Ludgate and the organization of the prison,

is the crowded bedroom, with the prisoners lying about in rags between the beds; the noisesomeness of the prison; the dirt and the noise and the stench of it; the drinking whenever there was any money; the idleness; the frying and boiling over the fire all day long; the wretchedness of some, the recklessness of others, the hopelessness of all; and for those who had neither money nor work, the pangs of hunger and the debility and low vitality of the half-starved.[1]

And it is just that, that *The Metamorphos'd Beau* rather adequately supplies; though in some respects the presentation is in lighter colors than Besant's humanitarianism might have approved, for it would be difficult to find a more real-istic and impartial account of the conditions of the prison and the attitude of the average man towards the institution than that hidden beneath the involutions of Ward's style.

In pattern *The Metamorphos'd Beau* might well have been an extension of *The London Spy* or included as one of the monthly parts. Ward employs almost exactly the same tech-nique: the narration of a personal experience, interlarded with anecdote and surprisingly detailed observation, related to his readers in the disarming innocency of a loquacious pedestrian.

Ward begins by assuring his readers that the visit was quite accidental. He had been drinking healths in the cabin of the *Royal Britannia* with an old seafaring friend, who was anx-ious after his long voyage to ogle the ladies of St. Paul's. Pro-ceeding down Fleet Street, they quite by chance encounter one of the guards of Ludgate at whose suggestion they decide to forego the ladies of St. Paul's for a visit to the famous prison—after all who knows what old acquaintance they might find there buried in oblivion. Having made their de-cision, they approach the postern lined with guards, and their guide, Bulldog, shouting loudly to the turnkey, gets them promptly admitted. To the right as they enter is a reception room for visitors, but the travelers turn left to a large hall designated as the "Rules" room. Here a dozen or so of the inmates are engaged in a game of cards, with the stakes a cup of "Sir John Parsons."

In another room, designated as the "Lumbry," or "Lumbree," poor men from the charity ward are standing at the grated window, begging-boxes in hand. All day long they beseech the passers-by on the street outside, "Pray remember the poor Prisoners. The Lord in Heaven Bless you, Remember the Poor Prisoners. A great Number of poor Tradesmen, and Women, Confin'd for Debt: Good Christian People, bestow your Charity on the Poor Prisoners." A generous citizen passes by, "The Lord in Heaven Bless you, Sir. The Lord Jesus Christ reward you, Sir. Christ Bless you, Sweet Lady." Three times a day in this same room under a full assemblage of the ragged mob the boxes are checked by the steward, and the profits divided.[2] One-fourth of the taking goes to the beggar and three-fourths to the general account of the ward. It is in the "Lumbry," too, that the general election takes place monthly. Here the steward himself is elected from among their own number by the prisoners;[3] here rules are made and enforced by the inmates. Here, too, on Sunday the "Kettlepot" boils the weekly stipend of chumps donated by the Butchers' Company to the poor men in the charity ward.

As the visitors again enter the corridor from the "Lumbry" room, a score of prisoners hurtle downstairs with two of their fellows in tow. There is much shuffling and shouting. "Open the Nut-Crackers! Open the Stocks!" And a moment later Ward and his friend observe the mob visiting justice upon the offenders.

Next the visitors inspect the Lower Ward, characterized by their guide as the most comfortable one in the prison. Here beds and clean linen, as well as conveniences for dressing meat, are available to those who have money to pay for them.[4] On the master's side up one flight of stairs is the Chapel Ward, so called from its proximity to the prison chapel, the latter "very Decent and Handsome beyond our Expectation." Up another stairway they enter the Charity

Ward, a long, dark room without chimney for either cooking or warmth, where the majority of the prison's inmates are crowded at night and lie shuddering on the cold floor in their rags. Here each newcomer, Ward tells us, is informed of the presence of a tyrannical "Monsieur Shawny" who demands of each novitiate an eighteen pence fee for floorage. A mythical personage invented by the prisoners, he could nevertheless, in case the fee were not immediately forthcoming, assume a reality sufficient to steal the coat, waistcoat, or stockings of one who slept on the floor.

On the top floor Ward finds a handicraft room (abandoned according to Besant by 1710) more "Lightsome" and with a good "Prospect from the Window over St. Georges-Fields." Here "Joseph the Carpenter" and "Stitch the Taylor" are hard at work, like so many "Faries." Next to the room is the prison seraglio, a lockup for the infirm and feeble-minded, where they find an old matron "Chain'd by the Leg and Hand-Cufft" in a room whose stench is sufficient to demand the "Essence Bottles" of the guests.

Ascending to the "Leads" on the roof of the prison, they find some young men at ninepins, and others viewing the adjacent villages and the distant Thames. To Ward's surprise among them is an old friend, a Mr. M——, known both to him and his seafaring friend Harry. After mutual exclamations and embraces, the visitors dismiss Bulldog and Mr. M—— assumes the role of guide and host. The party now moves off to the private wards, where the individual chambers "were pretty tollerable, bating the Sash-windows," some men having their own furniture "handsome and genteel," and "quart Pots with Lids to them, and Dishes that bore 'em Company," a proof "that good living was no Stranger there."

The greatest single attraction of the prison, Ward and his friend have still to see, and the party adjourns downstairs to the drinking room in the cellar. As they leave the private ward a bell is rung loudly, and they hear the cryer announce search for a man missing from his habitation since yesterday at five o'clock in the afternoon. The visitors proceed. Down a steep and narrow stairway—which Ward comments on as contradictory to the Biblical broadway that leads to destruction—they enter a veritable "Sodom," dark, dampish, crowded, stinking, and noisy. Much shouting and quarreling is going on among the prisoners. An old weather-beaten fellow in a ragged gown is droning out a melancholy song of old King Lud. Another raps out an oath at him. The old man replies he has "born all the Offices of the House," and is the senior of his ward. One rails at the hostess for continually overscoring and never quite filling his pot when she serves him.

What the Devil do you mean? Do you think I was born Yesterday? . . . S'Blood I can prove you have got four Shillings, and a Meal for you and your Husband, by an Apple-Pye that stood you but in two, and yet all this is nothing.

Over in a corner a fight breaks out between one "Bloody Nose" and another blade, designated as the "Lover," over the affection of a brazen hussy in a "red Top-knot." Oaths are followed by blows. The prisoners shout and huzza. Just as the confusion reaches its height, the watch arrives, calling orders for strangers to depart. Ward and his friend, Harry, take leave of Mr. M——, who, still hoping for a day of redemption, seems jolly enough at the moment.

Though Ward ends on a note of pathos and leaves the impression with his readers that he was somewhat saddened by the fate of his friend, the account is in no sense severely critical of the conditions in the prison. Elsewhere he has spoken out boldly against the injustice of a law which penalizes a man for debt and at the same time denies him the opportunity of discharging his obligation and freeing himself of the penalty.[5] Even in *The Metamorphos'd Beau,* of course, he attacks the exorbitant fees demanded of the prisoners, and certainly no aspect of the eighteenth-century prison was as vicious as that of farming out the management to unscrupulous knaves and scoundrels.

On the whole, however, the picture is drawn lightly. Ludgate was one of the better prisons. Ward's primary purpose at the moment was to interest his readers, not to arouse them. A certain immunity to poverty and brutality undoubtedly accompanies too close an association with both. Ward saw the prison, one suspects, quite as many of his contemporaries saw it. It was an evil institution, corrupt in its administration, and needlessly brutal and unsanitary. But so, unfortunately, was much of the world outside the prison. Ward, too, had once faced the danger of imprisonment for debt.[6] At the moment he was getting along. Having promised to see his friend again, he concludes his sketch by quoting from *Hamlet.*

> Then let the stricken Deer go Weep,
> The Hart Ungall'd go Play;
> For some must Watch, while some do Sleep;
> Thus runs the World away.

Ward in his account of Ludgate, much as in that of Bedlam, presented his readers with one of the grimmer sides of London life; in many of the trips written during the years 1699 to 1700 he was content, as he had been earlier, with depicting its more pleasant aspects. At the turn of the seventeenth century the recreational and workaday worlds were curiously interwoven. Much of the business of the city was carried on in coffee-houses and taverns. Much of the produce of the entire country was marketed at fairs. In London a morning at Change was regularly interrupted for a dish of coffee at Jonathan's. In the evening the citizenry gathered at the coffee-houses and taverns, the apprentices played football in the streets, the more fashionable literati and the beaux foregathered at the theatre. During the summer on every Sunday and holiday crowds streamed out of the city to the watering places or plied up and down the Thames on numerous excursions. In the winter the same crowds thronged the music houses and bear-baitings, the gambling dens and the lotteries.

The amusements of Londoners had, of course, been a traditional subject of satire for centuries, and in Ward's own day the characters, the topographical poems, the journeys in verse and prose, the songs and ballads, devoted to the characterization of Hampton Court, Islington Wells, and the many spas and fairs at which the Londoner idled away his summer, are almost innumerable. Ward's contribution to the

about-town-and-amusement literature lay in his adaptation
of the subject materials to the basic pattern of the trip. For
him—at least so it appeared to the reader—it was the relation of a personal experience, and the narrative element almost always dominates the more formal characterization of
place. Ward's accounts are at once more detailed, more intimate, more chatty and informal, than the rigors of verse or
the demands of more formal satire would have allowed.
It is in this respect that they are more readable, more graphic
and exciting, and deserve in a degree the success which attended their publication.

Two localities in and about London to which Ward devoted individual trips are those of Deptford, Greenwich, and
Charlton at the time of the annual fair, and Islington or
New Tunbridge Wells. The latter had been discovered by
Sadler in 1683 and designated as *New* Tunbridge Wells in
deference to the famous wells in Kent. By 1699 they had
become a popular watering place much patronized by the
citizens of London and already the subject of numerous
satiric attacks.[7] Ward's *A Walk to Islington, with a Description of New-Tunbridge-Wells and Sadlers Musick-House* is
really not a trip, but a verse satire in which he describes an
afternoon's sojourn there in the company of a young woman
from London. It will serve to show how closely the burlesque characterization of place in the trips is related to the
current satiric topographical poem. On the other hand *A
Walk to Islington* possesses many of the characteristic features of the trip: the dominance of the narrative element,
the minuteness of detail, and the informality of the account,
particularly at moments in which Ward emphasizes the narrator's acquaintance with people described.

According to Ward the entrance fee was threepence a
person. Beyond the gate were walks bordered by lime trees
and benches to accommodate the strollers, outhouses for
lotteries and raffling, booths for coffee-drinking and back-
gammon, and a large shed to accommodate the dancers. All
of London seems to have had representation in the hetero-
geneous crowd. There were beautiful ladies in satin gowns

and headdresses of lace with dancing-school manners, shop-girls from Change, courtesans arrayed in old remnants collected from brokers, bewigged beaux whose shoulders were as white from the powder as those of a barber, sharpers with cards in one pocket and false dice in the other, apprentices who sought only the accomplishments of dancing and singing, and, as Ward asserts, mistook lewdness for wit.

When Ward and his companion become hungry, they enter Sadler's Music House for cheesecakes and custard. From the security of the crowded gallery they gaze at the dancers below—bullies, bailiffs, prizefighters, sweetners, shop girls, and strumpets. Drawers are dashing hither and yon, crying "Coming, sir! Coming." A lone fiddler scrapes out a tune. An impertinent young miss of fourteen does a sword dance. A clown by the name of Thomas, whom Ward recognizes as a former acquaintance, entertains the crowd with jugglings and contortions.

Of the two items under discussion at the moment, however, *A Frolick to Horn-Fair, with a Walk from Cuckold's Point through Deptford and Greenwich* is the more interesting and largely so because of the greater amount of personal narrative. Horn Fair, so-called according to Philipott "by reason of the great plenty of all sorts of winding horns and cups, and other vessels of horn there bought and sold," [8] was held annually on the eighteenth of October, and in Ward's day it was still customary for Londoners to celebrate it by a burlesque procession proceeding by water to Greenwich, thence overland through Deptford to Charlton. Accordingly on the morning of the eighteenth Ward and a companion—this time a married woman of the town who had invited him, he would have us believe—repair to the Mermaid Tavern in Billingsgate, where they fortify themselves against the coolness of the trip by water with a dish of fish and a drink of canary. From the tavern window they observe the crowd. Citizens and their mistresses swarm near the waterside. Watermen wrangle for their fares. Apprentices and shop girls stow "themselves as close in a Boat together, as they do in a Cheap-side Ballcony, at my Lord-Mayors-Show." On the water is an "Innumberable Fleet of Oares, Skullers,

Barges, Cock-boats, Bum-Boats, Pinnaces and Yawles, some Going, some Coming."

When Ward and his companion join the crowd and embark on the river, their boat immediately becomes engaged in the customary hallooing and interchange of watermen's billingsgate. Ladles seem to have been standard equipment for the fair and were now put to use by those in the boats, who tossed ladles full of water at one another "till the Passengers were many of 'em as wet, as a Turbulent Woman just taken out of the Ducking-Stool." "I wonder," asks Ward's companion, "the Magistrates of the City do not take some care to prevent these sad Abuses upon the Water; for 'tis a shameful thing that Civil People should be call'd thus out of their Names." "Prithee," Ward replies, "never mind 'em; for if my Lord M[ayor] were here himself, they'd be as ready to call him Cuckold as they would any body else; and he would not know which way to help himself, but must put it up as we do, there's no Remedy."

The boats discharge their passengers at Cuckold's Point, but before Ward and his companion begin the walk through the fields to Deptford, they warm themselves at the ancient tavern, where in former days,

the Troop of Merry Cuckolds us'd to Rendesvouz; Arm'd with Shovel, Spade, or Pick-ax; their Heads adorn'd with Horned Helmets; and from thence to March, in Order, for Horn-Fair, Leveling the Way as they go, according to the Command of their Leaders, that their Wives might come after with their Gallants, without spoiling their Lac'd Shooes, or dragling their Holiday Petticoates.

As a good journalist Ward has the hostess of the tavern conveniently relate a risqué story concerning the origin of the fair. In King John's time, so the story ran, a water mill stood where the house now stands. The king, often coming to hunt there, took a fancy to the miller's wife and once in the midst of an amour was surprised by the angry husband, who feigning not to recognize his royal guest, threatened to throw him into the millpond. To procure his release the king promised to the miller a grant of all the land he could see from the window, providing that once a year on the eighteenth of October he walk to the farthest boundary of his estate with a pair of "Buck-Horns on his Head, attended with all his Family." Washing his eyes carefully, the miller looked hard and saw all the way to Charlton Hill. "With this piece of History," Ward continues,

we were mightly please'd, the Woman herself showing a great deal of Zeal in the belief of the same; which indeed I swallow'd without Chewing, as the Mob does the Political Reports of State, or an Ignorant Congregation does the Hum-Drum Doctrine of a Dark Priest.

Ward and his companion elect as a route from Cuckold's Point to Deptford to go by the way of "New-Dock," currently much on the tongue of Londoners. Passing by "a long Range of little Cottages, at the Doors of which sat abundance of Dutch-Buttock'd Lasses, with Sea Handkerchiefs about their Pouting Bubbies, . . . some Knitting, some Spinning, and others picking Okum," they arrive at the dock "reported by Competent Judges to be able to receive 200 sail of Large Ships." Beyond the dock in the open fields are a group of West-Indian Creolians cooking a porker over an open fire. Deptford itself is a village of wood houses all in one mold, as if by an act of parliament. Pretty women, wives and sweethearts of mariners who have gone away to the East Indies, are standing in the doorways and at the windows. Shops open into the street, "but a Brandy-Bottle, and a Quartern, a Botcher mending of a Canvas Doublet, a few Apples in a Cabbage-Net, a Peel-full of Deptford Cheese-cakes, an Old Waste-Coat, a Thrum-Cap, and a pair of Yarn Mittings" are the "Chief Shows that they made of their Commodities." At the upper end of the town is the famous hospital erected for decayed masters and their widows by Trinity House, "very Pleasant and Commodious as to the Building and Situation," but rather to be dubbed "Pinch-Gut-Colledge, than an Hospital," since the poor pensioners on the miserly allowance of twelve shillings per month are required to find "Meat, Drink, Washing, Fire, Cloths, and all the Necessaries of Life." [9]

Crossing through the fields to Greenwich, Ward and his companion encounter numerous knots of London apprentices still armed with ladles—the latter now serving as weapons of offense, a knock on the elbow of an unsuspecting bystander being the chief diversion of the crowd. At Greenwich the fair is in full progress. Ward has, however, remarkably little to say about it, and nothing at all complimentary. Held near the church and begun by a sermon, it was still the rudest fair in all England. For sale were chiefly shoes, pattens, leather breeches, horn tops, and baubles. "Every Fool was become a Tom-Ladle," he writes, and on the heath beyond the actual fair itself "every Bush was made a Fence to a Furmity-Kettle." A favorite rendezvous for the mob from Spitalfields and Clare Market, the fair swarmed with beggars and thieves. " 'Tis a Sanctuary for Ill Manners," he concludes, "a Protection of all Rudeness, an Encouragement to Wickedness, a Revelling of young Libertines, a Looking-glass of Confusion, hurtful to good Manners, and hateful to all Good Men."

II

Few trips written during the years under consideration possess greater interest for the modern reader than *A Step to Stir-Bitch-Fair, with Remarks upon the University of Cambridge* and *A Step to the Bath, with a Character of the Place,* since both of them deal with subjects rarely treated in the journalistic literature of the day. The former is only one of Ward's numerous contributions to the literature on fairs, but is the only one devoted to a rural rather than a metropolitan fair. In part seven of *The London Spy,* for instance, Ward had supplied his readers with an account of an afternoon's visit to May Fair. In parts ten and eleven he had devoted some sixteen folio pages to a description of the larger and more important St. Bartholomew's Fair, a subject to which he returned for a somewhat lengthy description in one of his later political poems, *Hudibras Redivivus, or a Burlesque Poem on the Times.*

It may be well to remember that by 1700 the fairs—metropolitan and rural alike—had lost much of their mercantile character. At May Fair, so called because it was held annually from the first to the sixteenth of the month, the first three days were given over to the selling of cattle and leather but the remaining thirteen were devoted exclusively to drolls, puppet shows, and lotteries.[10] At Bartholomew Fair much the same thing had taken place. Though the original charter had called for a fair of three days devoted to "the Sale of Live Cattle, Leather, and other Wares and Merchandise," the time had been extended after the Restoration to a period of fourteen days, "a season," to quote from a contemporary account,[11] "of the utmost Disorder and Debauchery, by reason of the Booths for Drinking, Music, Dancing, Stage-plays, Drolls, Lotteries, Gaming, Raffling, and what not." Even a fair devoted to the produce of its own district, such as the hop fair at Sturbridge, had its accompanying carnival, its sutlers' booths, its drinking dens, its raffling and gambling quarters.

It is true that the contemporary accounts were written for the most part by satirists,[12] whose business it was to dwell upon the vices and iniquities, or at least upon the fair's more picturesque and licentious aspects. For contemporary records, other than those of the satirists, one must turn to the handbills advertising the sights and amusements,[13] or to the denunciations and petitions to civic authority on the part of those who sought the curtailment or suppression of the fairs. In all cases the evidence is in substantial agreement. The fairs had to a degree become hotbeds of thieving and gaming, of lewdness and debauchery. Music houses, boozing-kens, puppet-shows, drolls, "Flying Chariots," rope-dancers, and the exhibition of monstrosities had choked out the earlier exchange.

If the writers are almost unanimous in their condemnation, however, there is abundant evidence that much of the London citizenry did not share in the view, for few events in the city were more ardently attended. With the arrival of the twenty-third of August the entire city seems to have turned to Bartholomew Fair. The theaters in the city were closed, the actors having "translated" themselves to their booths at the fair. Barkers and the distributors of handbills cried the sights of the fair through the city. Hackney coaches and chairs did a thriving business carrying citizens to and from Smithfield. The apprentices crowded thither in droves. Beaux and fine ladies in damask and laces mingled with footmen and the strumpets from the city. Coarse sailors and drovers gambled with city butchers and tailors. Members of the nobility attended on occasion, and in 1717 the royal prince is reputed to have gone to Southwark Fair incognito.[14] Indeed it is doubtful if any factor played a more important role in attracting visitors to the fair than the visitors themselves. The infectious atmosphere of a crowd, the excitement of hundreds bent on holiday, the fever of promiscuous intermingling and interchange were alone sufficient inducement.

Of the rural fairs in England none was more widely known or more frequently attended by Londoners than the great hop fair of Sturbridge, held annually from August 24 to September 29 in an open field near Barnwell Abbey, two miles east of the university town of Cambridge.[15] On the east side of the open fields ran the river Stour, from which the fair took its name. The northern extremities were bounded by the river Cam. For a full month at the end of each summer the cornfields lying within the angle created by the rivers were covered with acres of hops, hundreds of bales of wool, pens of cattle, and great piles of skins and leather. Nearer the river the traders and professional entertainers from London pitched their booths.

For in the latter respect Sturbridge, in spite of its center in trade, was not unlike Bartholomew. Following the brewers, the wool merchants, and the leather-dealers from London had come the goldsmiths and booksellers, the braziers and pewterers, the milliners and hatters, the mercers and drapers. In the wake of trade had come the sutlers, the music houses, the puppet-shows, and the drolls. With the amusements came the hangers-on, the sharpers and gamesters, the strumpets and trulls. Then Sturbridge Fair, too, had become fashionable, and many a Londoner, much as Ward himself did, journeyed thither for no other reason than to see and to be amused.

It was in the year 1700 that Ward apparently made the journey which provided him with the experience he records in *A Step to Stir-Bitch-Fair.* As in most of the trips the interest is less directly centered in a description of the fair, than it is in Ward's own experience, and the account is worth dwelling upon at some length because it illustrates Ward at his best in his comments on traveling conditions and the university town as well as the activities of the fair.

Having heard much about the fair, he begins, and the weather in 1700 being unusually pleasant and dry, he took it upon himself to make an excursion thither for his own amusement. Electing to travel by coach, he repaired to the Green Dragon within Bishopsgate, and presently found himself bound for Cambridge in a "Dirty, Lumbering, Wooden Hovel" drawn by six "thin-Gutted Tits." The coach was crowded and the passengers found themselves "wedg'd as close in one by another as a Barrel of Red-Herrings, or Wheat-Ears in a Tunbridge-Pye." Among them were two sempstresses, a performer's widow on the way to join her husband, a small child and its nurse, and an old gentleman on the way to visit his son at St. John's.

The first stop along the road was at Ware. Here, at the Sign of St. George, the travelers were refreshed with a dinner of eels, served in as many ways as a Frenchman cooks frogs. After dinner they were shown the great bed of Ware, ample enough to lodge a "Troop of Soldiers" and much talked about by all those who never travel "beyond the bounds of the home Circuit." Here, too, they engaged in the ceremony of being sworn upon a great pair of horns at the cost of twelve pence per person lest they undergo the ridicule of the whole house for the breach of old custom. In the evening the coach had arrived at Barley, where the passengers put up at the Old Pharaoh Inn, famous for its "Stout Elevating Malt-Liquor under the same Name." Amusing to Ward's readers must have been the "Blunt Conversation" of the landlady and the author's exchange with her of some Petronian yarns.

In the morning, the coach rattled on through Saffron-Waldon, where Ward asserts the air was so heavily laden with the odor of the flowers that he felt distinctly enlivened. Gossip reports, he goes on to say, that the air is so efficacious that people by merely passing through the town have been

cured of the jaundice. A mile out of the village they passed
a huge structure known as Audley-End, so stupendous that
it seemed "with the License of a Traveller, almost as big
as London" itself.[16]

As they entered the city of Cambridge, they saw students
in black and purple gowns strolling along the street, some
with "meagre Countenances," others thoughtful, still others
as "Plump and as Jolly as a painted Bacchus bestriding a
Canary Butt." Ward stopped at the famous inn "distinguish'd
by the Sign of the Devils Lap-Dog in Petty-Cury." Not the
least among the attractions here, was the beautifully plump
and gracious landlady who rewarded the sly gownsmen as
they came in with "either a Kiss, a Kind Look, or a cup of
Comfort." Refreshed by a cup of canary, he continued his
observations. "As for the Town it self," he writes,

it was so abominably dirty, that Old-street in the middle of a Winters
Thaw, or Bartholomews-Fair, after a Shower of Rain, could not have
more occasion for a Scavenger, than the miry Streets of this Famous
Corporation; and most of them so very narrow, that should two Wheel-
barrows meet in the largest of their Thorough-fares, they are enough to
make a stop for half an hour before they can well clear themselves of
one another, to make room for Passengers.

The colleges stand "without side the Town," he continues,
"which, in plain Terms is a Corporation of Ignorance, hem'd
round with Arts and Sciences, a Nest of Fools, that dwell on
the Superfluities of the Learned." Of the twelve colleges the
most interesting to Ward is Trinity, whose "commodious
Library" and "spacious Quadrangle" seem beyond comparison. The next most notable building is King's College
Chapel, famous for its "admirable Architecture, much after
the manner of Henry the Seventh's Chappel at Westminster,
if not finer and larger." Ward prefers the older buildings;
"their Aged Walls, and Obsoleteness of their Structure,"
he concludes, "procure Veneration from all Spectators, and
seem'd to me more Noble in their Ancient Uniformity, than
others disagreeably enlarg'd with additional Novelties."

The next morning Ward set out for the fair. He chose to
walk the two miles to Barnwell Abbey, though he tells us
he could have ridden thither for a matter of threepence in

one of the numerous hackney coaches, which having carried down their quota of traders from London remained for the duration of the fair, to ply between Cambridge and Barnwell. At the fair he found a multitude of gentry, scholars in black and purple gowns, tradesmen, hawkers, pedlars, whores, pickpockets, and thieves. In a wooden edifice constructed by the corporation of Cambridge and known as the Proctor's Booth sat the vice-chancellor of the university or his deputy, to preside at all cases that arose involving the conduct and behavior of the university scholars.[17] In a second edifice sat the mayor of the corporation or his deputy, assisted by the elders of the town, to preside in all cases involving the conduct of trade and the behavior of the laymen. Ward does not refer to any misconduct on the part of the students, but if one may judge by the official proclamation or "cry" of the fair there probably were many opportunities for the vice-chancellor's court to function.[18] No scholar was allowed to carry weapons to the fair. Moreover, the students were specifically commanded to "make noe fray, cry out as shreking, or any other noise, by which insurrections, conventicles, or gathering of people may be made in this fair." According to the "cry" all strangers were commanded to leave their weapons at their inns on pain of forfeiture and punishment. Ward, however, makes no mention of the fact and it is possible the rule was uninforced.

The most important article of trade was hops and Ward refers to the vast quantities which had been brought in from the adjacent counties. Near the river were Dutch markets of "red and Pickled Herrings, Salt-Fish, [and] Oysters." Next to them were stands dispensing pitch, tar, and soap. Beyond the latter lay the boozing-kens, known locally as "Lyn-Booths," and farther on up the hill the vendors' shops for punch bowls, spoons and porridge dishes, the pewter ware and jewelry. Proceeding up the hill, Ward arrived at "Garlick-Row," each side lined with slit-deal "Tenements" occupied by sempstresses, perfumers, milliners, toymen, and cabinet-makers, chiefly frequented by "Powder'd Beau's, Bushy Wig'd-Blockheads, Country-Belfa's and Beautiful Bury Ladies."

Beyond the top of the hill the fair stretched out into a

street known as Cheapside, one side of which was given over to wholesale linen drapers, silk-men, iron-mongers, leather-sellers, and tobacconists. On the opposite side stood the sutlers' booths, much frequented by London citizenry, the latter immediately distinguishable by their "Calves-Leather Boots" and the bloodiness of their spurs. To the rear of the booths was a large space designated as the "Duddery," filled with great quantities of wool in enormous bags called "pockets." In the midst of the wool fair stood the old weather-beaten pulpit in which the rector of Little St. Andrew's, Barnwell, performed his ancient right of reading prayers and preaching to the assemblage on each Sunday during the fair.[19]

At night, Ward relates in conclusion, when all the booths of the fair are shut up by "Skewering two Hair-Cloths together," the merrymakers perform an ancient prank. Seeking out the "Freshmen" of the fair they force them one by one to be christened. The act consists in beguiling the innocent victim into a sutler's booth under the pretense that one of his friends wishes to speak to him. Once they have attracted the victim inside, the merrymakers send for "Lord Tap," an old gentleman who goes about the fair armed with "Spiggots and Fossets." Then choosing two of their members to stand god-father, they force the victim to kneel, swear him upon the horns, dub him with a bawdy name, and, after "Lord Tap" has recited the ceremonial rhyme and rung a bell over his head, bid him arise. For his initiation the victim pays sixpence to "Lord Tap" and four or five shillings as a treat to the assembled company. Forever after the candidate is a free and full initiate of the great Sturbridge Fair.

As a fashionable watering place the city of Bath had not reached in 1700 the fame it was to attain in the following decade under the leadership of Beau Nash as "Arbiter Elegantiarium!"[20] Already, however, hundreds of Londoners journeyed thither each summer, and Ward in becoming a "fool in Fashion" and making the journey, recorded for his readers in *A Step to the Bath* an experience already common to many.

This time the journey began at the Saracen's Head in Fri-

day Street. Having made reservation on Monday's coach,
Ward repaired to the inn on Sunday evening in order to be
on hand for the early departure. Fellow passengers turned
out to be a Bristol merchant, two gentlewomen sisters, a wife
and widow, and their maid. Leaving at an early hour, the
coach arrived at "Cole-brook" in time for breakfast at the
Sign of St. George. From there the route led through Reading and Theal to Newbury, where the party stopped for the
night at the Sign of the Lion.

En route the passengers regaled each other with songs and
stories, a device which Ward uses to extend the narrative
matter. It is worth remarking, though, that the stories are
handled with a certain appropriateness to the design, and in
their emphasis upon personal experience lend considerable
reality to the tellers as well as to the journey itself. They are,
whether purely fictional or not, realistic yarns with practical
middle-class endings not inappropriate to the tellers. More
often they are concluded by an asseveration on the part of
some member of the group, such as, "A Friend of mine was
an Eye Witness of this, and knew both the Husband and
the Wife."

The supper at the Sign of the Lion was of "Yorkshire"
price. The trout cost "a Lease of Crowns"; a shoulder of
mutton and a plate of "Gerkins," six shillings; rolls and a
nipperkin of brandy, three and six; with two shillings more
for a treat to the coachman. Refreshed in the morning with
a pot of chocolate prepared by the women passengers, the
party proceeded to Marlborough, where the rocky descent
into town jolted the coach severely enough to break the
merchant's bottle of Nantz. This provides Ward with a convenient jest at the expense of the corporation, for when he
protested, as he tells us, the danger and inconvenience of
the road to the mayor, the latter replied, so he asserts, that
the repair of the road would inevitably ruin the town since
innumerable wheelwrights, farriers, and surgeons depend
upon the accidents of the road for a livelihood.

Beyond Marlborough the route led over a down, noted
for its "Flocks of Grey Weathers," where the party was
frightened by the appearance of a troop of light horse on

the right whom they took first to be highwaymen. Within
a few miles they reached "Sandy-Lane" road where the going
"was so Damnable heavy, that two mile in three hours was
an Extraordinary Journey." Stopping to dine at the Sign of
the Bear in Sandy-Lane, they continued the journey over a
rocky, narrow, and uneven road.[21] Just as the passengers
were about to request the coachman to be allowed to alight,
he informed them they were already within sight of their
destination, and less than an hour later they arrived in Bath
at the White Hart Inn.

The remainder of the account Ward devoted to the city
of Bath. Leaving the ladies—of whom he would have us believe he became somewhat too fond—confined to their rooms
for two or three days while they awaited the arrival of their
baggage from London, he joined some masculine acquaintances at the Three Tuns. After a glass or two of Bordeau and
Sherry Ward and his friends turned to an inspection of the
baths.[22]

First in the survey is the King's Bath, where Ward found
a crowd of some fifty persons accompanied by their numerous guides and attendants. Some were busy drinking the
waters, others were bathing, still others were being carried
back to their quarters in chairs. A somewhat larger crowd
was in attendance at the more fashionable Cross Bath to
which the quality resorted for pleasure rather than for any
curative purpose. Here beautiful ladies were wading in the
pool, their floating Japan bowls "freighted with Confection-
ery Knick-knacks, Essences, and Perfumes" gently pushed
ahead of them by their attendants. Standing by in admiration
were a crowd of beaux who occasionally disported themselves in displaying their own accomplishments of diving
and floating. In the gallery spectators feverishly observed
and commented on the conduct below.

Promptly at five the bathing ceased for the day. "Half-Tub
Chairs, Lin'd with Blankets" now were as much in demand
"as Coaches at the Play-House." With the baths deserted, the
crowd moved to the "Grove." Here raffling booths and
Royal Oak lotteries amused the sojourners in the city along
with backgammon, basset, and ninepins. Ward and his friend

paused for a moment to watch an important match at bowls. "Fly, fly, fly, fly; said one: Rub, rub, rub, rub, cry'd another. Ten Guinies to five, I Uncover the Jack, says a third. Damn these Nice Fingers of mine, cry'd my Lord, I Slipt my Bowl, and mistook the Bias."

In the morning of the second day Ward and his friends amused themselves in a famous coffee-house, where "Nonsense [was] banded to and fro like a Shuttle-Cock" and "last Nights Intrigue Whisper'd with abundance of Caution." Ward wins a snuffbox at a raffle for a guinea. From the coffee-house the survey continues to Hot Bath, chiefly notable, he remarks, for the row of old crutches hung up in memory of miraculous cures. On Friday evening he escorts his widow, now resplendent in London finery, to the public ball at the Town Hall, a biweekly event on Tuesdays and Fridays. Brawny beadles stand at the door to keep out the mob. Inside there is good music and excellent dancing. Refreshments of sweetmeats and wine are distributed by numerous attendants. On Sunday Ward and his friend attend services at the Abbey, "a very Ancient Cathedral piece of Antiquity" badly in need of repair and "crowded as Pauls."

'Tis neither Town nor City, yet goes by the Name of both; five Months in the Year 'tis as Populous as London, the other seven as desolate as a Wilderness. . . . The Baths I can compare to nothing but the Boylers in Fleet-lane or Old-Bedlam, for they have a reaking steem all the year. In a word, 'tis a Valley of Pleasure, yet a sink of Iniquity; Nor is there any Intrigues or Debauch Acted at London, but is Mimick'd there.

III

In the trip lay Ward's initial success. In the pages of *A Trip to Jamaica,* the monthly parts of *The London Spy,* and the minor trips of the period he had established himself as a journalist of considerable initiative and originality. The form had been peculiarly suited to his own genius. He was always more effective in prose than in verse. Not particularly well-read or adept in the more traditional satiric patterns, and almost wholly free of any didactic purpose, he had been forced to rely heavily upon the element of his own experience. To that he had brought an observing eye, an interest in colorful detail, a facilely loquacious prose, and a sensitivity to reader-interest which was to distinguish his work for over a decade.

His efforts during the years 1699 and 1700, however, were not solely confined to the new genre he himself had succeeded in creating. As any enterprising journalist might, he had tried the old along with the new, and numerous items appeared from his pen—without reference at the moment to his political efforts—in a more traditional vein.

Early in the year 1698, for instance, he had published *Sots' Paradise, or the Humours of a Derby-Ale-House,* a satiric poem in the Hudibrastic vein. In March of the same year he had written an account in verse of a tiger-baiting which had taken place at the Cock Pit on the afternoon of the ninth of the month, entitled *The Cock-Pit Combat, or the Baiting of the Tiger.*[23] Another broadside, *O Raree-Show, O Pretty-Show, or the City-Feast,* had followed hard upon the lord mayor's day celebration in November, presenting the reader with a burlesque account of the progress from Guildhall to Westminster and the installation dinner.

In the spring of 1699—almost a year earlier than the trial at the Guildhall reported in *The London Spy*—Ward had dipped into the case of the wits versus John Partridge, the astrologer. In *The World Bewitch'd, a Dialogue between Two Astrologers and the Author,* he had presented a burlesque account of the quarrel between Partridge and his papist rival, George Parker, in which both men recapitulated the charges they were hurling at each other in their own writings. Allowing Parker to score off Partridge effectively, he had warned the former to quit himself of the unseasonable title of Jacobite, and then added on his own a few "Infallible Predictions of what will happen in this Present Year, 1699." This in turn had led to a periodical publication burlesquing Partridge begun by Ward's friend and associate, Tom Brown, in October of the next year, entitled *The Infallible Astrologer: or, Mr. Silvester Partrige's Prophesie and Predictions of what shall Infallibly happen in, and about the Cities of London and Westminster, for every Day this Week,* and continued by Ward beginning with the eleventh number (January 6) as *The Infallible Astrologer: or, Mr. Silvester Partridge's merry Inteligence*. The pamphlet, as well as the eight numbers of the periodical for which Ward was responsible, indicate his early interest in the now famous attack on Partridge, and establish for him some share in the credit generally given to Brown as the chief precursor of Swift.[24]

A more extensive departure from the trip into the realm of verse satire was *A Journey to Hell, or a Visit Paid to the Devil,* parts i and ii of which were published in 1700. Ward had always, of course, assumed the conventional cloak of the satirist. His justification for *The London Spy* had been "to Expose the Vanities and Vices of the Town, as they should, by any Accident, occur to my Knowledge, that the Innocent might see by Reflection, what I should gain by Observation and Intelligence, and not by Practice or Experience."[25] His real object, however, had been to sell. His primary purpose had been to divert, not to reform his readers, and it was probably not so much a change of mood as it was the nature of the material which now drew him into satire, for *A Journey to Hell* was quite obviously inspired by Sir Roger L'Estrange's popular paraphrase of Quevedo's *Los Suenos*.[26] Taking no more than his general idea from the *Visions,* however, Ward set out upon his own attack. Foremost among those deserving derision were the dissenting ministers, the apothecaries and physicians, sixpenny wits, impudent printers, pirating publishers, pettifogging lawyers, and cheating vintners of London. Before part iii had gone to press, Ward's opponents had already begun to reply, and Ward was apparently dissuaded from continuing. Quevedo's satire, however, may well have served later to give greater social impetus to his writings.

Before the year was out, he wrote *Labour in Vain, or What Signifies Little or Nothing* (1700). Though in form it bears no relation to the *Visions* whatever, the spirit is essentially that of *A Journey to Hell*. Its sixteen pages are a humorous and often quite pointed commentary on the futility of the poor man's endeavor, embellished by personal anecdote and current rumor, containing among other things a spirited attack on the customary treatment of debtors.

By the autumn of 1700 Ward's reputation was assured. In a little over two years he had supplied his bookseller with twenty-five sixteen-page pamphlets in prose, four broadsides, a half-dozen pieces in verse, and a weekly periodical—not to mention his political efforts which will be taken up later. As early as February of this year his publisher, John How, whose fortunes had steadily risen with Ward's, offered his readers *A Collection of the Writings, Hitherto Extant, of Mr. Edward Ward,* the first in the long series of collected writings extending to the time of Ward's death. The man once unable to pay his Leicestershire host had come into his own.

Ward must have been immensely pleased and flattered by his own success. "Pray Sir gratifie my desire (if you can) with the Name and Character of the Author of the London Spyes," wrote an inquiring reader to *The Post Angel*.[27] "I have no Acquaintance with this Author," John Dunton replied,

but I find by a Title prefix'd to his Writings, that his Name is Mr. Edward Ward: As to his Character, he is a Gentleman of Grays-Inn, and his Writings declare him to be of a Comical Temper, and that his Faculty lies very much in Satyr, and Burlesque: . . . They that wou'd know more of this Ingenious Author, must read his Works, which are sold by Mr. John How in Rams-Head-Inn-Yard, in Fenchurch-street.

Ingenious Ward, [Dunton was to write on another occasion] . . . He was truly born a Poet, not made, not formed by industry; and (which is a great service to a man that follows the calling of an Author,) his Muse is never subject to the curse of "bringing forth with pain;" . . . He is a man of a peculiar style, and his Works are in great esteem.[28]

Ward's enemies, too, testified to his popularity. *Sot's Paradise, or the Humours of a Derby-Ale-House,* already in its third edition in the year 1700, drew a reply from the outraged ale-sellers entitled *The Paradise of Pleasure, or an Encomium upon Darby-Ale.* Who is the author of *Sot's Paradise* to turn "Traytor and Runagado" to that which has done him such "eminent Service"? More than one production, the author writes, Ward owes to the assistance of ale.

It was *A Journey to Hell* which moved his opponents to a personal attack. In his assault upon the apothecaries and physicians Ward had made reference to the quarrel then raging between them over the dispensary. He had left no doubt about it that if one were forced to choose between quacks, the physicians were the lesser of two evils. It was the apothecaries who chose to reply. *The Devil's Journey to London, or the Visit Repaid Ned W—d* (1700), "Written by an Apothecary," attempts to pay off the score against Ward, and the bitterness of its attack testifies to the weight attached to Ward's participation in the quarrel. The devil comes to London, is directed to Gray's Inn, and finally arrives with the porter's aid at the garret door:

> The Devil's got a Pounding at the Door,
> He raps at first, and then he soundly beats,
> Within Ned W—d, he through the Key-hole peeps,
> Expecting Bayliff, Debtor, or some Whore
> He Pox't, and Bilk't a day or two before;
> To bring her Bully, to her just Defence;
> Or Grays-Inn Porter to kick him from thence.

Finding him the devil continues:

> The best of Places, that in Hell can be,
> I have Reserv'd, and do intend for thee;
> Grieve not poor Ned for if the World does Frown,
> In Hell I will for all thy Spying Crown:
> Thou art Newgates Joy. Tiburns only Glory,
> Thou has outdone all that went before thee.

A second reply, *The Shoemaker beyond his Last, or a Satyr upon Scurrilous Poets, especially Ned W—d,* bears the earmarks of having been written by a churchman. It is at once more learned and more violent in vituperation. His grievance is the scribbling fever of the age, but Ward in particular arouses his ire.

> Upon the Lawreat of this gang I'll fall,
> For their Presumption he shall pay for all;
> I charge you fairly to stand on your Guard,
> No favour will I show you foolish W—d, . . .

How long have you a Poet been I pray?
Or who was it that put you in that way? . . .
You know no Pardon is allow'd a *Spy*, . . .

Thou sole Promoter of deformed Vice,
Pray what's the Moral of *Sot's Paradice?*
The *Walk to Islington*, the *Trips* you make
Abroad? And *Journey to the Sulph'rous Lake?*
None as I know of.

But the knowing journalist which Ward had turned out to be may only have been reassured by the attack and its attending publicity. The author of *A Trip to Jamaica* and *The London Spy* had himself become grist for the journalist's mill.

V

Hot-Brained Quarrels

As if they thought ill Language glorious,
And hot-brain'd Quarrels meritorious:
Hudibras Redivivus, Part 1 (1705)

WITH WARD'S REPUTATION as a writer daily becoming better established, it was inevitable that sooner or later he should become engaged in the political and religious quarrels of the day. The subservience of literature to politics is a marked characteristic of the period. Sometimes this alliance came about simply because men of letters felt compelled to give expression to their own convictions. At other times writers deliberately courted the favor and patronage of individuals or of powerful political groups, largely for protection and monetary reward. For a third group this relationship reflects no more than their own journalistic acumen in meeting the demands of readers avidly concerned with political and religious issues.

As for Ward, he was by birth and inclination both Anglican and Tory and his writings, whatever the issue or the occasion, reflect his own deep-seated prejudices. Whigs to him were anathema. Dissenters were grasping tradesmen and lying hypocrites, enabled by the odious practice of occasional conformity to usurp the offices of government. Low-church Anglicans in their toleration of dissenters were betraying their church and the true faith. Papists were misguided and dangerous zealots, who, owing to their political reverses, were at the moment comparatively helpless.

Even so it is probable that Ward was at times less concerned with the principles involved than he was with the opportunity offered for the ready sale of broadsides and pamphlets. That is to say, he was primarily a pamphleteer and not a politician. It is not to say, of course, that his preferences did not lie deep or that he did not maintain a consistent attitude on the issues he upheld. It is, indeed, Ward's dogged adherence to the high-church position with an unquestioning loyalty to the dictates of political faction that is the really distinguishing mark of his writing. Better men than he on occasion challenged their own leaders and parties; more obsequious writers sometimes managed to serve both sides in spite of, or in doubt of, the alignment of their own interests. But, to paraphrase Prince Hal's remark to Pointz upon an occasion, never a man's thought in the world kept the roadway of political faction better than Ward's, and there are few more adequate records of the prejudice, the unreasonable fears, and the violent hatreds which swayed the eighteenth-century reader than Ward's writings.[1]

Barely a month after his initial success with *A Trip to Jamaica* Ward issued his first distinctly political effort. Under the title of *Ecclesia et Factio, a Dialogue between Bow-Steeple Dragon and the Exchange Grasshopper* he published a versified attack on moderation and the practice of occasional conformity. In December of the same year, 1698, when a rebellious parliament under the leadership of Robert Harley voted to reduce the standing army to seven thousand men and William was forced to dispense with his Dutch Guards, Ward issued a broadside deriding the troops and generally revelling in the Tory triumph. *The Dutch Guards Farwel to England* he followed up with another broadside on the failure of the land bank, entitled *A Hue and Cry after a Man-Midwife, Who Has Lately Deliver'd the Land-Bank of Their Money*. In March of the next year he brought out another dialogue, *Modern Religion and Ancient Loyalty*, again lamenting the low esteem to which the church had fallen. Before the summer was out he was to suffer his first suppression, though from what seemed at the moment an unexpected quarter.

The first aim of *The Weekly Comedy, as it is Dayly Acted at most Coffee-Houses in London*, a weekly periodical begun on May 10, 1699, was diversion. Its purpose, similar to that of *The London Spy,* was to entertain by depicting, in caricature and burlesque, the citizenry in their places of pleasure and resort. As such most of the satire was directed at newsmongers, quacks, projectors, sharpers, disbanded soldiers, land-bound mariners, and canting dissenters. In the eighth number, however, Ward turned his attention to the current election of sheriffs in the city of London, and two weeks later the periodical came to an abrupt close.[2] Two epilogues later appended to a reprint of the ten numbers leave no doubt about its discontinuance.

Ward might have taken warning, but he apparently did not. Titles plainly indicative of his political bias continued to follow. In 1701 he published *The Kentish Fable of the Lyon and the Foxes, or the Honesty of the Kentish Petition Made Manifest,* obviously an attack upon the justices and grand jury of the quarter sessions of Kent, who, along with other freeholders of the shire, sent a petition to the House of Commons in May rebuking the Tory-dominated house for seeking to impeach the members of the Whig ministry responsible for the Partition Treaties.[3] In November of the next year he brought out another dialogue, *Bribery and Simony, or a Satyr against the Corrupt Use of Money,* once more attacking the low-church bishops and clergy.

For the moment conditions were favorable for the Tory journalists and pamphleteers. The Act of Settlement, assuring a Protestant succession, was passed in 1701. In March 1702 William III died and Queen Anne was known to be inclined favorably to the church and the Tories. Moreover, the elections of 1702 increased the Tory majority in the House of Commons. The favorable turn of affairs proved a signal for a general attack. A bill against occasional conformity passed the lower house in 1702, and though defeated in the House of Lords, it was reintroduced the following year. High-church and Tory pamphleteers and journalists rushed into the fray. Whigs and dissenters, in turn, were aroused.

Ward's role in the controversy which followed must at some points remain the subject of conjecture. Discretion demanded anonymity. And it is not always easy to determine at a much later date who of a dozen minor writers was responsible for each attack and counterattack.[4] The evidence for Ward's authorship in some cases, however, is clear; in others the probabilities are heavy. In 1704 he published *Helter Skelter, or the Devil upon Two Sticks. A Comedy, as it is Spitefully Acted between High-Church and Low-Church, in most Taverns about London,* a burlesque dialogue not inaptly characterizing the tavern conversation of the embittered partisans. This he followed up with *All Men Mad, or England a Great Bedlam,* another comment on the controversy with particular reference to the low-church bishops who had again helped to defeat the bill against occasional conformity in 1703. There is little doubt, too, that he was at least in part responsible for the libelous attack on the dissenters, *The Secret History of the Calves-Head Club, or the Republican Unmask'd,* first issued in January 1703 and reissued annually thereafter for over a decade—a powerful political bludgeon, the discussion of which will be reserved for a later chapter. Nor can there be any question concerning *The Dissenting Hypocrite, or the Occasional Conformist* (1704) which centered its attack on the principle of occasional conformity and the Whig journalists, Tutchin and Defoe. Again in 1703 the bill against occasional conformity failed only because of its defeat in the House of Lords. In 1704 the fight became more embittered and prolonged when the Tories, under the leadership of William Bromley, sought to attach the bill to the land tax in a desperate endeavor to secure its passage. The debate in parliament produced its complement in news organs and journals. Tutchin and Defoe, the editors of the two leading Whig journals, *The Observator* and *The Review,* fought tirelessly. Charles Leslie and James Drake launched two new Tory journals, *The Rehearsal* and *Mercurius Politicus,* in its support. When the weekly newsheets were no longer able to carry the load, the journalists resorted to pamphlets. The pulpits in turn supported and provided material for the pamphleteers. Though the bill was defeated once more, the controversy continued to rage throughout the following year.

Ward's contribution in *The Dissenting Hypocrite* is a characteristic one. Sensing an opportunity for a fast-selling pamphlet, he turned an earlier argument of Charles Leslie's, *The New Association* (1702), into a doggerel poem—as he characterizes it—delighting his readers with his rhymed diatribes against his rivals. The focal point of his attack is the dissenter's practice of attending the Anglican church in the morning and the meetinghouse in the afternoon.

> Conform and not, Conform's a Fiction;
> In Practice a flat Contradiction.

he writes in a couplet indicative at once of his best powers and the source of his inspiration.

How much encouragement Ward received from members of the high-church party is unknown. Tutchin in his reply to *All Men Mad, or England a Great Bedlam* accused him of fighting from behind "Stone Walls," cognizant of his own immunity.[5] It is apparent, however, that Ward never became a party scribe in any role comparable to that of Swift and Defoe, though he, too, exercised a certain political function. Swift and Defoe addressed themselves to a relatively intelligent audience. Ward disseminated the policies of the growing Tory faction among the lower classes, heaped prejudice and odium upon the opposition, stimulating the rabble to an open expression of their hatreds. What monetary reward there was came from the timeliness of his journalism and the violence and derision of his attack.

As the controversy over occasional conformity continued, Ward found even greater opportunity to be both timely and derisive, and in August of 1705 he launched the first number of his most ambitious and widely-known political effort, *Hudibras Redivivus, or a Burlesque Poem upon the Times*. Unlike *The Dissenting Hypocrite* this was not a mere repetition of another's argument. As Ward foresaw it, *Hudibras Redivivus* was to be a long poem issued in parts at monthly intervals. Its subject matter would depend from month to month upon the nature of the immediate controversy and the behavior of the Whigs. For the framework of the poem he could assume the role of a reporter journeying about town, commenting upon men and events, much as he had done earlier in *The London Spy*.

As an imitation of *Hudibras,* Ward himself had the decency to confess that it would fall short of the original, though he probably hoped otherwise. "Tho' I have made bold," he writes,

to borrow a Title from one of the best Poems that ever was publish'd in the English Tongue, yet I would not have the World expect me such a Wizard, as to be able to conjure up the Spirit of the inimitable Butler, who has left behind him too noble an Original for the greatest Hand now living to exactly copy.[6]

Nevertheless, "the Heat and Madness of our pious Incendiaries" give a "like Opportunity for the like Chastisement," and Ward had read his model well enough to know "such Satyr to be most acceptable, that tickles as it hurts."

Among the Tory poets of Queen Anne's day no dead worthy was, of course, more universally admired or more widely imitated than Butler. Oblivious of Butler's disdain for the inconsistencies and hypocrisies in the conduct of all parties and factions, they saw in *Hudibras* only a galling reproof of the Presbyterians and Independents, delivered in unusually pungent and rollicking verse. To imitate Butler meant for Ward, and for his contemporaries, to imitate in as far as possible the verse of the original while spinning out interminable diatribe and invective in condemnation and mockery of the appearance, behavior, and writings of one's opponents. For the thread of narrative in the original they substituted current episodes in the factional strife, imitations of coffee-house and tavern debate, and travesties of the enemies' sermons and pamphlets. For the verbal eccentricities and the ingenious rhymes of the original, which Butler's followers found themselves unable to imitate, they substituted a vernacular of their own, more colloquial and often equally racy.[7]

The result in the case of Ward was in no sense disastrous. The imitations, of course, fall far short of the original. Nevertheless, the emphasis in Ward upon the depiction of scenes and personages currently important provides an air of direct satire and realism which many readers find wanting in the original. Moreover, the octosyllabic measures, even in the hands of a less able technician, retain some of their spirited gaiety, and the colloquial language itself is not out of keeping with the greater realism and more direct imitation of life. Where Ward's imitation suffers most is in his attempt to repeat the rather long and discursive argumentative passages of his model. He had no talent, such as Butler had, for travestying the stupid inanities of religious and political debate. His attempt to do so is apt to be wearily repetitious and extraordinarily dull. He is at his best, as one would expect him to be, where he chooses rather to depict men and events. Here there is often an abundance of realistic detail, an energy of movement, and a vividness of language that must at once have entertained and intrigued his readers.

The opening number of *Hudibras Redivivus* presents a not inaccurate picture of the querulous times. Everywhere one goes political principles are the subject of heated controversy. Both parties are calling names. To the Whigs the Tories are "Tackers," "Parkenites," "Jacobites," and "French Abettors." To the Tories the Whigs are "Calves-Head men," "creatures of Titus Oates," and "Tantivity boys." In the coffee-houses and taverns the Tories are busily reading *The Rehearsal* and *Mercurius Politicus.* In the same coffee-houses and taverns, or in those directly across the street, the Whigs are feverishly pursuing *The Observator* and *The Review.* Arguments flare up into quarrels. Hot words are followed by blows. The disgruntled loser stalks off in sullen anger. The pulpit echoes the debate. Sunday after Sunday the sermon turns on the issue. Especially is this true of conventicles, Ward would have us believe, where

> Their Guides, those scantify'd Projectors,
> Turn Sermons into *Gazette*-Lectures.

As for the people, they are utterly confused:

> Some, of a Self-will'd, thwarting Nature,
> Seek Heav'n by Way of *Observator,* . . . .

> Others with zealous Labour scan
> The Pious Works of Prophet Dan,
> In Hopes, that thro' his Merits, they
> May steal to Heav'n the *shortest Way.*

In the second number Ward's perambulations take him among the bookstalls. They are piled high with political pamphlets and satires. A recent arrival among them is the notorious *A Memorial to the Church of England,* which later writers have assigned to James Drake. Beyond question, the pamphlet was the most outspoken and violent attack upon occasional conformity and toleration published during the days of the controversy. Ward apparently did not know the author. Neither could he foresee that the pamphlet itself would become the subject of an investigation by parliament, to be followed by a prosecution of the publisher. He himself thinks the pamphlet,

> An honest High-Church Book of Merit,
> Tho' written with a Low-Church Spirit.

It is to Ward's credit that he recognizes the book as needlessly ill-natured and vituperative. His comment is an illuminating appraisal of the pamphleteering standards of the day:

> For he that writes in such an Age,
> When Parties do for Pow'r engage,
> Ought to chuse one Side for the Right,
> And then, with all his Wit and Spite,
> Blacken and vex the Opposite. . . .
> Scurrility's a useful Trick,
> Approv'd by the most Politic.
> Fling Dirt enough, and some will Stick.

By the time Ward was engaged in writing part IV, parliament had again convened. Early in the session Lord Haversham made a speech in the House of Lords attacking the Whig government in its prosecution of the war, and made, moreover, the provocative proposal that the house address the queen on the subject of inviting the heir presumptive to reside in England. To the speech, after it appeared in printed form, Defoe replied in the pages of *The Review* and

in a number of pamphlets.[8] Ward relates how he heard both
Haversham's and Defoe's pamphlets hawked on the street
like "pick't Sallet" at a halfpenny each. Buying one of Defoe's
pamphlets, he reads it.

> At last I found, instead of Answer,
> Mere dull Scurility and Banter;
> Which shew'd no Honour could restrain
> The scoundrel Freedom of his Pen.

But Tory zeal in the summer of 1705 finally overreached
itself. In the end the queen, upon whose support the Tory
statesmen and pamphleteers had depended, became exasper-
ated. The elections returned a Whig majority to the house.
When a stubborn minority once again took up the cry that
the church was in danger, the matter was debated in the
House of Lords, and both houses concurring in the opinion
that the church was in no danger, the queen issued a proclamation for the arrest of the author of *A Memorial to the
Church of England,* as well as a timely warning to others.
For the moment even Harley turned away from the pamphleteers and journalists he had earlier abetted.

Ward's chagrin at the turn of affairs and the behavior of
the ministry and queen knew no bounds. In the January
number of *Hudibras Redivivus* he gives expression to a
thinly disguised diatribe against the queen, accusing her of
speaking fine words but of failing to support them with
action:

> But that which makes the Church-men wonder,
> And strikes them worse than Bolt of Thunder,
> Is that an E[nglish] H[eart] of Oak,
> Who, like a Friend, so kindly spoke,
> Should put upon them such a Joke,
> And make 'em by Experience find,
> That Woman's Words are only Wind. . . .
> Fair Promises avail but little,
> Like too rich Pye-crust they're so brittle,
> They seldom signify a Tittle.
> Good Deeds become an E[nglis]h H[ear]t
> Fine Words don't countervail a F[ar]t.
> Heroic Actions are alone
> The Glories of a Camp and Throne.

At the same time he bitterly denounces the Whigs and dissenters in terms which seem openly to court reprisal.

According to Hearne,[9] Ward was taken into custody for his remarks as early as February 7, 1706. *Hudibras Redivivus,* however, continued to appear regularly in spite of the remonstrance, though not without some qualms on the part of the author. On April 11, according to Lutrell,[10] Ward once again "for writing reflecting pamphlets on several ministers of state," had his "appearance recorded in the Queens bench court."

It was a severe summer for Ward's friends as well. As early as April William Pittis, whom Ward had taken occasion to praise in *The Dissenting Hypocrite,* had been fined forty marks and sentenced to stand twice in the pillory, as well as to find security for a year for having contributed a defense of *The Memorial to the Church of England.* Dr. Joseph Brown, who later along with Pittis and William King contributed complimentary sonnets to Ward on his adaptation of Cervantes, suffered the same sentence in May for outspoken attacks upon the lord keeper and Harley.[11]

On June 13, when Ward himself was arrested for being the author of *Hudibras Redivivus,* he pleaded guilty to the charge and awaited his trial. He was sentenced on November 14, and the matter was duly recorded for his readers in the current issue of *The London Gazette:*

Edward Ward, being convicted of Writing, Printing, and Publishing, several Scandalous and Seditious Libels, (Entitled, Hudibras Redivivus; or, a Burlesque Poem on the Times) highly Reflecting upon Her Majesty and the Government; was likewise on Thursday last fined for the same by the Court of Queen's-Bench 40 Marks, and ordered to stand in the Pillory on Wednesday next at Charing-Cross for the space of One Hour, between Twelve and Two in the Afternoon, with a Paper on his Head denoting his Offence; and also to stand in the Pillory on Thursday next near the Royal Exchange in Cornhill in like Manner: And, before he be discharged out of Prison, he is to give Security for his good Behavior for One Year.

Hudibras Redivivus had, however, continued throughout the summer, though with a somewhat altered emphasis. Parts x and xi, both issued in June, are devoted to a harmless description of a Whitsun holiday crowd and to a congregation of Quakers meeting in a "Slit-deal Tabernacle" near the Bull and Mouth Tavern in Lombard Street. The twelfth and concluding part of Volume I, as well as parts I and II of Volume II, which he now entitled *Hudibras Redivivus, or a Burlesque Poem upon the Humours of Town and Country,* are devoted to a description of a mountebank on Tower Hill. Later numbers record further perambulations about the city. Parts III, IV, and V are given over to a description of Smithfield Rounds, Bartholomew Fair, and the neighboring shops; part VI to the lord mayor's day parade; part VII to the festivities on the eve of November 5.

The numbers issued while Ward was awaiting his sentence are for the most part free from political reference. It was impossible, however, for him to forbear an occasional jibe at his opponents, who at the moment were laughing loudest if not longest. When the mountebank is dispensing his fabulous pills and enumerating the catalogue of cures, Ward includes an account of the "Pilula Fanatica," which relieves all users from worries of conscience,

> And qualifies their Minds to take
> All sorts of Oaths for Interest Sake.

And when the lord mayor is on his way to Westminster, Ward comments on the fact that the usual pageants have been suppressed.[12]

> They're Popish Jimcracks, out of Season;
> Abominations, that displease
> The Saints in pious Times like these,
> And by the Dolts, are held to be
> Full as prophane as Poetry.

The arrival of November 5 provides him with even more serious concern, since the people of the city are once more celebrating the day more fervently than they do January 30. Bells ring in the morning; at night the mob fills the street with noise and shouting. As he is going towards his own room at six, Ward sees boys stealing sticks and tubs for a bonfire. Others beg pence from passers-by to purchase faggots. Windows are lighted (from cellar to garret) by rush and cotton candles. The mob comes to a dark house, and, calling out, "Jacobite," falls to banging the doors and the closed shutters with staves. With dire threats of violence and mouth-filling imprecations upon the householder the mob moves on. Shortly, a ragged group return with an effigy of the pope, rattling their clubs above their heads and kicking dirt from the miry puddles to disoblige each other. A little sooty chimney sweeper makes an obscene gesture at the effigy and the crowd roars an huzza. This is the manner, Ward comments, that the Whigs have of encouraging fear of the Tories. They hold their own by shouting popish fears and crying "Jacobite" at every election.

Parts VII–XII of the second volume of *Hudibras Redivivus* were not issued until 1707. In the closing numbers he had bethought himself of equally effective though less offensive subject material. *The History of the Grand Rebellion* by Edward Hyde, the Earl of Clarendon, had been published in 1704. Under the guise of a coffee-house debate, Ward now launched into a versified adaptation of Clarendon's history of the rebellion and the principles of '41. It was an inexhaustible source of material with the additional advantage that one could not be prosecuted for poetizing history. Long before he concluded his account of the martyrdom of Charles, the second volume of *Hudibras* had come to an end, and though part XII promised a continuation, the project of versifying Clarendon's history had undergone a considerable modification before it finally appeared in 1713.[13]

Ward had been punished, but he had not recanted. When he published a second edition of *Hudibras* in 1708, all of the twenty-four parts now being assembled, he revised the affront to the queen by reconstructing the most offensive line,[14] but in a special "apology" prepared for the occasion he repeated his general charge. Once more enumerating his original motives, he concludes, "these are the chief Motives that first put me upon the following Task; and if I am blameable therein, I hope it will still prove an error on the right side."

II

By the close of the year 1706 the Tory heyday for pamphleteering and journalism was temporarily over. The queen, with her forces engaged in a costly continental war, was forced to rely heavily upon a Whig parliament and ministry for its prosecution. For three years, until 1709, the high-church and Tory cause seemed to be lost. Late in the year 1709, however, in the arrest and prosecution of Dr. Henry Sacheverell, the Whigs overreached themselves much as the Tories had done in 1705. Once more the Tory journalists and pamphleteers rose to the attack.

Dr. Sacheverell had preached his offending sermons on August 15 at the Derby assize and on November 5 in St. Paul's. In December he was impeached by the House of Commons and a trial in Westminster Hall was arranged for February 27. On the night of the second day of the trial, March 1, the London mob out of sympathy for Sacheverell and the high-church party stormed the protestant meeting-houses of the city. Ward was himself a not unsympathetic onlooker. He, too, was for Sacheverell; and the London mob was finally demonstrating its hatred for the dissenters, a hatred he himself had helped to nourish. At any rate the scene that unfolded before his eyes was grist for the mill. Hard upon the occasion he produced a long narrative poem in five parts, *Vulgus Britannicus, or the British Hudibras,* an eyewitness account of the mob's activities from the gathering in Temple Bar to the ensuing debates in the coffee-houses, following the mob's dispersal by the queen's guards.

Since the task Ward set himself in *Vulgus Britannicus* again, much as in *Hudibras Redivivus,* depended upon observation and burlesque characterization—at which he was something of a master—rather than upon any analysis of the issues involved, it is in its own way fairly effective. He knew the London mob, having followed its behavior on more than one occasion, and he provided his readers with an interesting and lively—if not an impartial—picture of the activities. For Ward there was something beautifully ironic in the behavior of the mob. It is the Whigs, so he reminds his readers, who

believe in democracy and the voice of the people as the
"Source of All Authority" in government. It is the Tories
who have always held the rabble unable and unfit to exercise
either judgment or restraint. Now the very element which
the Whigs regard as their source of authority has turned
upon the Whigs themselves, and in that very turning has
demonstrated the incapacity for rational and civil behavior
which the Tories have always attributed to "our Good
Sov'reign Lords the People."

As for the mob, it is merely an aggregation of irresponsible
beings, just as the Tories have always insisted it was. Most
of its members are,

> Spew'd out of Alleys, Jayls, and Garrets,
> Grown sturdy with Neckbeef and Carrots;
> Some liquor'd well with Foggy Ale,
> Others with Glorious Mild and Stale;
> Informers, Lab'rors, Brothel-Keepers,
> Pimps, Panders, Thieves, and Chimney-Sweepers, . . .
> Unletter'd, Rascally and Base,
> A Kingdoms Danger and Disgrace.

The mob, according to Ward, first gathered impetus and
direction at a meeting near Fleet Ditch, and from there
moved out along the street,

> Well arm'd with Oaken Stick and Club,
> The Scepters of the Sovereign Mob,
> In Loud Huzzas proclaim'd their Coming,
> On Stalls and Bulks with Truncheons Drumming.

Each alley added its quota, ragged and disheveled vagabonds
pouring out of the hovels and cellars. Tramping through the
street members of the mob jostled each other, exchanged
blows in "Common Jests," and beat their oaken cudgels
against posts and doorways. Dogs fled whimpering along the
street, afraid of the cudgels and the brutal gelding knives.
Coaches were halted by men clamoring at wheel and bridle
until the frightened passengers contributed a shilling or half
crown. Steadily the crowd moved out through Ludgate to
St. Dunstan's. There with huzzas and shouting they escorted
the doctor to his coach. According to Ward, Sacheverell be-

sought the mob to disperse, but they insisted upon accompanying him.

> Thus did the Priest in Triumph Ride,
> With Legions shouting by his side, . . .
> Which startling Noise, like Winters Thunder,
> Fill'd many List'ning Ears with Wonder.

On the evening of the first day of the trial there was tumult and shouting in the streets. A large bonfire blazed in Temple Yard around which the mob congregated. On the second night the mob again filled the street; the clamor was more pronounced. Towards nine o'clock the sacking of the meetinghouses began. First to fall was the meetinghouse of Dr. Burgess in "Little Amsterdam." Ward describes the rifling of the building. Pews were torn up, doors and windows wrenched from their fastenings, the wainscoting was torn off the walls, pulpit and clock were broken into fragments. Members of the mob shouldered the debris and made off to nearby Lincoln's Inn Fields. There the materials were piled up, ignited, and burned. Even the personal belongings of Dr. Burgess were carried off, his household stuff, his cordials, his pipes, and tobacco. Bystanders watched the mob at work; women went to see the consecrated pews and pulpits thrown into the fire. The mob circled the burning pile, shouting and huzzaing, waving their broomstaves and cudgels aloft, jostling and beating each other.[15]

The job well done, the rioters held council and decided to divide for the rest of the night's work. One group moved off towards Nevel's meetinghouse in Fetter Lane, another towards Dr. Taylor's meetinghouse in Hatton Garden, a third towards Blackfriars. Whispers and rumors were abroad. Some said they were plotting to burn all the dissenting churches in the city. Others said not only the churches, but the homes of all prominent Whigs. Panic and terror spread throughout the city. The government became alarmed; a hurried council was held at the Old Cockpit in Whitehall. It would have been logical to call out the train-bands, but Ward remarks that most of them were already members of the mob itself. Informed of conditions, the queen ordered out her

ROSPECTUS LONDINENS

H-CENTURY LONDON
us engraving

PANORAMA OF EIGHTEEN

From an anonym

own horse guards. Ward describes the dispersal. Mounted guards suddenly appeared in the street, riding hard upon the mob. Pillagers, cut off in their retreat, dropped their encumbrances and fled into unguarded alleys and cellarways. Some, petrified with fear, stopped in their tracks and cried for mercy. Others loudly protested that they were only onlookers. Laggards were brought down with the flat stroke of the sword. Unfortunate ones were trampled by the horses. Those unable to flee were surrounded by the guards and turned over to constables and watches to be hurried off to the compters. Finally the streets, earlier filled with shouting and huzzaing, were silent as tombs.

In the morning the beating of drums and the marching of halbardiers called out the train-bands. Many a cobbler, porter, and prentice, Ward remarks caustically, now turned soldier to quell a mob of which he himself had been a member eight hours before. The train-bands were always the subject of ready humor for the satirist. Ward describes how,

> every Willing Hero laid
> His Business by, to whet his Blade;
> And scour his Firelock, and his Barrel,
> Upon this unexpected Quarrel;
> That he might come himself, or Hire
> Some Man as Brave, that durst to fire
> A Musquet that should do no hurt,
> And never start at the Report;
> But stand in Wet or Windy Weather,
> At Corner Post an Hour together;
> And boldly guard it in the Night,
> That none should reel or stagger by't;
> Without first showing to the Guard,
> Good reasons why he drank so hard;
> And that he was no Mob tho' mellow,
> But a good honest Drunken Fellow.

In spite of Ward's burlesque, however, the train-bands kept order in the city streets for the duration of the trial.

From the streets the agitation moved into the coffee-houses and taverns. Charges and countercharges were exchanged over the ale glasses. The doctor himself had openly courted the mob. Prominent Tories had been seen feeing the rioters.

Healths to the doctor and the church were rebuffed by healths to the revolution and the protestant succession.

> Hawkers, like Wild-geese flew along
> In Trains, and cackl'd to the Throng;
> Stretch'd wide their Threats, and strained their Vitals
> To tempt both Parties with their Titles.

On March 17 the trial was over. Sacheverell had been found guilty by a majority of seventeen votes. His sermons were to be burned in the presence of the lord mayor and the sheriffs of London and Middlesex. He himself was to refrain from preaching for a period of three years. The sentence was felt to be ridiculously mild. Once more the crowd gave vent to its feelings and bonfires and illumination greeted the night.

On April 9 three prisoners taken during the dispersal of the mob were arraigned on a charge of high treason in the sessions house in the old Bailey—Francis Willis, a footman; Daniel Dammars, a waterman; and George Purchase, a sheriff's officer. Willis was acquitted. Dammars and Purchase were found guilty and accordingly sentenced, though the sentences somehow were never executed. In the report of the proceedings in the *State Trials* [16] one Ward appears as a witness for the defense. He testifies that about eight o'clock on the night of March 1 he went into the city and saw a great crowd of people, some carrying the two irons which bore up the top of Dr. Burgess' pulpit which he immediately recognized. Is it too fanciful to suppose that the name has reference to Edward Ward, journalist and pamphleteer, even then collecting materials for scenes he was later to describe?

The trial of Sacheverell, though nominally a victory for parliament, alienated from the Whig cause both queen and citizenry. The elections in the summer of 1710 returned a Tory majority to the house. The Whig ministry gave way to Tory appointments. Under the reaction the bill against occasional conformity now passed both houses. Within the year the Tory leaders, Harley and St. John, had risen to positions of prominence and power. Under their guidance secret negotiations for peace were begun with the French. When they had been carried through to a successful conclusion in 1713, Robert Harley had become Earl of Oxford, and St. John, Viscount Bolingbroke, in reward for their services to the kingdom.

The three years from 1711 to 1713 were halcyon days for the Tory journalists. Ward, though busily engaged in the digest of Clarendon's history and other journalistic activity less directly political, found time to celebrate the rising power of his party in five numbers of *The Poetical Entertainer, or Tales, Satyrs, Dialogues, and Intrigues, Serious and Comical,* a periodical issued at irregular intervals during the years 1712–13.[17] To the queen he addressed "An humble Offering to the best of Queens upon the Consumation of Peace." To Bolingbroke he wrote "A Congratulatory Poem to a certain Gentleman lately Honour'd by her Majesty." To the despairing and angry Whigs he shouted derision in songs, satires, and epigrams.

Unfortunately, however, the Tory triumph itself was short-lived. No sooner had the treaty of Utrecht been signed in April 1713, than dissension broke out between the two leaders, Oxford and Bolingbroke. A year later, when Queen Anne died, the Tory party had been broken into fragments and the day of the Tory journalists and pamphleteers was definitely over. Even as the queen lay dying the final act of the Tory debacle was taking place on the streets of London, and the triumphal return of Marlborough provided Ward in *The Republican Procession or the Tumultuous Cavalcade* with an opportunity for another derisive attack on the opposing party.

Marlborough, victor of Blenheim and Ramillies, having been dismissed from his office as captain-general of the English forces in 1711, had a year later retired to the continent, awaiting a change of sentiment in England. With the Tories in control there had been little hope for such a change at the time of his retirement. They had found his ambition and avarice—so they asserted—an insurmountable barrier to peace. Working carefully, the Tory ministers had undermined his influence with the queen. A parliamentary commission had examined his accounts and found him guilty of accepting bribes from the contractors of bread for the army, as well as guilty of withholding pay from the continental troops in his employ.

As already indicated, however, the winter and spring of 1713–14 had seen far-reaching changes in England. With the Earl of Oxford and Viscount Bolingbroke alienated in a struggle for power, and the queen rapidly failing, Bolingbroke himself is said to have accused Oxford of inviting Marlborough to return to England. The duke insisted later that both men had corresponded with him relative to his return. At any rate, early in July the Marlboroughs had left Antwerp for Ostend, where they had been detained by contrary winds. On August 1, the queen having died the same day, they arrived at Dover, and began their progress to London. As the Marlborough party approached Southwark on the morning of the fifth, Sir Charles Cox, a member of parliament from the borough, with a company of grenadiers and two hundred citizens on horseback met the party, and escorted it into the city amid the plaudits of a cheering and enthusiastic crowd. At the last moment a public welcome of bells and a salute of guns had been withdrawn by the officers of state, but the action was insignificant in the cheering and shouting that echoed through the streets. When the escort withdrew from the party at St. James's a parting volley was fired in salute. With the queen lying dead at Kensington it was—whether deliberately chosen or not—an odd moment for a triumphal entry.[18]

This is the account furnished us by history. Ward's is a burlesque account of the procession and the character of the escort. It provides us with some interesting sidelights on the state of the public mind and the journey itself. Ward himself had earlier sung the praises of the duke, but the antipathy of the Tory party to the captain-general had long since changed the heart of many an honest layman, and Ward now repeats the current rumors and prejudice.

Quite fittingly his poem opens with a eulogy to the queen. Then he turns to the fear felt among many of the Tories that the return of the duke is not without secret design. Marlborough had requested before his self-imposed exile to be made captain-general for life. More than one honest citizen now feared he had come to demand the title of lord-protector as well.

> However, aiming to aspire
> As high as Monarchy, or higher,
> And fancy'ng he could rule the State,
> As well as Noll of ancient Date,
> By Zara's Management he reckon'd
> To be an Oliver the Second,
> Fore-knowing that his wife Directress
> Would make an excellent Protectress,
> Or prove a very useful Wife
> To a Lord General for Life.

At any rate their arrival and entry Ward cannot but consider as an insult to the queen and the country. Turning to the description of the almost royal procession through Kent, he describes the duke distributing largess to the rabble to change their hisses into shouts of joy. At Kent Street-End the company of guards awaits the party. Foremost among them rides Sir Charles Cox,

> a Brewing Knight, notorious
> For Actions foolish and inglorious.

Next to him come the citizens on horseback, whom Ward describes man for man: a cobbler, a preaching tailor, a coal-merchant, a Ludgate mercer, a doctor, a leather-seller, a brewer

> Who curs'd the Queen before Her Death,
> For which, to his eternal Shame,
> He paid Marks Forty for the same;
> Yet afterwards was heard to rail,
> And say if Curses could prevail,
> He would be glad at such a Rate
> To curse away his whole Estate.

Among them, too, is Dr. Burgess.

> Next these a Lecturer of Note,
> A preaching Scandal to his Coat . . .
> That his whole Parish, to his Shame,
> Is nick-nam'd Little Amsterdam.

As the procession winds through the streets, numerous incidents take place. According to Ward, Sir Charles Cox had arranged for one of his apprentices to be among the crowd in the street and to address the party with a speech

> In praise of Quixote and his Dame
> Who stopp'd their Coach and heard the same,
> Giving five Shillings, as a Token;
> To him, by whom the Words were spoken.

When the procession is crossing London Bridge a Tory "Esculapian" at the sign of St. George upbraids the entourage from the door of his shop. Sir Charles Cox, riding before, tries to silence him by threatening to strike him with the sword, whereupon the apothecary darts behind his door, seizes a fire shovel, and dares him to come on. Cox riding on, the mob accompanying the procession replies with "dirt-grenadoes" and hurling the missiles among the shelves and pots plays havoc with the shop. In Gracechurch Street a bulldog hearing the drums becomes excited and attacks one of the men, dragging both horse and rider to the ground before the angry mob draws him off and kills him. At Temple Bar one of the wheels of the duke's carriage breaks and the heavy box slumps to the ground. A captain of the train-bands, waiting with his guard to welcome the procession, must needs dismount to help right the coach. Superstitious members of the crowd shake their heads thinking the misfortune an ominous one, and Ward makes much of the incident. Having been transferred to another coach, the duke and duchess proceed to Holywell House.

The account is crudely offensive. Ward, no doubt, meant it to be so. Only the uncertainty of the times must have allowed the author to escape with impunity. In the characters of the various members of the procession he had attacked prominent men of the city with libelous invective. He had been unsparing, too, in his criticism of the duke and duchess. His purpose had been to deride the triumphal entry; for many of his readers and friends he must have amply succeeded.[19]

It was the last of Ward's relatively effective political satires.

Earlier in the same year he had finally completed the first two volumes of *The History of the Grand Rebellion . . . Digested into Verse,* his most ambitious, though futile, political project. The two volumes, as well as the last one issued in 1715, were adorned with a series of eighty-five plates "Engrav'd by the best modern Artists," from original paintings by Vandyke, More, Dobson, Johnson, "and other Eminent Painters." The project, we are told, cost well over five hundred pounds, a sum out of all proportion to its merit. Ward characterized the venture as an "unprecedented Poem . . . troublsome, tedious, and unprofitable" to himself; and the title-page, as if the publishers themselves had been in doubt of Ward's ability to digest the great Clarendon, reminds the reader that the volumes are "useful for all that have, or shall buy the Lord Clarendon, or other Historians of these Times."

Rarely again was Ward to address his readers on problems of state.

VI

The Pious Regicides

These are those Pious Creatures that make a wry Face at a Puppet Shew, yet can justify cutting of Throats; that think a Play-House profane, and vindicate Regicides.[1]

The Secret History of the Calves-Head Club (1703)

To COMPLETE the record of Ward's political writings from the year 1698 to 1713, it is necessary to turn our attention to one more item generally associated with his name. *The Secret History of the Calves-Head Club, or the Republicans Unmask'd* was an anonymous pamphlet first issued in 1703 and republished annually thereafter throughout the period under consideration. It was first assigned to Ward by Walter Wilson in his *Memoirs of the Life and Writings of Daniel De Foe;* and later students of the period have almost invariably accepted the ascription.[2] That Ward was responsible for *The Secret History* as a whole, however, remains exceedingly doubtful. The question of authorship is complicated by the nature of the publication itself, and though there is little question that some part of the responsibility belongs to Ward, the nature of the evidence for such an ascription will become clear only as we examine the various editions of the work itself.

Purporting to unmask a profane and blasphemous society of dissenters who on January 30 assembled to drink a health to the pious memory of Oliver Cromwell and his associate regicides, *The Secret History* ran in its first edition to twenty-two quarto pages and consisted of a "Preface," seven pages of prose entitled "The Secret History of the Calves-Head Club," and a series of "their Anniversary Thanksgiving-Songs on the Thirtieth of January, by them called Anthems."

According to the preface, apparently prepared by the publisher, the intent was admittedly political. "It is hoped," he writes,

that this Publication may give a Check to the Evil of the Example, and destroy the Continuance of the Practice, or at least give fair Warning, and take away the Pretence of Surprize from those, who shall proceed to insult the Government in so Saucy and so Villainous a Manner.

Much in the same vein, he had earlier stated the case for the publication of the collection and suggested, at least by implication, the source of the anthems themselves. "The following Collection," he begins the preface,

has been so industriously handed up and down, where it was thought it would be well received, and confirm those Principles which too many have unhappily sucked in, and raise the Confidence of those who were thought too bashful for their Party, that some honest Men have thought, that there could be no more effectual Remedy for the Mischief it might do, or any surer Way to stop the Career, than a Publication.

Something of an account of the history of the society as well as its ceremonial is presented in the portion designated as "The Secret History of the Calves-Head Club." The account is, of course, based upon hearsay and rumor, but the author—as had the publisher in the preface—attempts to disarm the reader by suggesting that his own good nature made him

look upon it as a Fiction upon the Party, till happening in the late Reign, to be in the Company of a certain Active Whigg, who in all other Respects was a Man of probity enough; he assured me, that to his Knowledge 'twas true; that he knew most of the Members of that Clubb, and that he had often been invited to their Meetings, but that he had always avoided them.

To the probity of the Whig the author is further indebted. The club, so the Whig reported, was founded by Milton and "some other Creatures of the Commonwealth" in opposition to Bishop Juxon, Dr. Sanderson, Dr. Hammond, and "other Divines of the Church of England" who had met privately on each anniversary of the martyrdom, and "compil'd a private Form of Service for the Day, not much different from what we now find in the Liturgy." During the Restoration the club had been compelled to proceed with a good deal of caution, but under the more liberal regime of William they had met "almost in a Public Manner" without the slightest apprehension.

From another gentleman "who about Eight Years ago, went out of mere Curiosity to see their Clubb" the author of "The Secret History" learned that the meetings were held at no particular house, but moved from place to place as convenient, that an ax was usually hung up in the club room as the "Principal Symbol," that the chief item on the bill of fare was "a large Dish of Calves-Heads dressed several ways," that after the removal of the tablecloth an anniversary anthem was sung and a large "Calves-Skull" filled with wine was passed from guest to guest, who drank off a brimmer to the pious memory of the regicides, and that all in turn then contributed to a collection for the mercenary scribbler who had contributed the anthem. "I have taken care," the author concludes,

to set down what the Gentleman told me, as faithfully as my Memory wou'd give me leave; and I am persuaded, that some Persons that frequent the Black Boy in Newgate Street, as they know the Author of the following Lines, so they know this account of the Calves-Head Clubb to be true.[3]

Succeeding the account in "The Secret History," the pamphlet concludes by reprinting a series of "anthems" purported to have been sung by members of the society in the years 1693 to 1697.

Apparently proceeding to three editions within the year, *The Secret History of the Calves-Head Club* reappeared in 1704 under the label of a fourth edition. This, in addition to the earlier material, carried an ironical dedication "to the Grave and Worshipful John Tutchin," charging him not only with encouraging the club but with acting as "Secretary to the abominal Society of King-Killers."

By the time the fifth edition appeared in 1705 the existence of the Calves-Head Club was accepted by the Tories as definitely proved, and the widespread rumor of a "Drinking Plot" in the borough of Southwark aroused Whigs and dissenters to their own defense. The actual facts in the case are none too clear, but the nature of the rumor can be followed readily enough in the pages of the rival Whig and Tory publications, *The Observator* and *The Rehearsal*. In the issue of *The Observator* for February 10–14 Tutchin refers to the fact that a tailor in Southwark has been taken up for drinking a health to the regicides on January 30. *The Rehearsal* for February 10–17 also makes reference to the story and charges Tutchin directly with attending the lecture at Salters' Hall on the day in question and afterwards joining a "Calves-Head refreshment in Southwark," where members sang anthems and drank suitable healths "to the Pious Memory of that Noble Britain who Struck the Stroke, and Cut off the Head of that Anti-Christian Tyrant, etc."[4]

To "Lying, Libeling Lesley," Tutchin replied in *The Observator* for February 21–24. No such health had been drunk and the entertainment had not been held during the day but in the evening. The accusation against the tailor had been brought by one Goody Strumm at whose house the party met, but the tailor's house having been searched in turn, nothing had been found but an eighteen-year old musket, so that the report

came to a Cods-Head Story at last: for when the Calves-Head would not do, they found the Gentlemen had din'd at an Ale-House upon Salt Cod and Eggs, and then they turn'd it that way, as if the Cods-Heads had been Emblematically struck off, hereupon the Fishmonger was examin'd, and it appear'd that the Cods had no Heads.

To the additional charge of Leslie that at both Salters' and Pinners' Hall the memory of Charles I had been insulted by the singing of the psalm

> This was the mighty Work of God,
>   This was the Lord's own Fact;
> And it is wond'rous to behold
>   With Eyes, that noble Act.
> This is the joyful Day indeed,
>   Which God himself hath wrought;
> Let us be glad, and joy therein,
>   In Heart, in Mind, and Thought,

Tutchin replied that Mr. Barton's, rather than Hopkins and Sternhold's translation, had been used and the psalms were those of Matthew xi. 6 and Luke vii. 23. In *The Rehearsal* for March 10–17 Leslie once more returned to the matter, reiterating the charge of the psalms, and concluded with an additional bit of gossip he had picked up. After the services the party had been entertained at Squire L——'s, where they had discussed the day, the sermon, and the song, and one of the witty parsons had remarked that he would have preferred to have chosen for his text, John xi. 23, "Lord by this time he stinketh, the words of Martha to our Saviour."

The Secret History of the Calves-Head Club for 1705, of course, contained no reference to the Southwark story, though it carried several "large additions," i.e., "A Vindication of the Royal Martyr . . . written in the Time of Usurpation, by the Celebrated Mr. Butler, Author of Hudibras"; "A Character of a Presbyterian . . . by Sir John Denham"; "The Character of a Calves-Head Clubbman"; and a new series of anthems for the years 1697 to 1699. The sixth edition, which followed in January of 1706, however, contained "An Appendix to the Continuation of the Secret History of the Calves-Head Club" which recounted the Southwark incident as further evidence of the society's actual existence. No new information about the incident is furnished the reader unless one accepts as authentic the rather ludicrous explanation offered by members of the congregation at Salters' that the selection of the 118th Psalm owed itself to "the Ignorance of the Clerk" who had "made choice of the very same Stanzas at the Burial of his own Wife, when her Funeral Sermon was preach'd."

A seventh edition of *The Secret History* appeared in 1709, an eighth in 1713. Tutchin having died some years before, the ironical dedication is replaced in the 1713 edition by "An Epistle to the Worthy Members of the Calfs-Head-Club," reiterating the general charges and warning the society to disband lest it furnish the author "with new Matter against the next Thirtieth of January." In this edition the "Appendix to the Continuation of the Secret History of the Calves-Head Club" is supplemented with an account of "Remarkable Accidents and Transactions at the Calves-Head-Club," a new series of "incidents." Fortunately, however, the "Remarkable

Accidents" are not all as solemnly laid down as are the accusations of Leslie in *The Rehearsal*. It is obvious that the author or authors of *The Secret History* have become somewhat weary with their perennial denunciations. The "Remarkable Accidents" will now include adventures both "Serious and Comical," and more than one of the stories indicate that political pamphleteering has been superseded by divertissement.

With the death of Queen Anne and the rise to power on the part of the Whigs the cry of "Calves-Head Club-Man" slowly lost its usefulness. A lone edition appeared in 1721, but no "new Matter against the next Thirtieth of January" had been found to include in its pages. From a small pamphlet of twenty-two quarto pages in 1703 it had grown to an octavo volume of over two hundred pages. For a full decade it had retained its popularity and each recurrent January it had served to discredit a political foe.

The violent political bias of the pamphlet of course demanded anonymity on the part of both author and publisher at the time of its publication. Whether or not Edward Ward had anything to do with *The Secret History* depends upon the nature of the original materials, as distinct from those the publishers compiled from other sources. Had Ward acted for the bookseller [5] his own authorship would have been confined in the first edition to the account under the title of "The Secret History." To later volumes he might have contributed the dedication to Tutchin in the fourth edition, "The Character of a Calves-Head Clubbman," the "Reflections" upon anthems, and "the Appendix to the Continuation of the Secret History" in the sixth edition, and "An Epistle to the Worthy Members of the Calf's-Head-Club" and "The Remarkable Accidents and Transactions" in the eighth.

There is considerable variation in the spirit as well as in the manner of the materials so catalogued, but at least two of the items bear the unmistakable imprint of Ward. Even to the casual reader the "Remarkable Accidents and Transactions" both "Serious and Comical" concluding in nearly every case with a series of verses on the subject, are strik-

ingly similar both in spirit and manner to *The London Spy*
and to *The History of the London Clubs,* as we shall see
presently. "The Character of a Calves-Head Club-Man," too,
makes abundant use of similes and metaphors which the
reader of Ward recognizes as extraordinarily characteristic.
Of the Calves-Head Club member the author writes,

It is as easy a Matter for a Man to take an Elephant by the Snout, and
throw him over his Back, as a Fox does a Goose, as it is to convince him
of any stated Opposition to his own partial Sentiments. . . . When he
disputes his Principles, he is as hot as Pepper, as biting as Mustard, and
as sour as Vinegar. . . . He is an impatient Angler, who thinks it best
fishing in troubled Waters; and hates Peace and Quietness, as much as
a poor Debter does the Sight of a Bayliff, or a Country Farmer a wet
Harvest.

It is possible that Ward may have contributed the remaining articles under consideration as well, though they are decidedly less characteristic. The account of the origin of the
club under the title of "The Secret History" is, for instance,
ingeniously disarming and suggests a subtlety and restraint
not elsewhere found in Ward's writings. On the other hand,
the dedication to Tutchin, the "Reflections" upon the anthems, and "the Appendix to the Continuation of the Secret
History," in the sixth edition, may well have been contributed by him.

The nature of the successive issues of *The Secret History,*
however, suggests that a number of writers rather than a
single author may have been responsible for the production.
More logical than the assumption of Ward's responsibility
for *The Secret History* in its entirety, is the supposition that
the unknown publisher, or publishers, may have solicited
the talent of a number of Tory writers, and that Ward was
among them. At least one other factor—this time an external
one—points towards Ward's responsibility in the matter. In
1717 Ward, writing the preface to *A Collection of Historical and State Poems, Satyrs, Songs, and Epigrams,* published
as Volume V of the *Miscellaneous Writings,* tells us he had
originally intended to give an account of all his past writings,
but that upon a second consideration, finding himself under
a necessity "of not owning several unlucky Brats, of whom

I am the true Father, I thought it safest to defer the Catalogue
I intended to a fairer Opportunity." It is difficult to conceive
to which of the writings that have subsequently become
known as his this might apply if not to parts of *The
Secret History.* There could have been no doubt in 1717
about his authorship of *Hudibras Redivivus,* for which he
had earlier been sentenced to the pillory. There could have
been equally little doubt about *Vulgus Britannicus.*[6] The five
numbers of *The Poetical Entertainer,* in which he had attacked prominent members of the Whig party, *The Republican Procession,* and the attack on Bishop Hoadly in *The
Tory Quaker, or Aminadab's New Vision in the Fields,* are
all included in the volume then in the process of publication.
On the other hand one gathers that *The Secret History of
the Calves-Head Club* was still under fire. With the Whigs
fully in control of the government it might have been ill-
advised and even dangerous to admit authorship of so
potent an attack.

A question of considerable interest to the modern student
is whether or not such a society actually existed. It is possible that no such mysterious meetings took place on January 30 anywhere except in the minds of the Tory pamphleteers, who found the "Calves-Head Club" an effective political
bludgeon.[7] Recently scholars have been inclined, however, to
accept the possibility that the story of the club's existence and
activity was not, at least in its entirety, a mere fabrication on
the part of political opponents. It is not likely, of course, that
any society, of such extensive proportions as the authors and
publishers of *The Secret History* would indicate, existed
among the dissenters, nor is it within the realm of possibility
to suppose that Milton played any role in its organization
whatever. On the other hand it is not difficult to see how a
society of the kind, as well as wide-spread rumors of its existence, might have arisen.

January thirtieth was a sacred day, celebrated throughout
the entire kingdom by parliamentary proclamation, in honor
of the martyrdom of Charles I. On that day sermons throughout the entire kingdom rehearsed the sufferings of the king

and hurled dire imprecations at all sympathizers with the
cause of the Commonwealth or the principles of revolution.
It is only reasonable to suppose that men who found little
sympathy with the fervor of the public celebration and who
were in principle opposed to undue emphasis upon the royal
prerogative may have on occasion, singly or in groups, de-
rided the zeal of their contemporaries. In that case rumors
of the event might gradually spread through society and
lay hold upon the fertile imagination of the man in the
street. In the coffee-house and tavern the rumor might grow
to enormous proportions. All of the insignia and ceremonial
of the Calves-Head Club would shortly be known and the
profane hymns chanted in horrified whispers.

   That there was at least some such basis in reality for the
common man's belief in the existence of the society is indicated by writers other than the authors of *The Secret History.* Samuel Wesley was a dissenter who later conformed to
the Anglican church. In 1704, being involved at the moment
in a quarrel over an earlier letter on the educational policies
of dissenting academies, he published *A Defense of a Letter
Concerning the Education of Dissenters in their Private
Academies.* In it he relates an incident which took place in
the year 1693 before his own change of heart. "I happened to
be with some of my former acquaintances," he writes,

at an House in Leadenhall-street or thereabouts, in the Year 93. all of
'em, as I remember, were then Dissenters, except one, and he has since
left the Church of England. Their Discourse was so fulsomly lewd and
profane, that I could not endure it; but went to the other side of the
Room with a Doctor of Physic, who had been my Fellow-Pupil at Mr.
Morton's, and to whom I owe that Justice, to declare he likewise dis-
lik'd the Conversation. A little while after we went to Supper; but then
the Scene was chang'd, and they fell a railing at Monarchy, and blas-
pheming the memory of King Charles the Martyr, discoursing of their
Calves-head Club, and producing or repeating some Verses on that Subject. I remember one of the Company told us of a Design they had at
their next Calves-Head Feast, to have a Cold Pye serv'd on the Table, with
either a Live-Cat or Hare, I've forgot whether, enclos'd: and they had
contriv'd to put one of their Company who lov'd Monarchy, and knew
nothing of the matter, to cut it up; whereupon, and on the leaping out of
the Cat or Hare, they were all to set up a Shout, and cry, Haloo! Old Puss!
—To the Honour of the Good Old Cause, and to shew their affection to a
Commonwealth.[8]

THE OLD EAST INDIA WHARF AT LONDON BRIDGE

From a painting by Peter Monamy

Tom Brown, too, had asserted the existence of the society as early as 1702 and boldly proclaimed John Tutchin, the editor of *The Observator,* as its secretary and chief promoter.[9]

The nature of the hearsay, rumor, and half-truth responsible for the belief in the existence of the society is nowhere more clearly presented than in *The Secret History* itself. Before the appearance of the pamphlet "The Calves-Head Club" was a political epithet tossed about among the warring factions, without, one takes it, any significant amount of credence. With its publication the belief in the existence of the society suddenly crystallized. The "unmasking" of so wicked and profane a society must have been regarded as something in the nature of a publisher's scoop. The specious sincerity with which the existence of the society is asserted, the disarming deference to their materials on the part of both publisher and author accounts to a large degree for the success of the attempt. The former expresses himself as hesitant to expose the villainy of his opponents and as being driven to it only by the violence of their own party rancor. The author humbly submits that the source for his information was himself a Whig and a former member of the society. The collected anthems, so the publisher asserts, have been handed up and down among those in sympathy with the Commonwealth until he thought there could be no more effective remedy for the mischief they might do, or any better way of stopping their career, than by their publication.

As a matter of fact, evidence to support the existence of a group or society whose activities lent credit to the rumor of the Calves-Head Club, is nowhere more clearly found than in the songs themselves. One may say with a good degree of certainty that they are not fabrications by Ward or any of the other authors. Whether or not it is true, as the publisher asserts,[10] that they were written by Benjamin Bridgewater, who "was largely rewarded by Members of the Club for his pains," many of them are apparently authentic songs and were actually written to be sung by sympathizers with the cause of revolution. One of them, for instance, is identified by Wesley as the song he heard in 1693.[11] Another, "A Psalm sung the 30th of January, 1696," was reprinted in *Poems on Affairs of State* (1703),[12] and interesting variants in the text indicate that the song was transmitted orally and does not owe its origin or preservation solely to its appearance in *The Secret History*.[13]

By far the greater portion of *The Secret History,* however, is given over to the promulgation of rumor and hearsay. We have already seen how the edition of 1706 made capital of the incident in Southwark as additional proof of the actual existence of the society. "The Remarkable Accidents and Transactions at the Calves-Head Club" appended to the seventh edition of *The Secret History* in 1713, one of the two items obviously written by Ward, is an entire series of "incidents" arranged chronologically according to the year in which they occurred from 1705 to 1712. To one interested in following through the gossip and hearsay upon which the belief in the existence of the society continued to flourish, they present an interesting sidelight upon political conditions and the state of the public mind during the latter years of the reign of Queen Anne.

It is unnecessary at the moment to run the gamut of the entire seven years. Part of the material for the year 1712, however, ably reflects the nature of the incidents which gave rise to the belief in the existence of the society, as well as the kind of incident a belief in the society could create. On January 26, a market day in the borough of Southwark, "a carrionly Slink, or at least a Rainbow colour'd Calf" was brought into market and straightway condemned by the inspectors, Moses Web and John Gun. Instead of ordering it burned immediately, however, the inspectors contrived out of dissenting principles, so the account runs, to postpone the execution until the thirtieth, when in a public bonfire on Margaret Hill "the Head and neck were burned apart from the body." Witnesses at the fire becoming incensed, Robert Marshal, William Rubidge, and Thomas Havergil informed against the inspectors and had them summoned before John Lode, Walter Cook, and William Overman, justices of the peace for the county of Surrey, where they were convicted of a misdemeanor, bound over to quarter-sessions, and there fined twenty marks and imprisoned until the money was paid and they had found security for their good behavior.

At the trial one William Stevens had asserted under oath
that when members of the crowd attempted to dissuade
Web from burning the carrion upon so improper a day, Web
had answered him, "That he would roast the Head for Doctor Sacheverell's Supper."

Much of the material retold in "The Remarkable Accidents
and Transactions at the Calves-Head Club" both "Serious
and Comical" is, however, less worthy of report. Its nature
would indicate that Ward had wearied of the undue solemnity with which he had reiterated his earlier charges against
the dissenters. At moments he was certainly more anxious
to entertain than to expose, and there is a good deal of evidence that towards the end he himself, as well as the more
intelligent of his readers, was perfectly conscious that to
some degree he was engaged in perpetrating a hoax. At any
rate it was the humor of some of the current stories, rather
than any danger to the state, that interested them.

For the year 1709, for instance, he relates a story of an
eminent bookseller near Leadenhall Street, who, having forgotten the date, inadvertently allowed his cook to serve him
calves-head for dinner on the night of January 30. The cook-
maid afterwards tossing the remnants into the street outside
the door, the neighbors became suspicious and reflected "with
no little Severity upon the Bookseller's Reputation." Finally
a leatherseller of the neighborhood heard of it, and coming
to satisfy himself of the truth of the story found his own
spaniel eagerly engaged over the scraps. "A Pox take you
Chops for a Fanatic Puppy," the leatherseller is reputed to
have shouted, "after all the expensive Education I have given
you, under Tim the Cobler, are you turned Regicide?" In
mock solemnity Ward concludes the account by an elegy
upon the poor dog who had been forced to pay the penalty
for his rashness.

> Alas, poor Dog, 'twas very hard,
>   A Halter should dispatch thee hence;
> Methinks one Puppy might have spar'd
>   Another for a first Offence.

One final incident, included in the material for the year
1712, is worth recounting, since it relates an attempt upon

the life of Oxford rarely recorded. On Tuesday, November 4, the penny post brought to the door a package directed to the lord treasurer, who, upon opening it as far as the packthread would allow, discovered a pistol. The box thereupon was removed to a window and the packthread untied with the utmost caution. Inside, the pistol, ready primed and cocked, was so arranged that, discharged by the person opening the box, it would set off, by means of quills filled with wildfire, two inkhorns charged with powder and ball. Fortunately the amateur bomb was dismantled without damage. No doubt—according to the account—the incident was only one more example of the outrageous behavior of members of the Calves-Head Society.

Out of such material, it is safe to say, much of the lore of the Calves-Head Club had originally grown. Undoubtedly there were dissenters who throughout the period of royalist dominance withdrew among themselves out of a common sympathy and out of a desire for protection from the ardent participants in the celebration of the royal martyrdom. There some of the bolder and more daring spirits among them may have on occasion composed and sung the songs in derision of Charles I and his execution. Fears and rumors multiplied. The story of the existence of the society began to be whispered in the coffee-houses and taverns. Politicians noised it abroad. A firm belief in the existence of the society served to create "incidents"; the "incidents" themselves serving to substantiate the belief in the minds of the people. In the public's acceptance of the existence of the society, however, *The Secret History* played by far the most important role. And so thoroughly had it accomplished its purpose that a festive imitation of the reputed calves-head ceremony caused a public riot in the streets of London nearly fifteen years after the last edition of *The Secret History* had appeared on the bookstalls.[14]

VII

Man and Manners

Therefore, since it as essentially relates to the Comforts of the Life of Man, to know what other People are, as well as what he himself should be, I thought it no Ill Task to Communicate to the World what knowledge of Mankind I have gather'd from my own Experience.

"The Preface," *A Journey to Hell* (1700)

THE MAJOR PORTION of Ward's writing during the reign of Queen Anne was non-political in character, however, and his own fortune as a journalist was far less dependent upon his political efforts than was that of many of his contemporaries. The years from 1700 to 1712 were for him particularly busy ones. His "name was up"; his wares sold. Volume after volume appeared on the bookstalls. Judged either by the number of titles or by the accumulated pages of his writings, no writer in England during that decade—with the exception of Defoe—out-published him. It is true that many of his writings were of an ephemeral nature, that they were often obscene, and that they now seem at times needlessly prolix and dull; still, he had a steady hand upon the pulse of a growing reading public. He knew their appetites and tastes. If it is apparent that he shamelessly catered to a certain grossness and vulgarity inherent in the crowd, it is equally true that he demonstrated once and for all that a scribbler, a mere Grubstreet wit, could, without the support of a political faction or the patronage of the rich, earn a livelihood with his pen.[1] "As for my own part," he writes,

I thank my Stars, I had the happiness of knowing the World a little too early, ever to be much deluded with fair promises, or to wast much time in precarious Dependencies upon such persons, who are ready enough to give you their Hands, and to flatter you with their Tongues, when their Hearts are far from you; so that, I have rather chose to apply myself closely to that Talent, which Providence has given me for a comfortable Subsistence.[2]

His success lay in his knowledge of rudimentary psychology. He knew how to catch the eye of the man in the street with provocative titles. He knew, too, how to inveigle him into buying the book with an intriguing preface. "If anybody should wonder," he once commented,

> why I couch'd some of the Poems under such surprising Titles, I must needs tell 'em, I borrow'd my Method from our Moorfields Conjurers, who use their utmost Art to put on a terrible Countenance, that every body that gazes on their Outsides may think the Devil is in 'em; and they undoubtedly find it a very useful Policy; for I have commonly observ'd, that he thrives the best, and has his Door most crowded, that can look most frightful.[3]

Having persuaded the readers to buy, he knew how to divert them through page after page of the text, providing, of course, their tastes were not too squeamish, and they were willing to "wave their Judgments to give room for their Good Nature." "Here's pleasant Poetry for the Youthful, that Love the Jingling of Rhime"; says his bookseller, advertising Volume II of the writings,

> and Merry Prose for the Graver Christian Reader . . . Here are Amorous Intrigues to Oblige the Ladies; Tales, Jests, Flirts, Puns, and Conundrums, to tickle the Fancies of the Witty; Also Rambles, Drunken Frolicks, Squabbles, Rangles, and Rencounters, to please Nocturnal Tiplers.[4]

But it was Ward himself who most accurately characterized his own writing. In the preface to *The Fourth Volume of Writings,* having presented the purchaser with his customary denial of malicious intent and specific reference, he concludes pointedly, "I'll engage a Man cannot go Twenty Yards in any Street in London, but he will meet some Original or other, whose likeness he will find so well preserved, that he may know them by their Pictures."

It is a surprisingly frank remark, and summarizes in simple fashion the essence of his success. It was his forte to describe the world he knew. His success with *A Trip to Jamaica* had taught him the market-value of humorous invective and satiric burlesque. His later experience with *The London Spy* had shown him the abundance of material that lay at his own door or in a neighboring alley. In a sense all his later work, even the political writings in a measure, are a repetition and extension of that pattern. Readers then, much as now, were interested in the representation of their own environs and society. They loved to see themselves and to laugh at their neighbors in the half-serious, half-indecent, jocular characterizations of one who knew their own world and spoke their own language. They awaited anxiously—one is led to believe —and conned with relish the phrases of one who often wrote with more daring and greater earthiness than they themselves spoke.

More popular with Ward during this period than the prose trip was the character, a genre which had enjoyed a considerable vogue nearly a hundred years earlier. The brief, pithy delineation of what one today might call types of personality had been introduced to English readers by Joseph Hall's *Characters of Virtues and Vices* in 1608. In Hall, where the characters were closely modeled upon those by Theophrastus, the emphasis had been upon the abstract virtue or vice, and the purpose, a moral one, since the sketches were to serve for "exhortation and dissuasion." Among his successors who were less moral in their approach than Hall, the character had become less and less concerned with abstract definition. In Sir Thomas Overbury, *Characters or Witty Descriptions of the Properties of Sundry Persons,* and in John Earle, *Microcosmography,* the character had become chiefly a description of an individual or type, and the primary concern of the author had become the foibles and idiosyncrasies of men rather than abstract principles of virtue and vice. From Hall's early concern with the general patterns of behavior, such as "The Wise Man," "The Honest Man," "The Flatterer," and "The Slothful," the interest among later writers moved to such types as "An Affectate Traveller," "A Braggadochio Welshman," "A Roaring Boy," "A Raw Young Preacher," "A Pot-Poet," and "A Tobacco-Seller."

Quite in line with this general development had been the broadening of the genre to include place and institution as well as person.[5] Earle had, for instance, included among his characters that of "A Tavern," "A Bowl-Alley," "Paul's Walk," and "A Prison." Lupton included that of "Saint Paul's Church," "The Bridge," "Cheapside," "Paris-Garden," and "Play-Houses."[6]

Moreover, as the subject had veered toward the unusual and the eccentric, the style had tended toward the satiric and the burlesque. Hall had expressly forbidden his readers to laugh except in bitter disdain, but both Overbury and Earle sought to amuse as well as to chasten the evildoer. In time the emphasis came to be less and less on the penetrating insight with which the author beheld the truth of his subject and more and more upon the style itself—the ready phrase, the amusing metaphor, and the witty conceit—and the character itself became increasingly concerned with the externals, with the appearance and behavior of a man, his stature, his customs, and his manners.

This complete shift in emphasis and concern is nowhere more apparent than in Ralph Johnson's *The Scholar's Guide from the Accidence to the University* (London: T. Pierrepont, 1665) in which he sets down the fundamental rules for the writing of characters, as they were conceived in the year 1665.

1. Chuse a Subject, viz, such a sort of men as will admit of variety of observation, such be, drunkards, usurers, lyars, taylors, excise-men, travellers, pedlars, merchants, tapsters, lawyers, an upstart gentleman, a young Justice, a Constable, an Alderman, and the like.
2. Express their natures, qualities, conditions, practices, tools, desires, aims, or ends, by witty Allegories or Allusions, to things or terms in nature, or art, of like nature and resemblance, still striving for wit and pleasantness, together with tart nipping jerks about their vices and misscarriages.
3. Conclude with some witty and neat passage, leaving them to the effect of their follies or studies.

With the revolution of 1688 and the rise of an intense interest in political party, the character, along with other literary forms, had been superseded by—or adapted to—political pamphleteering and imitations of *Hudibras*.[7] In 1698, largely under the impetus given to the form by the *Caractères* of

La Bruyère in France, a new translation of the characters of Theophrastus appeared on the English bookstalls.[8] This was followed within a year by a translation of the *Caractères* of La Bruyère under the title *The Characters, or Manners of the Age,* and in 1702 by *The English Theophrastus, or the Manners of the Age, being the Modern Characters of the Court, the Town, and the City,* an adaptation of the genre to the local scene. Almost immediately the character in prose and in verse became again one of the most common forms exercised by poets, journalists, and essayists alike.

Ward, of course, had made use of the character as early as 1698. As we have already seen, the early numbers of *The London Spy* had included on occasion a description of individuals encountered, closely resembling the character, and the fifteenth number was entirely given over to the form. Moreover, it is true that *The London Spy,* as well as many of the trips, are in themselves a kind of character, in which the locale or the institution becomes the subject. In all of them, however, the characterization of place or institution remains subservient to the motif of the trip or journey. In the writings after 1700 about to be considered the character has become the dominant pattern.

Ward made use of his earlier experience. The weakness of the character whether isolated or in a series, lay in its essentially static quality. In *The London Spy* he had discovered the method of enlivening the formal presentation of character by the association of the character with place, by a dramatic introduction, and by the use of appropriate dialogue. Now that the current interest permitted, he could turn all these to account.

In the first series of writings to be considered it is the presentation of character through dialogue which is the basic pattern. The use of dialogue as a literary device had, of course, a tradition quite as ancient as that of the character, and one considerably more familiar to the average reader. In Ward's own day the colloquy had peculiarly lent itself to the discussion of controversial issues, and proved a device easily appropriated by the pamphleteers and journalists. In periodical literature its chief use had been in the question and answer method of L'Estrange and Dunton, where it provided an exchange between reader and editor.[9] In Ward the colloquy serves less as a medium for the expression of the author's ideas, however, than it does as a means of character portrayal, and again suggests his debt to the dramatic rather than to the Socratic tradition.

Both Ward and his readers were familiar with the theater; if not with the more fashionable playhouses of the city, at least with their counterpart—the drolls and pantomimes of Bartholomew Fair. To the latter Ward devotes considerable time in both *The London Spy* and in *Hudibras Redivivus,* amply demonstrating his familiarity with the dramatic gusto and the racy, colloquial language of the Smithfield shows. In revising the ten numbers of *The Weekly Comedy* before including them in *The Third Volume of the Writings,* he arranged them as a drama in three acts, though this may have been little more than a ruse for avoiding prosecution in reprinting a satire suppressed in its original form. In 1705 he published a Bartholomew droll entitled *Honesty in Distress but Relieved by No Party, a Tragedy, as it is Basely Acted by Her Majesty's Subjects upon God's Stage the World.* Though it does not seem likely that in either case they were written to be reproduced upon the stage, they serve to illustrate Ward's familiarity with the dramatic medium which he currently brought to bear in the presentation of character in dialogue.

Ward's earliest attempt in presenting the character in dialogue is *The Insinuating Bawd and the Repenting Harlot* (1699), a conventional account of the innocent maiden, misled by the counsel of an older friend and seduced and betrayed by an Inns of Court gamester. It is an unsuccessful poem, though his bookseller tells us of a certain clergyman who not only bought it and read it, but expressed himself to the effect that if all the women in London were to read it, the poem would work a greater reformation among them than forty sermons. In 1704 he continued the experiment with *Female Dialogues, or Ladies Conversations,* a series of prose conversations on marital fidelity, the theater and meetinghouse, the smoking of tobacco and the drinking of Nantz. The characters presented are "Madam Wheybeard, an Old Lady, who had Marry'd a Young Gentleman, and Madam Morecock, a Young Lady, who had Marry'd an Old Gentleman," loving sisters in affliction, as Ward characterized them; "Madam Antipope, a Great Sermon-Hunter, and Madam Pitlove, a Frequenter of Plays"; and "Madam Le Nantzy, an Old Maid, a Smoaker of Tobacco, and a Great Lover of Cold Tea, and Madam Manlove, a Buxom Widow who lately Buried her Husband." *Female Dialogues* is more readable than *The Insinuating Bawd,* primarily because it is in prose, which Ward invariably handled with greater flexibility and freedom than verse.

Female Dialogues in turn was no more than a prelude to a more ambitious project. In 1708 Ward began a series of dialogues concerning the married state, bringing out six of them under the title, *Marriage Dialogues, or a Poetical Peep into the State of Matrimony.* Within two years he had extended the number to fifty-four dialogues and presented his public with *Nuptial Dialogues and Debates: or an Useful Prospect of the Felicities and Discomforts of a Marry'd Life Incident to all Degrees, from the Throne to the Cottage.*[10] This he dedicated to "The Worthy Gentlemen of the County and Corporation of Leicester" in return for the gracious hospitality and "many Civilities" extended by the home folk to the rising young author of London when he had visited them some time before.

Nuptial Dialogues and Debates hardly merited the dignity of the dedication or the popularity it subsequently achieved.[11] The gallery of characters is an extensive one: the prudent wife and extravagant husband who "beggars" her children; the fumbling libertine who delights in annoying his pert young wife by talking about his past "skirmishes"; the wealthy woman married to a man of inferior fortune; the generous husband and his parsimonious wife; an "old drolling Gentleman with a Carbuncle-Nose, and his merry Tallow-fac'd Lady"; a blunt old gentleman and his "fantastical Lady, who, between forty and fifty, had made her a colour'd Furbelo'd-Scarf"; an old "prodigal, new-sworn Constable and his young noisy Wife" who challenges his authority; a generous city "Mechanick" and his stingy wife who locks up the cupboard "to keep the Victuals from his Apprentices"; "King Avery, the Pirate, and his Indian Princess at Madagascar"; a "Great Commander and his Lady, upon his Arrival from the Wars," an obvious reference to Marlborough. The characters, however, are not as well conceived or as ably presented as those in a series to which we shall presently turn.

Inherent in the verse dialogue is a certain inadequacy in the unity and fullness of the portrait. Ward is at his best when he concerns himself with the appearance and behavior of his subjects and with the presentation of typical situations. Here he was divorced from any direct comment by the narrator and from the use of situation, as well as handicapped by the exigencies of meter and rhyme, which served to restrain his use of metaphor and simile and the racy, colloquial idiom of the streets.

The popularity of the *Nuptial Dialogues and Debates* lay in the topics discussed rather than in the characters. To a marked degree they concern themselves with questions similar to those presented to the *Athenian Mercury* for discussion by its readers, and demonstrate the interest of the middle class in problems of thrift, profligacy, the relation of man and wife, the education of daughters, the treatment of apprentices, religion, and dress.[12] Ward's attitude in the "Moral Reflections" appended to every dialogue are consistent with the general middle class view. The extravagant husband and the tippling wife ought to be restrained; the wife should still try to please though the husband be tyrannically severe; the young girl should be taught domestic duties rather than sent to the dancing school; the apprentices are most profitable when kindly treated. For his readers this moral suasion may well have outweighed the inadequacy in the presentation of characters.

A happier attempt of Ward's to present character through dialogue, this time in association with the characterization of place, was *The Weekly Comedy, as it is Dayly Acted at most Coffee-Houses in London,* the first of two periodicals under a strikingly similar title, already referred to in the chapter on political writings.[13] *The Weekly Comedy* has three facets rather than one, but certainly its political bias is the least important. Of first importance are the characters themselves, whose names are suggestive of their trades and behavior. The tradesmen, for instance, are represented by the merchant, Truck; the dissenting tailor, Cant; and the turncoat, All-craft. Among the sharpers are Snap, a quack by the name of Plush, and a projector, Whim. Present, too, is the city beau in Prim, the lawyer in Squabble, the sailor and soldier in Log and Snarl, the poet in Scan-all, and the newswriter in Scribble. As the issues of the periodical succeed each other, the character of each comes out more and more sharply.

In the opening number it is Scribble, the newswriter, who dashes into the room, and, in reply to the chorus of "What news?" from the others, relates for a solemn truth the discovery by some mariners of an island off the coast of Ireland, where,

the Natives, I am inform'd, are such a diminutive Race of Tom Thumbs, that the Discoverers first took 'em to be Children, till they came near enough the little Mortals to discern their Beards; none of 'em exceeding the height of a large Coffee-Pot, and yet, as 'tis said, are such Little, Brisk, Nimble, Hot-Mettled Fellows, that they no more fear a Man of twice their Bigness, than a Knight Errant does a Monster . . . their Sheep are no bigger than English Rabbits, but very delicious Food; their Wooll being Cole-black, and their Horns white as Ivory. Their Cows are all Milk white, with Nut brown Tails; and are so very large that their Dairy-Maids are forc'd to stand bolt upright upon a Buffet-stool to milk 'em. Their Horses are shap'd like our Grey Hounds, but as Tall as Asses, their Bodies of a Dun colour, with a White List down their Backs, but their Mains and Tails are finely dappled, every single Hair being of divers Colours. Their Mastiff Dogs are no bigger than Guinea-Pigs; and yet, like the People, are of that Courage, they will Fight the Devil.

The story, of course, reminds one of the famous travels of Gulliver,[14] but Ward's satire, unlike Swift's, is directed primarily at the news-writer, Scan-all, and at the preposterous yarns which circulate among the denizens of the coffee-house as news. Before Scribble, upon his first announcement, is allowed to proceed with his story, he is interrupted by Cant, the hypocritical dissenter. "Pray, Mr. Scribble, what is it? I hope no ill design against the Government. I vow I am ready to faint, for fear it shou'd be something to the Injury of our Religion, or the Dishonour of the Church." He in turn is interrupted by Log, the Mariner.

Prithee, Friend, hold thy Tongue . . . I have seen more Salt Water than ever thou hast done. I have known all these Irish Seas thou talkest on, ever since I was scarce big enough to Pump Ship . . . And I am certain if any such Island had been thereabouts, I should have seen it some time or other; But I'll hold thee a Bowl of Punch, to a Pipe of Tobacco, there's no such Place you talk on, unless it's lately dropp'd out of the Clouds, or risen from the bottom of the Sea.

Scribble confirms the truth of his story by saying it appeared in *The Post Boy,* whereupon Cant affirms, "Nay, then I am as well satisfied it's Truth, as if I had read it in Partridge's Almanack. For all true Protestants ought to believe that Paper, as readily as a Turk does the *Alchoran.*"

In the later numbers of the periodical Scribble dashes in again and again with his news. Now it is of a comical incident in Hackney; then again of "one of the prettiest Adventures by way of Wedlock" from "Spittle-fields." Once he dashes out as abruptly as he enters to secure the story of an incident in King Street, near Guilford, where Snarl reports he saw three post boys mounted upon hackneys annoying a newly-wed bridegroom by the blowing of horns.

In one of the later numbers it is Prim, the beau, who holds the center of the stage. Snarl has just demanded to know if any one could inform him whether the king of Spain "be dead or no." Replying in the affirmative, Prim exasperates the captain by his precious manner and refined niceties of speech. Snarl flies into a rage. Prim apologizes profusely and then, turning to the drawer, gives vent to his own wounded dignity. "Here, Boy, you Slovenly Rascal, bring a clean Napkin, and wipe this Tobacco Dust off the Table, and not let a Gentleman sit like a Puppy in a Chimney Corner, amongst Dust and Ashes."

Whim is allowed to characterize himself. "A man of our Business," he says, "ought to have as many Notions in his Head at once, as there are Cogs in the Wheel of a Wind-Mill, if it be only to keep his Faculties in Agitation; for if ever he suffer his Brains to cool, his Conceits all die like Salamanders." At the moment he and All-craft have a wonderful invention, an engine capable of making periwigs "after the Newest French Mode," which with the assistance of two men "to Draw, Size, and Curl" will do as much work as fifty laborers. Prim becomes interested at once and makes an appointment with the two projectors for ten o'clock the next morning at Pontack's to look at a special wig made from the model.[15] The next afternoon he drops back into the coffee-house wearing the new wig, for which he informs his curious friends he paid the ripe sum of fifty guineas. It is Snarl once more, who puts a damper on his spirit as he sums up in expressive, if vulgar, phraseology the ridiculous appearance of the excessively long and heavy wigs fashionable at the time. To him Prim appears "like an Essex Calf peeping out of a Thicket of Brambles, or like the Fundament of a Peacock with his Tail spread; for I can scarce see any part of your Face but your Mouth for Periwig."

There is a good deal of interest and humor in the characters and one is apt to be drawn too far from the business at hand. There is the mariner, Log, for instance, who in reply to Truck's question, reports that he had a good voyage, but a "Man's no more Expected for it, than if he had over-set the Navigation, and come into the Channel Keel uppermost." As it turns out, he has been discharged for cheating his employers, who would not allow his "Accounts for the Ships Expenses." Asked about his wife and whether or not a mistress would be more satisfactory, he replies in the negative.

You must know, we have a Custom at Sea every Saturday Night to Drink a Health to our Wives, and he that has never a one to Remember, looks as simply, d'ye see, as a Maid at a Gossipping, when the Marry'd Women are talking Bawdy. Besides, we that are Married Men, have always the Honour to Drink first of a Bowl.

Nor does any one disparage the weight of his argument.

The success of *The Weekly Comedy,* however, does not lie wholly in the characters, but also in the characterization of the coffee-house itself, which Ward achieves through the coming and going of his dramatis personae; through their business with each other, through their asides to the drawers,

and through their insatiate demand for news. Already quoted
has been the remark to the drawer by Prim as a sequel to
his quarrel with Snarl. On another day Plush, the quack,
who has been treating Snap for a venereal disease, comes in
and orders a dish of sage tea and the newspaper. As he sits
reading, Snap comes over to him and asks him for the news.
"I know not what is in 'em yet," Plush replies,

for I have but just begun my Lesson, which, indeed, I Read as much for
Fashions sake, as for Information; for he that sits by himself in a Coffee-
House, without a News-Book in his Hand, looks as awkwardly as a
Mourner after a Corps, without a sprig of Rosemary.

It is Ward's creation of atmosphere which is important
here and difficult to convey: Snarl's surly interruptions,
matched by the obsequious niceties of Prim; Cant's objections
to Snarl's profanity; Scan-all's furious attempts at dashing
off a reply to *An Encomium upon Parliament;* the quarreling of Plush and Snap over the former's bill; Scribble's
eternal dashing hither and yon in the search for news stories.
It is the liveliness and energy of the picture—a quality characteristic of the coffee-house in real life—which here provides
the background for a group of characters, certainly one of the
most lively and animated in Ward's writings.

VIII

Citizens, Soldiers, and Seamen

'Tis true, the Picture is but half drawn, and only the unagreeable Side
is expos'd to our Reflexions: But if this seems Injustice, when ever the
Gentlemen who are criminal in the Matters here lay'd to their Charge,
will change their Sentiments, I'll promise to turn Satyr into a
Panegyrick.
                                            Mars Stript of his Armour (1708)

I N THE PREVIOUS chapter we considered the character as
presented through dialogue. In many of his writings,
Ward, however, adhered more closely to the traditional
form. In *The Wealthy Shopkeeper, or the Charitable Citizen*
(1700) he traces the life of a tradesman-citizen from his birth
in the country to his death as a rich alderman in London.
Though it purports to be the study of a type, the poem is remarkably individual in its portraiture. Ward identifies the
citizen as a son of a yeoman or parish priest, who was
brought up to the city at the age of fifteen and apprenticed
to a London merchant. From there he traces his life through
his days of apprenticeship and marriage, to the setting up of
his own shop when he settles down to the thrifty life of a
tradesman, watching his outlays, attending Change, joining
a meeting, spending his evening at the coffee-house, reading
the *Gazette* and *Review,* and meddling in the affairs of state.
After twenty years he is looked upon by his neighbors as a
substantial citizen, an honest man, and a sharp dealer. He
goes to church twice every Sunday, says long prayers at his
meals, and hears his youngest apprentice read a chapter from
the Bible every night before he retires. He hates extravagance,
never treats his neighbor beyond a dish of coffee, and is
known to wrangle over a farthing at his club. Aspiring to
office, he becomes a churchwarden, and immediately there

is a gallery added, an organ raised, or a steeple mended, so that he can be buried with a stone indicating he was church-warden when the repairs were made.

Worth ten thousand pounds, he assumes an air of importance. He nods gravely to his neighbors. He dines with aldermen. In hope of a bequest he is chosen governor of the Blue Coat Hospital. Life has become a routine. He rises at five. Donning slippers and a gown, he descends to the counting-house and considers the management of his projects. At eight he breakfasts on toast and cheese. Descending once more, he chides his apprentices and charges the eldest with the affairs of the day. After that there is a visit to the neighboring coffee-house for news; dinner upon the jot of twelve, a nap till one, and then a visit to Change. At three he is at Lloyd's Coffee-House reading letters, buying and selling. Before six he is back at the shop where he demands to know all that has gone on, who has been in and out, and what business has been done. From there he goes to his club, where, over a halfpint, he talks trade, religion, and affairs of state, not at such length, however, that he has not time for a dish of coffee on his way home, where eating a light supper, he talks smuttily to his maid, and retires before Bow Bell rings nine.

Still busy with his petty routine, he is overtaken by age and the gout. When he dies, he leaves £500 for a plot of ground, £2000 to build an almshouse, £10,000 to endow it, £500 to beautify the monument, £200 to the Blue Coat Hospital, £10 to each man servant, £20 to his maid, £300 to the parish poor, and a new gown and cassock for the parish priest.

It is a full portrait, exceptionally specific and concrete. No wonder that in the second edition the first forty-eight lines giving the details of his birth and coming to the city were replaced by general moralizing upon the character of a covetous man, obviously to remove some of the features which might have served to identify the subject and perhaps incriminate the author.[1]

In *The Reformer, Exposing the Vices of the Age* (1700) Ward presents his readers with twelve additional characters

of the city: "The Vitious Courtier," "The Factious Hypocrite," "The Precise Quaker," "The Covetous Miser," "The
Prodigal Son," "The City Letcher," "The Insatiate Wife,"
"The Amorous Maid," "The Beau Apprentice," "The City
Mob," and "The Country Squire." Many of them he was to
repeat in his more complete galleries later on. Two of them
supplement the picture of the tradesman-citizen already
presented.

The portrait of "The Insatiate Wife," for instance, might
well serve as a picture of the second or third wife of "The
Wealthy Shop-Keeper." She is a woman much younger than
her husband, who, in view of the latter's concern with the
routine of his business, is forced to find her own gaiety and
entertainment or to live a restricted life within her own
doors. From two to four every afternoon, while her husband
is upon Change or at Lloyd's, she stands in the shop window
admiring the "Pritty lovely eyes," the "Handsome nose," or
the "well-Shap'd Leg and Body" of the passer-by. Impatiently
waiting for six o'clock prayers, she dashes off dressed in her
best with a prayer book in her hand, often, however, visiting
her gallant under pretext of going to church. In either case,
she returns in time to kiss her husband demurely good night
before he retires.

"The Beau Apprentice," too, might find a place in the
tradesman's shop, though probably not for any length of
time. He, though he cleans his master's shoes on weekdays
and carries the family Bible after his master to church on
Sunday, apes a beau in his heart, powders his hair or his periwig, and runs off at every opportunity to St. James's Park or
a playhouse. On a holiday, decked out in his bravest attire, he
strolls in the fields or watering places, where, if he finds the
dolly he is hoping for, he courts her by quoting phrases from
a play or *The London Spy*, which serves him for compliment or banter.

It is in *The London Terraefilius, or the Satyrical Reformer*
and *The Modern World Disrob'd, or both Sexes Strip'd of
their Pretended Vertues* that Ward presents his readers with
his longest parade of the citizens of London, both tradesmen

and quality. The first, published in the form of a periodical, was issued in six parts from July 1707 to April 1708. The characters depicted include almost every conceivable kind of pedestrian on the London streets. It is as if the author sat down inside a tavern window and catalogued the passers-by. In the preface he shouts his warning:

Satyr, at present, is my Tallent: for Stubborn Folly and Habitual Vice must be Corrected with Severity, therefore stand off Knave, have a care Fool, Fly Hypocrite, hide Harlot, run Libertine, chaw Bully, skulk Bawd, lope Skellum, for I am just now going to lay about me like a Country Cudgel-Player.

The manner, too, bears witness to the situation. As each subject comes along, Ward addresses him directly, as if the pedestrian could hear him, or as if he were rapt in a monologue for the entertainment of a friend. "You are Welcome to Town, Sir Quorum Keeble," he greets the country squire before he presents his character. "Here comes a Neat Prim Fellow for you," he comments to his friend, as he introduces the beau. "Pray observe Captain Cog yonder, Strutting along to the William and Mary, with a Tall Footman after him, like a Highland Scotchman," he continues.

And the portraits follow each other in the casual sequence suggested. A city official who, after worshiping for forty years at a conventicle, now attends services in the Church of England to enable himself to hold office, is followed by the country squire come up to town for the Easter term, who, having left his family in the country, spends his time "high Eating at Noon, a Whore and a Bottle at Night, the same repeated *De die in diem et de Nocte in Noctem*." A sea captain with a "Bottle Nose" and a pair of "Trumpeter's Cheeks" is on his way to a Wapping music house, having just taken his leave of his employers upon Change. A beau with a "Narcissus Countenance" and "Frenchify'd Habiliments" treads along the "Pav'd stones in Fleet-Street with as much Grace and Regularity as if he was crossing a Dancing-School," peeping into every Woman's face as a "Moorfields Star gazer does into an Eclipse." A surly philosopher with a "Calves-skin Companion in his Pocket" heads for a coffee-house, which he will empty with his "Essences and Entities." A pirating Printer, "Mr. Obolus Snap-Copy," hurries by with a bag full of farthings on his way to "Pater-Noster-Row to buy damaged Paper, in order to wrong somebody or other of, perhaps, ten Pounds to get ten Shillings." An early morning drunk leans against a post so drunk by eleven he "can not set one Leg before the other without Stumbling." A lady of quality swims home in her chair, "like a Sick-Woman in a Horse-Litter," having just taken leave of the "Ladies Punch-Club near St. James's." A train-band captain, "Hooped round with a Fring'd Sash," struts by with "Clock-work Strides" that delight the ladies. A "chaste Diana," secure in her own virtue and proud of her beauty, flaunts her sex everywhere, sits up a whole night with a beau in her bedchamber, unlaces her stays with a most vigorous lover, trusts herself up two pairs of stairs with a young student of law. A mistress of a flogging school in Moorfields, a "Sodomitical Succubus," who keeps the walls of her house adorned with bundles of flogging twigs in variously colored ribbons for her aged patrons, is being carried to Bridewell by a reforming constable, who broke open the door and surprised her with an old Tallyman.[2] The rods of bundles are carried after her by the constable's deputy and following after come a great multitude of huzzaing rabble.

Some of the portraits are done more fully. There is, for instance, the pewterer turned mechanic, so anxious to hear the latest news and so busy contriving new projections that he goes full trot to Change. *The Daily Courant* is bread and meat to him, though he insists in conning it aloud in the coffee-house and by mispronunciation makes half of it a new language. A great zealot, he would interrupt his very devotions if a hawker came by the door crying, "A New Mail from Holland," forthwith leaving "God and his Family to inquire what News that he might not be behind with the rest of his neighbours."

There is, too, "Sir Medicus Oculurum," the quack oculist, in his "Lac'd jacket," followed by his retinue—a Welsh coachman, a footman, and "an Æthiopian scare-crow for the Country People to gaze at."

Pray observe with what singular Vanity and Ostentation he steps cross a Kennel at the Head of his Equipage . . . with what ridiculous Pride he turns his Platter Countenance over his Porterly Shoulder, on purpose that his Ragamuffins may pull off their Weather-beaten Felts, that passangers may know by their Obedience who is the Master of the Vermin.

In the country he travels in a coach and four with his servants mounted on Smithfield hackneys, "Arm'd with Musquetoon and Blunderbus." Welcomed to the inn by the loud huzzas of the country people, he selects the best room, has the bells rung announcing his arrival, visits the mayor and invites the aldermen to dine with him, sends the bell ringers a crown, and gives a barrel of drink to the poor. By instruction, his servants sit in the kitchen and talk of his miraculous cures and knightly honors; he allows himself to be seen inside the window. The next day—and as long as their money lasts thereafter—he waits on the blind of the town, those with most money being treated first. Ward says that he himself as a schoolboy walked ankle deep in kennel dirt to delight his ears with the witty dialogue between the master and a notable merry fellow in a blue jacket.

It is at once the dramatic manner and the lively characterizations which interest one in *The London Terraefilius*. This is less true of *The Modern World Disrob'd, or Both Sexes Strip'd of their Pretended Vertue* (1708), where Ward devoted part i to the ladies and part ii to the men. Here the presentation in a formal series lacks the dramatic quality of *The London Terraefilius*. The subjects are not selected at random from among passers-by, nor is the emphasis upon the citizen and tradesman. In this case the subjects are members of "quality," and the characters, interestingly enough, revert to the earlier treatment of the genre as a study of type rather than a portrait of an individual. Ward, moreover, is unusually deferential in his preface. "I earnestly entreat you," he writes in part ii,

that you would not misconstrue any Thing that you find among the Male Characters, to the Injury of the Author, or the Dishonor of any Great Person now living; for I solemnly declare, that all those Images that seem the most bold, and may unhappily be thought, by injudicious Readers, to carry along with them a Kind of daring Presumption, are drawn from the Histories of such ambitious Gentlemen, who in former Reigns, have taken irregular Courses to advance their own Grandeur . . . [Here you may find only] Satyr, without Spite; Novelty, without Fiction; Pleasantry, without Levity; and an abundance of Truth, without personal Reflection: . . .

The characters on the whole add less to our visualization of London folk than those in *The London Terraefilius*. Some of them are, however, not without point and bear a certain semblance to life. On occasion, too, Ward manages to express a characteristic trait in rather neat and concise phrasing worthy of his betters, as when he characterizes "The Censorious Lady" as "the unhappy Eccho of other Peoples Failings," or "The Promisory Gentleman" as one who "never meets you, but he gripes your Hand, to the Detriment of your Knuckles." Even where he is less apt and more verbose there is a certain realism in his manner which is not without interest. One may compare, for instance, the following presentation of a "Gaming Lady's" conversation at the card table with Swift's satire on polite conversations.[8]

When she claps the King upon the Queen, she cries, "My Ladies, there's a Wedding" . . . When Pam wins the King, she Reflects upon the Favour that Knaves have at Court, and when Spades are led about, she smilingly recollects how she was dug out of the Parsley-Bed. When Hearts are play'd, she thinks of nothing but Love; and if Diamonds are Trumps at the same time she prettily observes, how the greatest Hearts, especially Female, are captivated by Jewels, and overcome by Riches.

Among the ladies Ward presents are two of especial interest. The first is a bluestocking. The female student is "a Mimick of a Scholar," who apes him in everything as nearly as possible in order to be thought an equally rational creature. Disdainful of her own sex, she is mortified by the trivialities of their conversation. She herself is never without a book and a mouthful of Latin phrases, for "She thinks it one part of Scholarship to speak hard Words, and another to understand 'em." Possessed of a smattering of French, she translates a novel in secret, then whispers it abroad lest others be unaware of her accomplishments.

The second "lady" is an actress who achieves her ambition of being kept by a courtier. By birth she is either a "By-blow" begotten out of wedlock and "put off in her Infancy with a small sum of Money, to be nurs'd up by the careful Wife of some indigent Taylor, or a poor Shoe-maker," or else she is lawfully begotten and "train'd up in some back Street or Alley near Long-Acre, by a jolly Porter, upon his hussifly Dame, who makes Mustard, crys hot Gray-peas, or keeps an Apple-stall." Her first training is to act as a nursemaid for younger children. Her second is to cry "Beef and Broth for some Boiling-Cook, among Journey-men Taylors" at noon for twopence a time. At twelve years of age she goes to market with her mother, guarding her mother's stall, and from thence it is only a short stop to crying "Nuts and Damsons in Bartholomew Fair." Pretty as well as impudent she is there picked up by some strolling players, who mislead her with extravagant promises. She is now Madame Betty to the apprentices and cook wenches. After that, by virtue of her face and her impertinence, she becomes in a short time a member of her majesty's comedians, where she pleases both as an actress and harlot. Now the mistress of an old lord, she is happily triumphant in her own career, until, desiring too much, she unwittingly discloses her flirtation with a young dandy, upon which the old lord casts her out. Finally, born in the cellar, she dies in a garret.

The portrait reminds one of an earlier work published by Ward. In 1703 he had written *The Rise and Fall of Madame Coming-Sir,* a prose character enlarged to biographical scope with a sequence in narrative suggestive of the novelette. Essentially a satirical portrait of the typical barmaid, *The Rise and Fall of Madame Coming-Sir* becomes at moments the rather pathetic story of the arrival in London of an innocent country girl who secures a position behind the bar of her brother's tavern, becomes the toast of the tavern-frequenters, and is the victim, finally, of her own pretty impudence. Both of the sketches under consideration to some degree anticipate in subject matter and treatment the more lively and humane chronicle of *Moll Flanders.*[4]

It is *The London Terraefilius* which remains Ward's most effective attempt at the presentation of unrelated characters in a series. By the casual sequence of personages, resembling as it does the chance accosting of one's fellows on the street, and by the dramatic manner of their introduction, he was to a degree able to overcome the inherent weakness of the genre. For his subjects he had sought out "such a sort of man as will admit of a variety of observations," canvassing the city from the sailors of Wapping to the courtiers of Westminster. They are, moreover, not inaccurately drawn. With only a casual glance at his subject he seems to have been able to catch a dominant line. Moving with the bold stroke of a caricaturist, he filled in his picture. Many of his phrases and situations are apt, as the quotations in the text will illustrate. Nearly all of them are graphic. The pewterer rushing from his prayers to a coffee-house upon the announcement of a new mail, the quack oculist stepping across the kennel at the head of his retinue, the mistress of a flogging school being carried to Bridewell with the hooting rabble at her heels, the beau gracefully stepping along the pavement stones and leering at the ladies—these are, after all, pictures from life. To one who is neither unduly distracted nor detained by the style, the justice of Ward's own comment is apparent: one could not have gone twenty yards in any street in London without happening upon an original.

It is in this sense that *The London Terraefilius* is less a list of characters than it is a panoramic photograph of pedestrian London, and so achieves a unity denied the more formal series. In two other series of characters, which we are about to examine, the search for unity and continuity provides an even more interesting innovation.

II

In 1706 Ward published the first of two strikingly similar pamphlets on the navy and the army, *The Wooden World Dissected in the Character of a Ship of War*[5] and *Mars Stript of his Armour, or the Army Display'd in all its True Colours.* Here he sought for interest and unity by selecting for his subject the various members of a single profession. This, to be sure, was a far cry from the earlier conception of the genre.

But just as the consideration of type had given way to that of individual, so the latter now gave way to an emphasis upon activity and profession. In *The Wooden World* and in *Mars Stript of his Armour* the characters are distinguished from each other not so much by their conduct and behavior as they are by their rank and duties within the profession.

The innovation, without any regard to its intrinsic merit, is a tribute to Ward's ingenuity. The identity of profession provided a new unity to what otherwise tended to be a series of unrelated portraits. Moreover, the emphasis upon activity rather than conduct opened up new possibilities in subject matter. The earlier character had been distinctly limited. As the genre had moved from its concern with the type to concern with the individual, it had increased its range. In much the same way its extension to a consideration of all members and ranks within a given profession increased its range over the earlier tendency to consider a single member of a profession as typical of all the rest. To the journalist in search of material the discovery of fourteen sailors instead of one was a page-filling boon.

It is true, moreover, that the subject matter of both *The Wooden World* and *Mars Stript of his Armour* was in itself something of a discovery by Ward. Neither the sailor nor the soldier had commonly been treated by the writers of characters. Overbury, indeed, includes the characters of both, but later writers of the seventeenth century seem generally to have ignored them. Ward had already made use of both the sailor and the soldier in the numerous sketches included in *The London Spy,* as well as including them among the dramatis personae of *The Humours of a Coffee-House.* It is unnecessary to assume, however, that their presence in either case owed itself to more than Ward's cursory observation of the world about him—a city to which neither soldiers nor sailors were strangers. The extended treatment of the sailor in *The Wooden World,* on the other hand, seems to have derived from additional factors, both literary and political. The figure of the blunt, homely sailor was familiar to the reader and play-goer of the time in the person of Manly, a character in Wycherley's comedy, *The Plain-Dealer,* whose name Ward appropriated for his dedicatory epistle. For two years, moreover, before the publication of *The Wooden World,* London itself had followed an extended controversy over the relative importance of the sea and land forces under the leadership of Sir Charles Rook and the Duke of Marlborough, a controversy finally terminated by the replacement of Rook by Sir Cloudesley Shovel. It seems more than likely, especially in the face of Ward's frequent charges of corruption in the administration of both the army and navy, that *The Wooden World* was an attempt to capitalize on the interest stirred up by the controversy.

Certainly one element of the pamphlet's popularity lay in the audacity of its exposition. To subject the entire navy to a burlesque and impertinent characterization of its members was at the moment to startle as well as to amuse the public. To pique the curiosity of his reader further Ward writes the account as if he himself were a sailor—one who knew too much about the vices and follies of his confederates and was yet willing to tell all. The dedicatory epistle to "all Worshipful and no Worshipful Gentlemen" he signed Manly Plain-Dealer. In the dedication and in an accompanying note to the reader, dated November 24 at Portsmouth, he explains his "purpose." As a sailor he had found it dull in port and had amused himself by the first idea that offered itself to his fancy, which was "to draw the Picture of the most glorious Piece of Creation, called a Tar." As for the satire, he had not designed to attack any one individual, since everyone knows there are always exceptions and "we have some Captains in the Navy, as much the Glory of our Isles as the Ships they Command." As for the performance itself, he recognizes it is slight and hastily done, but the reader need remember "it is but an Essay, nay only the first rude Strokes of a Novice," and at any rate he had been called away to the service 'ere he had finished.

The prefatory material is, of course, no more than a playful ruse. No one reading even the first character, that of "A Ship of War," could possibly have mistaken Ward's hand.[6] Here are all the similes he had already used to characterize a ship in *A Trip to New-England* and a few more after his most characteristic manner thrown in gratis. A ship is "a Wooden World fabricated by the frail Hand of Man," a "Noah's Ark," a "floating Castle," the "great Wooden Horse," the "New-Bridewell of Nations," a "Christian Sanctuary for non-solvent Debtors," the "great Bridge of the Ocean, conveying over to all habitable Places, Death, Pox, and Drunkenness"; and bringing back in return, "all foreign Vices that we are Strangers to in our own Country."

From the ship itself Ward turns to the sailors. The captain is a "Leviathan, or rather a kind of Sea God" worshipped more through fear than through affection, a man who relies more on his talent than upon book knowledge, which he accounts impertinent. He is an admirer of the saying that familiarity breeds contempt and so exacts "infinitely more Ceremony from his Lieutenant, than he will allow to God Almighty." Generosity is to him an unaccountable extravagance and compassion little better than a human frailty. The king allots him three parts in eight of any prize, but he grants himself the other five "to prevent foolish Fractions and Divisions." Let a half-starved sailor steal a pair of old shoes from him, however, and he will surely "drub the pilfering Cur to Death for it." He ships his menial servants as able seamen and so has his service free "from a Steward down to a Shoe-wiper." He makes wills for dying sailors and forging their names enriches himself with their pay.[7]

It was part of Ward's purpose to dwell upon culpability and fraud. To his cause, one takes it, he summoned all the current stories of chicanery and petty thievery the coffee-houses and taverns would yield. The graft of the commander is matched by that of the inferior officers. The ship's master is the "impartial Surveyor, of all the Ship's Provisions," who "if he fares not well by it, he may thank his own Honesty." The gunner "commemorates Gun-powder Treason, with a Treason upon Gun-powder," for he shortens his charge of powder, charges the king full price, and pockets the rest. The purser is so excellent an alchemist he can transmute rotten peas and musty oatmeal into pure gold and silver, enact miracles of turning water into wine, and with the captain's connivance make a profit for them both.

More able than the exposition of vice are certain of the characters in which Ward combines a rough, hearty humor with a vigorous phrase that serves to echo the characteristic behavior of his subject: The boatswain's badge of power, for instance, is his bamboo with which he has mauled "more White-coats than fell at the Battle of Blanheim." With it he enacts miracles, cures men of the scurvy, makes them take up their beds and walk, the lame skip, and "heavy-ars'd Fellows tumble up from below," contrary to the laws of gravity. He is most terrible in the captain's presence. His throat is still his best badge of authority. He can call every man by his name for he dignifies them all "with the Title of Dog, Rogue, or Rascal," and can "roar forth Death and Destruction upon the hoisting of a Water-cask." The sea chaplain is one who was brought up in the fear of the Lord, but had it well reasoned out of him at the university, and is now happy he did not stay on lest he might have grown "Pedant, and par'd himself into Stupidity." In the ship he holds forth not in the pulpit but by hanging his nose and arms over the back of a chair, while he harangues the seamen with old sermons of another's composing. He is infinitely better at the punch bowl than at preaching, and "a compleat Scholar, that's evident, because for these many Years he has given over all Study." The surgeon is an old barber with a shop the size of a sea chest, a few pots, a smattering of "Fustian Words and Phrases, whose true Sense he is more puzzl'd to lay, than to anatomize the Body of a fat Capon." He makes one and the same recipe serve a hundred ailments, for "there's no standing upon Niceties, he cries, with Fellows that have the Constitution of a Horse."

If Ward lays about him rather severely with the officers, he is on the whole sympathetic with the common sailor. "A sharp Blade indeed, if kept whetted with a good Diet," he writes. "He's a rare Dog under an honest Commander, and will fight everlastingly if he can but have Justice at the End of his Labours." His station is the forecastle where he and "his Brother Jacks lie pelting each other with Sea Wit." He loves short voyages as he loves short prayers. He views all things "as Sheep do the Stars, or a Cart-Horse what passes in Cheap-side, without any After-Thought or Reflection." On shore he is "the Primum Mobile of all Hurly-burlies, and the Terror of the Spittlefields Weavers." His favorite delight is a music house in Wapping [8] and next to that a public caval-cade, "where he makes a hellish Pother, and throws away his Hat among the dirty Crowd, out of pure Extasy." "In fine," he concludes,

take this same plain blunt Sea-Animal, by and large, in his Tar Jacket, and wide-kneed Trowzers, and you'll find him of more intrinsick Value to the Nation, than the most fluttering Beau in it . . . Our Ships of War are un-disputably the best in the World, and so might the Sailors be too; for all depends upon the Merit and Honesty of the Commander, who models everything as he pleases; and if he valued the Interests of his Country above an ill-got Estate, he might in one Twelvemonth make a Man of War the most beneficial, august, and delightful Habitation in the World.

The brief excerpts and summary will serve to indicate the content of *The Wooden World* and to show something of Ward's manner and style. The list of characters numbers fourteen, that of the lieutenant, the midshipman, the cap-tain's steward, and the ship's carpenter having been omitted here. The emphasis, as elsewhere in Ward, is primarily upon externals. There is little subtlety of distinction or any pro-found grasp of human psychology. The subjects whose char-acters he presents are distinguishable from each other not by any inherent difference in spirit but merely by their activity and rank. With the possible exception of the common sailor the personnel of the entire navy is made up of charlatans and knaves. Ward, of course, did not mean to ask his readers to accept his account at face value. His primary purpose was to entertain, hence the excess verbiage, the hearty and coarse humor, the rough and ready billingsgate of the dialogue.

As a matter of fact, few of Ward's characters are more ably drawn than those in *The Wooden World*. Characteristic of Ward at his best are the graphic pictures he presents of the men engaged in their various activities. The bellowing boatswain shouting his men up from below. The chaplain preaching with his arms and nose over the back of a chair. The sailors tossing their hats into the air at a parade. Fre-quently, too, the characterizations themselves are not inept.

The captain's regard for generosity as an extravagance and for compassion as a human frailty, the lieutenant's contempt for captains and yet his desire to become one, the chaplain's gratitude for having escaped the pedantry of the university are, as Ward puts them, telling remarks. The humor, to be sure, is hearty and boisterous, but to a degree not inappropriate to the subject matter. The carpenter, Ward writes, is "a knotty Piece of Timber, and the more you soak him, the tougher he grows." The common sailor ends each week in a debauch, drinks till he sinks on an old sea chest, and there remains dead as a doornail till roused by the boatswain's boom, "Get up, all Hands to Prayer, and be damned!"

It is not difficult to see why *The Wooden World* was a success. Four editions had appeared by 1711. Thrice more it was reprinted before the end of the century.[9]

The companion piece on the army, *Mars Stript of his Armour,* was first published in 1708. According to Ward himself, it owed its inception to the "universal Applause" with which the public had greeted *The Wooden World.* As that disclosed "the Miscarriages of our Fleet, the Insolence of our Naval-Officers, and the Miseries and Hardships of our Sailors before the Mast," so this will reveal "the Avarice or Negligence of our Commanders" responsible for the rout and defeat of the English forces at Almanza.

Though Ward fundamentally was only doing another series of prose characters, he was again able to catch a current interest by relating his account to the recent defeat of the English forces and by his pretense at exposing vice and corruption. "To make a Regiment fight well," he writes, "they must be pay'd and cloath'd well." It is from a sense of duty to his country that he has taken it upon himself to point out the "ill Actions committed by some Officers," who, if they object that the picture is but half drawn and only the disagreeable side exposed, might try altering their behavior, and he will accordingly turn his satire into panegyric. "There are Commanders," he finds it necessary to explain,[10]

who think it Murder, to surprize Men into the Service; who rule their Soldiers by Love, not Fear; who neither abuse their Inferiors, nor meanly cringe to those who are above them . . . who would no more wrong a Soldier of his Pay, or a Tradesman of his Debt, than they would affront the one, or desert the other in Time of Action; who, if it lay in their Power, would do good to all Men, and Injuries to none.

In spite of his introduction Ward had few concrete charges of brutality and corruption to present. What he had to say about the army, much as in the case of the navy, depended upon the current supply of coffee-house fiction and rumor. The one cogent comment he makes—one that he had already made elsewhere—was that the common soldier was fearfully underpaid.[11] Xerxes, he writes, once wept to see his army because he realized that a few years would wipe out its numbers. Now he would laugh as heartily as he once cried to see "the Folly of 100,000 Coxcombs, who venture their Lives for the poor Stipend of a Groat a Day!" Neither, for that matter, are the soldiers properly taken care of after they return wounded or broken in health—a matter he had commented on with some pertinence in *The London Spy*.

The characters on the whole are less ably drawn and less diverting than those in *The Wooden World*, as is frequently true when Ward tries to repeat himself. The series begins with an account of the "Captain-General," and the character of Marlborough is indicative of the fact that at the time of the writing Tory opinion was still solidly in support of the general. He alone, Ward writes, owes his preferment to merit, to "the Greatness of his Sense and Courage." He alone is free from the avarice and personal ambition universally motivating the officers.

As for the lieutenant and major generals, they secure their preferment by intrigue and solicitation rather than by merit. They are prodigal of promises but niggards in execution. They live in "Scarlet Luxury," and if "but two or three of our Country Gentlemen, who represent their respective Burroughs in the Senate, should peep into his [the major general's] magnificent Apartments, Lord bless us! What a Noise they'd make the next Sessions?" Each winter he leaves his post of command to bask in the luxury and sunshine of the court. The quartermaster enriches himself by the practice

An Eighteenth-Century Coach and Coach-Yard

From an engraving by Hogarth

of "transubstantiation" and can "make an Individual be Resident in forty several Quarters at a Time, and [himself] receive Contributions for each of them." A "colonel's," writes Ward in what must have been a personal attack, "is the best Post in a Regiment, or an honest Gentleman now living is very much mistaken." Let him thank heaven for an employment no astrologer would have guessed or predicted had he seen him "mount the Guard in Tangier, with a Brown Musket on his Shoulder, and never a Souse in his Pocket."

More immediately appreciated by Ward's readers was his character of a captain, who feels it a "thousand Pitties that we have Generals, who were never private Centinels." He has "a damnable Aversion to Learning and Sense, believing that either of them renders a Man effeminate and spoils his being a Hero." In charge of recruiting men, he will collect a parcel of poor tradesmen, entertain them at a tavern till they are drunk, cram a shilling in their pockets, and the next morning both he and the sergeant will swear they were fairly enlisted.

The characters of the chaplain and surgeon are again among the most vivid and picturesque. As for the former, he's equipped "a-la-Cavalier, more like a Soldier than a Priest," wearing a long wig, a sword, and a speckled neckcloth. The chaplain's proclivities to liquor and women he excuses by saying he must stand in with his people. Among men of learning he shows aversion to disputes, but among soldiers he is always a man of letters. The surgeon is one whose sign formerly read, "Shave for Two-pence, Bleed for Six-pence," and who now bleeds both the persons and pockets of an entire regiment. His customary proceeding with one who protests that his prices are too high is to toss his "Bargaining-Skull upon the table, shouting, 'There, my Master, on the Table is the Skull of just such an obstinate Person as your Self.'"

It is the private soldier, as it had earlier been the common sailor, who is the subject of the most apt characterization. "The Oaths of the private Men rattle louder than their Drums, and may be heard almost as at as great Distance as their Cannon." An army is "an Hospital, where you may certainly meet with a Cure for the Wounds of the Mind, however you endanger the Body." "Give a Soldier Victuals and Drink enough, and you need never fear his Fighting, but 'tis the Humour of an Englishman, [that] he loves to die with Money in his Pockets, and Meat in his Belly." " 'Tis true, they are not the best Christians; but no Men follow the Rule of not providing for Tomorrow, better than themselves." They are a very religious group and attend prayers each Sunday, then "decently rob, plunder, and ravish all the Week afterwards." The common soldier "thinks no more of his native Country, than that does of him; and with a stupid Insensibility, resigns himself to what ever happens, firmly believing his Condition can't be well worse than it is, either here, or hereafter."

Interesting as a departure from the traditional character, and even more interesting as an adaptation of the genre to questions of current concern, *The Wooden World* and *Mars Stript of his Armour* do not possess the realism of *The London Terraefilius* or *The Weekly Comedy*. Occasionally graphic and suggestive of the actual behavior and speech of the men, the characters at other times appear to be no more than mere forays of indecent metaphor and arresting innuendo. In this sense they add less to our knowledge either of the city or the age. They provide us, however, with the current rumors and half-truths, the unsupported stories of scandal and intrigue which circulated among the populace at a time when a growing portion of the citizenry was already wearying of what seemed a needless and interminable war. Ward's emphasis upon the activity of men and his discovery that the lives and behavior of ordinary seamen and soldiers were interesting to the populace was significant. Much as *The London Spy* had served to uncover the reader's interest in the local scene for the later essayists, so Ward's emphasis upon the common man and particularity of detail pointed the way for the novelist. Both Defoe and Smollett were later to benefit from the interest Ward had created in the humorous vagaries of the soldier and sailor.

IX

Tippling, Gossip, and Bawdy Talk

Their chief business is tipling, gossip, and bawdy talk.
The Secret History of Clubs (1709)

IN A STUDY of the character writings of Ward in the period
between 1700 and 1712, it remains for us to examine
briefly his most widely known, if misunderstood, attempt. Still busily engaged in the search for the new and the
interesting, he published in the summer of 1709 a thin
pamphlet entitled *The History of the London Clubs, or the
Citizens' Pastime,* depicting a series of six real and imaginary
clubs created or selected to unify his characterizations of
London folk. This he followed in the same year with
part II, extending the description to four additional clubs.
He shortly thereafter increased the number of clubs to thirty-
two, added a good deal of material to the first ten which he
incorporated in the new edition, and published the whole as
*The Secret History of Clubs . . . with their Originals and
Characters of the Most Noted Members thereof.* The word
"history" was, of course, no more than a device, but its use
has led later writers to a misapprehension of Ward's purpose
and to the repeated charge that though he professes to furnish his readers with an account of existing societies, the
clubs he depicts are wholly fictitious, as well as the product
of a somewhat prurient mind.[1]

The charge of pruriency may for the moment be ignored.
Ward on occasion could cater shamelessly to the baser appetites of his readers, but it is well to remember that there
were both readers and appetites. The presence of the readers
is attested by the number of editions necessary, throughout
the eighteenth century, to supply the popular demand for

the enlarged and final volume. The charge that the accounts are wholly fictitious on the other hand reflects a general misconception of Ward's purpose. In the years immediately preceding 1709, as we have seen, he had been engaged in the writing of prose characters, and each year from 1706 to 1709 had seen the publication of one or more series. He had been interested during those years in securing some device that would lend a degree of unity and reality to his characterizations. When he turned to the clubs under the pretense of relating their histories, it was no more than a similar attempt to unify his portrayal of London citizenry. The word club he used not in the narrow sense of an organized society holding stated and recurrent meetings in a chapter house, but in the larger and equally current sense of a gathering or grouping of citizens in terms of their activities and habitual places of resort.[2] In its narrower sense the club has, of course, consistently fascinated the social historian and occasionally made him somewhat over-zealous in his search for information. For Ward it is apparent that the word club was no more than a convenient device to give a background to his satire and the diverting yarns with which he entertained his public.

All this is immediately apparent when one turns to an examination of the "histories." Ward's original effort, *The History of the London Clubs, or the Citizens' Pastime,* part 1, was published early in the year. For his characters he chose six groups of citizens, sufficiently distinct in their activity as well as in the locale of their resort, to be designated by the word club. "The Yorkshire Club" is, for instance, the character of the horsetraders of Smithfield Market, of whom Ward had already given us some account in *The London Spy.*[3] "The Basket Women's Club" is a character of the rural housewives who each market day brought their well-laden panniers to Clare Market and naturally enough would in considerable groups refresh themselves at a neighboring tavern before setting out upon their return. "The Thieves Club" and "The Beggars Club" are similar descriptions of what were then familiar types in the boozing kens and congregating places near Fleet Ditch and the district of White Friars. "The Broken Shop Keepers Club" held near the mint in Southwark is the description of bankrupt tradesmen who gather there for "safe Retirement from the Revenge and Malice of the unmerciful Creditors."

To these characterizations of obvious London types, Ward added by way of introduction to the series an account of a pseudo-fictitious "Lying Club," held in several parts of the city and "now remov'd to a certain Tavern in Westminster." This was an additional device, lending reality to the grouping of his characters in clubs. It was responsible later, however, for the misapprehension of what he had set out to do. That there was less misapprehension among his immediate readers is obvious, and if there had been any tendency not to see through the design at the beginning, Ward's parting quip would have immediately clarified the issue. Having given an account of one or two of the "unconscionable" yarns of the society, he concludes,

In these sorts of Merry Jests and Extravagant Fables, the Rhodomantading Society used to spin out their Club Hours, judging the largeness of a Man's Sense by the Magnitude of his Lyes; which are now so common that they are got into every Tradesmans Shop, insomuch that scarce any Commodities can be purchased without 'em.

When *The History of the London Clubs,* part i, proved successful, Ward repeated his efforts. Four new groups of citizens he deemed worthy of characterization: the mountebanks and charlatans, always a good subject for satire and derision, here labeled "The Quacks Club"; "The Beaus Club" at Tom's Coffee-House near Covent Garden; "The Mollies Club," a diatribe against a current group of effeminate fops also satirized in *The Female Tatler;* [4] and "The No-Nose Club," a fictitious account attempting to divert the readers with the preposterous suggestion of assembling all those in the city suffering from a rather common ailment, if one may judge from the innumerable references in literature.

So far it is clear that Ward's principal purpose was to present his readers with satiric characterizations. The device of the club had served excellently to unify and lend body to the attempt. Twice he had purported to present an account of

an actual club in the narrower sense. The first one had delighted the readers with the "unconscionable" yarns told at
the Lying Club; the incongruous suggestion of the second,
the No-Nose Club, had come near to convulsing the ground-
lings. The device of the club had moreover been extraordinarily popular. It is obvious that any enterprising journalist
would have sensed an opportunity to carry the project
further. There were other groups of citizens whose activities
or, in some cases, whose vices would unite them sufficiently
for a composite character under the title of club. Other incongruous suggestions might prove equally diverting. Then, too,
as "The Lying Club" had not been entirely without foundation, so there were other societies and clubs in London
worthy of burlesque. There were even stories and rumors,
now he had broached the subject, of clubs and societies,
mysterious and comical, which had existed in earlier days.
These old stories, too, could be collected. They would all be
grist for the mill.

Within the year the larger edition was ready. A summary
view of its popularity is given us by the fact that it was reprinted in the following year, this time as *Satyrical Reflections upon Clubs,* and labeled by the publisher, J. Phillips,
as Volume V of the works "by the Author of the London
Spy." Ward incorporated into this larger edition all of the
material he had used earlier, expanding it as he did so. He
added the characters of twenty-two more clubs, bringing
the total up to thirty-two. For the occasion he prepared a
satirically ironical dedication and preface. "A Book that is
but big enough for the costly Dress of a Calves-Skin Doublet," he writes, "ought never to appear without Dedication
and Preface, for fear the World should Laugh at it for
receding from fashion." He will not, however, "sneakingly
beg your Favour, or anticipate your Judgment by a selfish
Commendation" of his own performance, "because extol-
ling the intrinsick worth of what you must buy before you
try, makes a Preface so like a Quack's Bill" that he abhors
the thought of it. Neither will he, as it is customary to do,
allege "the hurry of other Business, or the insufficiency of
Time" as responsible for his blunders.

If the preface itself is not sufficiently indicative of the ironical nature of the "history," we may consider for a moment the dedicatory epistle to that "Luciferous and Sublime Lunatick, the Emperor of the Moon." "I have humbly presumed," he writes,

to address the following History to your imperial Inconstancy . . . And as I expect Nothing but Moonshine to reward my Labours, in Case they are honour'd with your Highness Approbation, so I hope I shall have Nothing but a dark Night, to punish me, when I need a light one, in case I have disoblig'd you. Besides, as I have principally treated of the Madness of Mankind in the following Sheets so I thought the Lunacies of this World a proper Subject to entertain your Highness.

It is not Ward's fault if, after that, later historians misunderstood his design and purpose.

Some notion of how Ward incorporated earlier material into the later *Secret History of Clubs,* as well as an interesting revelation as to the source of much of the material, may be had by an examination of the revised account of two of the clubs. In his earlier "history" he had given, as we have seen, a rather fragmentary account of a society frequently bandied about in coffee-house gossip as "The Lying Club," with a few select yarns reputedly told by members of that organization. The account appearing in print had stimulated further gossip in the coffee-houses and taverns about the club's supposed existence and origin. Other tall yarns were recited as having been originally told by Sir Harry Blunt and his club.[5] With an ear open for what he could hear, Ward collected his materials for the more extended account. When it appeared, the earlier details as well as the yarns had multiplied.

In the earlier edition he had spoken of the club as an "Ancient Society reviv'd, held in several parts of the City, now removed to a certain Tavern in Westminster." He now gave the year of its origin as 1669, and the place of meeting as the Bell Tavern in Westminster. Moreover he could supply his readers with a set of rules governing the meeting of the club, as well as the story of its founding and Sir Harry Blunt's election to the chairmanship. The club owed its origin, so Ward's account runs, to a now famous dinner at which Sir Harry Blunt entertained some travelers from abroad. The food consisted of a large stewed carp, three brace of partridge and a leveret, and a "Butter'd Apple-Pye" for dessert. The talk, in view of the dinner, turned inevitably to hunting, and one of the travelers told of a boar-hunting incident in France. A second traveler replied with another yarn—which Ward had already told in the earlier account—of a fishing expedition in the East Indies. Upon the conclusion of the second story Sir Harry told one of his own. Being particularly expert with the longbow, he and his man had set out the day before for some sport in a wood in Surrey. Coming to a small river still empty-handed and sitting down for a moment to rest, he had spied a woodpecker on an apple tree across the stream. Taking aim for the sake of practice, he had discharged his arrow at the precise moment a huge carp had leapt clear of the stream, and the arrow shooting the fish through the head, nailed it and the woodpecker to the tree trunk. Later, having crossed the river to retrieve his game, he had stooped to pull a tuft of grass to wipe the blood off the peg of his arrow, and caught a young leveret by the ears, which kicking and clawing, he had hurled into a neighboring furrow with such force that it had killed three brace of partridge nesting there. His man, having sacked the game, shook the apple tree for refreshment, and a quantity of the fruit as well as the game, he had brought this day to dinner to convince them all that he scorned to tell less truth than another man.

At that point someone suggested meeting once a week, and the name of "The Travellers' Club" and "The Gentlemen's Club" having been passed over for "The Lying Club," Sir Harry was elected chairman. Among the rules agreed upon were the following: The chairman was to wear a blue cap with a red feather upon it or to be turned out of doors. Candidates for membership had to qualify by an acceptable yarn before being admitted. Any one who spoke a word of truth between the hours of six and ten without saying, "By your Leave, Sir Harry," would forfeit a gallon of wine of the chairman's choice. To any one telling a yarn so tall that the chairman found himself unable to match it, the latter was required to turn over the little blue cap and the chairmanship. Any one who missed a meeting was called upon at the next to tell four lies offhand or forfeit five shillings to the servants of the house.

A second club to which Ward added substantially in the expanded edition was that of "The Basket Women's," now called "The Market-Womens club." The addition is in the nature of a yarn about the drinking powers of the women, which Ward must again have picked up, as he had the materials of "The Lying Club," in the taverns and coffee-houses. A certain vintner in Cheapside, whom Ward identifies as famous for curing the toothache by staring at three or four candles through blue spectacles until he salivates his gums, got into an argument with a merchant over the question whether or not women drink more than men, and made a wager with the latter that he could secure three women who could empty a hogshead of claret before they slept or became ill. The terms of the wager having been arranged, the vintner hastened to Clare Market and invited to his shop three likely candidates—Bess Grundy, Moll Bunch, and a third, a substitute for Nan Toply, who at the moment had not yet recovered from giving birth to a child. The women, acquainted with the terms of the contest, ordered a dish of tongues and after two or three slices, requested a monteith and liquor. After a drink or two they called for their pipes and tobacco and settled down to the night's work, drinking, eating, and smoking by turns, and busily gossiping in the intervals. By five o'clock in the morning they had emptied the hogshead and called for a quart of mulled wine to settle their stomachs. At six they trudged off to market, to which their maids had brought their produce for the day. The merchant, still not recovered from his astonishment at their capacity, trailed them through Lincoln's Inn Fields, but beyond finding them merry and inclined to dance could discover nothing abnormal. "Come, Come, Girles," Grundy remarked on the way, "Drunk or Sober, always mind your Business."

Ward, of course, asked no one to believe that any of his stories had actually taken place. They were good yarns;

that was their justification. Something likely enough had taken place—something that had grown into gargantuan stature in coffee-house gossip and under the burlesque of his own pen. But that they were not to be credited, his dedication and preface had both given warning.

As for the rest of the thirty clubs whose histories are given, they fall readily into the categories already suggested. The majority are mere groupings of London citizenry according to their activities or their vices for the sake of the satiric character. Two others are in the nature of the divertingly preposterous suggestions already utilized in "The No-Nose Club." A half dozen others are pseudo-authentic accounts of older clubs whose materials were recruited from the still surviving accounts of coffee-house and tavern. At least nine of them are accounts of contemporary clubs and societies, compiled with greater and lesser degrees of accuracy. We may continue our study by examining a few of those under the first category not already mentioned in the discussion of the earlier edition.

"The Surly Club" was Ward's satirization of the language and behavior of Billingsgate porters, oarsmen, and lightermen, notorious throughout the city for their obscenity of speech. "The Split-Farthing Club" was an attack on the avaricious and miserly citizens of Bishopsgate Street, whose chief grievances were "Backward Tenants" and "high Taxes," and who spent much time talking about what to do with their money when they died, though not one of them ever gave sixpence to a poor relation. "The Wrangling or Hussel Farthing Club" was a similar attack on the dissenting tradesmen who spent their time in the coffee-house perusing the news and talking politics and national affairs. "The Bawds Initiating Club" was one more reference to the numerous houses of ill-fame and the practice of inveigling and betraying young country girls into their toils.

An example of Ward's grouping of subjects by their activities rather than by their vices is the picture he presents of "The Weekly Dancing Club" in St. Giles which is another example of his broad use of the word club, for he states

that any one paying the price of a sixpence admission was
entitled to enter. In the more common use of the term today
it was, of course, no club at all, but merely a place of entertainment and dancing, not unlike the night club of today.
The club was held over the "Cole-Yard" gateway into Drury
Lane, and the public dancing on Thursdays soon emptied
the eighteen-pence galleries at the theaters. Here one could
see, according to Ward, a motley crowd of rakes, apprentices, liverymen, thieves and gamesters, chambermaids,
punks, and loose widows. A brawny bully, equipped from
a second-hand shop in Long Lane with a flaxen wig fresh-
combed and powdered and a lace hat under his arm, escort-
ing a Gray's Inn seamstress in tawdry laces, old ribbons,
and black bugles. A lawyer's clerk accompanied by the
buxom daughter of a Chancery-Lane victualer. Masquerad-
ers in costumes borrowed from a music house in Moorfields.

The preposterous club was one of Ward's most fruitful
suggestions to the literary essayists. In the earlier edition he
had suggested "The No-Nose Club." Now he proposed "The
Club of Ugly Faces." [6] According to Ward it was founded
by a man named Hatchet, who longing for company invited
others of similar unfortunate physiognomy to join him, after
an arch butcher's boy in Newgate Street had asked him to
turn his huge nose aside while the lad passed with his tray
of beef. A third club, undoubtedly diverting for Ward's readers but rather too inelegant for our own tastes, was "The
Farting Club" held some thirty years since at a public house
in Cripplegate parish.

Ward's suggestions were ingenious and no doubt amusing
to a certain class of readers. The humor is coarse in its forthright exploitation of the grossly offensive, and there is no
motive for the delineation other than that of entertainment.
Nowhere are the limitations of Ward's powers and taste
more apparent. With Addison the preposterous club was to
become the expression of a refined and whimsical spirit play-
fully arraigning the oddities of man and his behavior; with
Steele it was to become the instrument of gentle raillery and
satire.[7]

In a few cases it is difficult to tell whether Ward is in-

dulging in a preposterous suggestion or deriding an actual
gathering of young and ambitious tradesmen eagerly aping
their betters. "The Mock Heroes Club," for instance, was
held at an alehouse in Baldwin's Gardens and was composed
of young clerks and shopkeepers, who addressed each other
by the title of some distinguished man in history. So An-
tonius Copywell and Valentius Drinkwater mingled with
the master of the house, one Don Quixote, and his tapster,
Sancho Pancho. It is not clear here whether Ward is merely
having fun—whether he is using the device to satirize the
pretentious air adopted by ambitious shopkeepers and the
younger fry of the law—or whether he is deriding an actual
society. The same is true of "The Knights of the Golden
Fleece," so-called because they met at the Sign of the Golden
Fleece in Cornhill, though, according to the account, they
later removed to the Three Tuns in Southwark. The club
was made up of tippling citizens and exchange brokers.
Names for the members were chosen by two godfathers
selected from the group, who bade the candidate arise, dub-
bing him the while whatever name came to mind—Sir Peter
Squabble or Sir Skinny Fretwell. Ward's purpose becomes
clearer as he describes their activities. The time, he writes,
was spent "Drinking plentifully; Smoaking incessantly;
telling Stories lamely; talking Politics wildly; disputing
Principles warmly; and at last to dwindle into lushious
Bawdy." And one need perhaps assume no more than that
it was a device to deride a group of men whom Ward de-
spised.[8] The names he avers they gave each other are themselves a part of the satire.

Of an entirely different nature are the clubs whose history
Ward relates out of the distant past. That memories of the
older clubs still lingered and that stories of ancient deeds
were rehearsed over the tavern bowl with a good deal of
awe and nostalgia for the glamorous violence of a bygone
era is indicated by Ward's reference to "The Man-Killing
Club" and "The Man-Hunters Club," similar in nature as in
name, though different in the degree of violence with which
they pursued their game. Ward relegates "The Man-Killing
Club" to the time of Charles II, and the account echoes deeds

attributed in the literature of the day to the Hectors and
Scourers. The fact, however, that eligibility for membership
in the club demanded an act of mayhem identifies the material as lingering legends of the older Elizabethan clubs,
such as, The Damned Crew, The Bugles, and Tityre-tues.[9]
It is interesting to see how the evil reputation of the older
societies lived on through the century.

"The Man-Hunters Club" bears the earmarks of having
been a somewhat more recent organization. The nature of
the club's activities reminds one again of the Scourers, and
since Ward's account antedates by only two or three years
a new recurrence of street terrorizing, this time identified
with the Mohocks, the account is significant. Certainly it
demonstrates how a group of young hellions out for sheer
fun, without any desperate intentions and without any
actual violence, can precipitate a fear in a populace that in
turn creates stories of slit noses, of chairs pierced by swords,
and of women ravished and rolled downhill in barrels.
The club, according to Ward, consisted of a group of wild
young rakes educated in Chancery Lane, "among the sober
Offices of the Law and Equity," who, meeting commonly at
a tavern near the Tennis Court Playhouse on the back side
of Lincoln's Inn Fields, began the sport in an attempt to
find a new and exciting diversion. The first man at the house
at night would constitute himself chairman and order the
next two or three out to beat for game in anticipation of
their later report for the diversion of the group. The two
or three "hunters" would hide themselves along the borders
of Lincoln's Inn Fields until they saw some person treading
along the pathway by himself, whereupon they would spring
to their feet and draw their swords, shouting, "That's he.
Bloody wounds, that's he!" Usually the person so surprised
would be frightened out of his wits, dash madly down some
near street or alley into an alehouse in despair of his life,
there to tell his story to sympathetic and horrified listeners.
If the person, however, proved sufficiently self-possessed or
courageous to draw and stand his ground, the "hunters"
would immediately sheer away crying, "It's not he!"

After a run or two the men would return to the house

and regale their fellows with their adventures, drinking and boasting about their deeds until midnight, when, if they were drunk enough as they stole home, it would be, "Hey-Boys for scowring the Watch, battering their Lanthorns, knocking up their Whores, breaking Bawdy-House-Windows, or any other mischief that happen'd in their way."

One cannot help wondering how much Ward's account, published in 1709 and reissued in 1710, was itself responsible for the stories and fears of the Mohock scare, current in the year 1712.[10]

A good many of the clubs, however, had a reality more substantial than coffee-house and tavern gossip. The existence of many of them is substantiated by numerous references in other writings of the period. Ward's description of "The Atheistical Club," a society of "Irreligious Profligates" meeting at an "eminent Tavern in Westminster," whose blasphemous conversation and jesting disturbed the God-fearing populace of London, curiously parallels, for instance, the alleged activities of the later Hell-Fire Club, for which an edict of suppression was ordered by the government in 1721.[11]

So, too, the reference to "The Scatter-Wit Club," a group of playhouse critics and wits meeting at the Rose Tavern in Covent Garden, is substantiated by an allusion to the club in an attack on William Walsh, entitled *On the Author of a Dialogue concerning Women, Pretended to be Writ in Defence of the Sex,* though we need accept neither Ward's sobriquet for the club—since the account is derisive—nor the indecent verses he ascribes to its members. Compare, for instance, Ward's statement that the club met near

to Apollo's Sessions-House, where our celebrated Wits are forc'd to take their Trials, and abide by the Judgment of a herd of Criticks, who assume to themselves the judicial Power of Damning or Saving any Stage-Author, according to their Prejudice or Partiality

with the following lines from the poem:

Near Covent-Garden theatre, where you know
Poets their sense, players their shapes do shew,
There is a club of critics of the pit,

Who do themselves admire for men of wit;
And lo! an arbitrary power assume
On plays and ladies both to pass their doom.[12]

The description of Tom Briton's weekly musical, which
Ward re-titled "The Small-Coal-Man's Musick Club," is another club for which there is substantial literary and historical evidence.[13] Tom Briton was an eccentric but honest
crier of small coal, who out of his love for music assembled
each Thursday a group of music lovers at his quarters—the
second floor of his coal shop next door to St. John's Gate,
Clerkenwell. Ward gives one of the early patrons of the club
as Roger L'Estrange, who had "a tollerable Perfection on the
Base-Viol," and states further that men of wit and quality
honored the musical society with attendance until the weekly
meeting became as well known as the Kit-Cat Club. Tom
himself was so unusual that many who saw him going about
crying coal considered him a nobleman in disguise; others
more accurately pointed him out as "a famous Small-Coal-
Man . . . a Lover of Learning, a Performer in Musick, and
a Companion for a Gentleman." Tom had made a good
collection of ancient and modern music, Ward tells us, and
collected in the routine of his business a handsome library,
not long before auctioned off at a considerable advantage.
The portrait is a kindly one; Ward implies that he was himself a patron of the club, and he includes in the account a
song he himself contributed to a Thursday musical.

Equally odd, and an interesting sidelight on the times, is
the account of "Sam Scots Smoaking Club," again undoubtedly an authentic picture, though the evidence at the
moment is wanting. Sam kept a music house at Temple Gate,
where he sold "Harps, Fidles, Minuets and Bories," and was
a great lover of the pipe and bottle. In the company of four
cronies—a linen draper turned dancing master, a Salisbury
Court barber, a graver, and a Scotch writing master—he
nightly made the rounds of the city taverns, and the group
soon earned for itself the sobriquet of the smoking club by
their capacity to consume a pound of tobacco an hour. On
more than one occasion an irate vintner would ask the five
men to move on when his other customers complained too

bitterly about the poisoned air. Far from discouraging the gentlemen the reproof only served to stimulate their activity until it became customary for them to enter a crowded tavern, and calling for pipes and tobacco, set about seeing how soon they could empty the house of customers.

Three of Ward's accounts relate to contemporary organizations of ornithologists, florists, and scientists. The first he characterizes as "The Bird-Fanciers Club" and the account itself is largely a description of the annual feast of the society, open to all who cared to buy a twelve-penny ticket to the dinner. A special feature of the dinner was the final course in which a huge bird pie, when cut open, liberated a host of canaries which became the prize of the crowd, who clambered over tables and chairs in an hilarious effort to capture their prey.

Quite similar is Ward's account of "The Florists Club" which met for its annual flower festival at the Sign of the Lion, near Hoxton Hospital, a house noted for its cheesecakes and Lincoln ale. Here the annual dinner was followed by an inspection of the flower display and by the judging and christening of new varieties produced by the ardent gardeners.

The scientists Ward characterizes under the title of "The Vertuosos Club," a convenient term throughout the century for members of The Royal Society.[14] Here Ward is treating of matters already familiar to us in the writings of Swift, who was no more kindly inclined to the projectors and inventors than Ward himself. Less ingenious than Swift, and on occasion even more indelicate, Ward succeeds, however, in giving to his account a homely and somewhat humorous realism not unworthy of his superior. "When they were thus met," he writes,

happy was the Man who could find out a New Star in the Firmament; discover a wry step in the Suns progress; assign new Reasons for the spots of the Moon . . . or indeed impart any crooked Secret to . . . puzzle their Brains, and disturb their Rest for a Month afterwards.

Among their projects Ward lists that of conveying Hampstead air into the city by subterranean pipes, that of making a ship sail into the teeth of the wind, and that of turning sea brine into fresh water. Indeed, he concludes, "the whole Company were so infected by an itch of Curiosity that if a Man funk'd a Pipe and could not give a Reason for the Blewness of the Smoak, he that ask'd the question would think him an unworthy Member of so Philosophical a Society."

It was, one suspects, with considerable malice aforethought that Ward concluded his volume with an account of the Kit-Cat and Beefstake Clubs. For more than one reason he felt unkindly towards the former. The Kit-Cat roster contained the names of many leading Whig statesmen, and since 1705 the club had begun to assume a distinctly political cast. Moreover, among the literary men of the day who belonged to the club were those whose writings were in considerable esteem, and it is not impossible that Ward envied them their reputation, as well as their easy access to a patronage denied himself. It is not necessary, however, to assume that Ward meant deliberately to distort the truth.[15] The statement that the Kit-Cat owed its origin to that "Amphibeous Mortal, Chief Merchant to the Muses" Jacob Tonson, who drew together a group of university wits whom he dined once a week in return for their writings, Ward borrowed from the account of the club by Sir Richard Blackmore.[16] Ward's error in assuming that the club was named Kit-Cat for the cook (Christopher) and his house (the Sign of the Cat and Fiddle) rather than for a cook whose name was Christopher Cat, is a minor one, and was at any rate a current story about the origin along with a half dozen others. The real point of Ward's attack lies in his characterization of the wits as an arrogant, self-centered group, chiefly interested in rehearsing their own merits, and in his attack upon their subservience to an ambitious, mercenary bookseller. It has been a matter of speculation among historians how Tonson managed for so long a period to merit and receive the esteem and friendship of the leading literary figures and statesmen of the day. No doubt, as Ward suggests, he found it a convenient business arrangement. If Ward is unfair, it is because he labors a point obviously open to question. Tonson probably did not play quite the important role Ward suggests. Certainly the club's existence depended upon something more fundamental than the bookseller's desire for fame and business. Neither did the wits and statesmen subscribe so supinely to his projects and judgments. Ward's final thrust, however, must have pleased rival booksellers. Tonson, he writes, "look'd but like a Bookseller seated among Lords, yet, *vice versa* he behav'd himself like a Lord when he came among Booksellers."

For the members of the Beefstake Club, Ward, on the other hand, had considerable regard, and one can see that he meant to play off these men who disdained the diet of pies for roast beef against the more aristocratic and delicate-palated Kit-Cats.[17] The meetings of the club were held in the King's Head Tavern in the old Jewry, and the picture Ward presents of the club in session is an intimate one. The chairman at the moment is Estcourt, the Irish comedian, who sits thrumming his silver gridiron with a "Screwtore-Key," turning a pun or Irish witticism over the handling of each bar. To Ward we are indebted for the story of the voluminous book, large as a bale of Dutch linen, lying open on a sideboard table in which the secretary was to enter for preservation each witticism and *jeu d'esprit* of the members upon a majority vote of those present. Estcourt, according to the account, was a great mimic who could take off any man's gesture and deportment, and amused himself and the club by imitating any member who was absent.

Ward's concluding remarks are vague. He tells us that the club left the King's Head, but he apparently did not know the place to which they had removed. We now know that by January 1 of the next year, Estcourt himself had opened the Bumper Tavern in James Street, Covent Garden, and the friends of the Beefstake were once more united.[18] For Ward, however, the account served its purpose.

> In a right Choice, we shew that we are wise,
> Who then can blame such Worthies, who dispise
> For noble Beef, that Childish Diet, Pies.

The Secret History of Clubs is a very valuable record. Life in the eighteenth century was singularly gregarious. It was at the tavern and the coffee-house that the city's business was carried forward. Tradesmen exchanged their wares and city merchants concluded their contracts over a cup of coffee or a bottle of claret. Stocks were bought and sold, laborers were paid their wages, apprentices were bound out to their masters or upon the completion of the seven-year contract celebrated their attainment of mastery. Physicians and surgeons held their consultations and prescribed for their patients; tailors took the measure of their customers for a new suit of clothes; booksellers engaged their hack writers and printers; lawyers rehearsed cases with their clients and witnesses. Wits and writers gathered to celebrate their publications and lingered over the wineglass to lay out new prospectuses. Editors of periodicals and newspapers dropped in to collect contributions or to collaborate with their colleagues. Officers of state and members of parliament gathered in clubs and coteries to discuss new stratagems and the prosecution of policy. All over London in coffee-houses and taverns, the birds of a feather flocked together. The young clerks and shopkeepers at an alehouse in Baldwin's Gardens, the tradesmen and brokers at the sign of the Golden Fleece, the horticulturists at the sign of the Lion near Hoxton, the beaux at White's, the critics at the Rose, and the wits at Will's. What would be more natural than that the journalist concerned with the contemporary scene should turn to the gatherings at the coffee-houses and taverns?

It is in this sense that Ward's contribution in *The Secret History of Clubs* is interesting. The pictures he presents are teeming with life. Men move and act uproariously and tell bawdy lies. They are bigoted and narrow, pronounced in their prejudices and tastes. They concern themselves with the petty and the nonessential, envying the successful rather than the virtuous. Under the influence of good food and drink and under the impetus of their own conviviality they expose themselves and many of the superficial aspects of the life they lead. More subtle and profound than Ward himself realized is the picture of the social impact, the jostling of man against man, the pulsing life and the energy of movement which pervades its pages. For his own readers the author's warrant was simply that he told them, sharply and pertly, what they had already heard, what they already knew.

X

A Preposterous Union

For Men of Sense must own 'tis better
To live by Malt, than starve by Meter.

The Hudibrastick Brewer (1714)

IN THE YEAR 1712 Ward was at the height of his success
as a journalist. In the interim of fourteen years since the
appearance of *A Trip to Jamaica* he had published well
over a hundred items, ranging in length from sixteen-page
folio pamphlets to a two-volume adaptation of *Don
Quixote* and the three-volume digest in verse of Clarendon's *History*.
Included among his writings had been seven periodicals,
two of them weeklies and six of them monthlies, several of
which extended their existence over a two-year period. Fifteen of the larger volumes, issued singly, have an average
length of over two hundred and thirty pages. Many of the
items were, of course, reprinted in edition after edition.
If such continuous activity had not exactly produced opu-
lence, it certainly on the other hand must have provided a
fair competence for the writer, and Ward must frequently
have felt that he had come into his own.

Late in the autumn of that year Ward turned taverner and
opened an alehouse at the "Great Gates in Red-Bull-Yard,
between St. Johns-Street and Clerkenwel-Green." His first
reference to the new venture is a rhymed advertisement for
his "celestial liquors," which appears in the fourth number of
The Poetical Entertainer:

There, on that ancient venerable Ground,
  Where Shakespear in Heroick Buskins trod,
Within a Good Old Fabrick, may be found
  Celestial Liquors fit to charm a God.

Rich Nectar, Royal Punch, and Home-Brew's Ale,
Such as our Fathers drank in Times of Yore,
When Beef, Fat Bacon, and salubrious Cale,
Were Food and Physick for the Rich and Poor.
Commodious Rooms, with Hampstead Air supply'd;
Obliging Usage for each civil Guest;
A Garden Spot, whose fertile Banks provide
Refreshing Salads to delight the Taste.
No Bacchanalian Ensigns at the Door.
To give the Publick notice, are display'd,
Yet Friends are welcome: We shall say no more,
But hope their Friendship will promote a Trade.

What moved Ward at the very height of his success as a
writer to turn tradesman, it is not too difficult to conjecture.
The career of a pamphleteer and journalist was frequently a
precarious one. John Dunton, who had once been the fairly
affluent editor of *The Athenian Murcury* in the nineties,
spent a good share of the succeeding decade hiding from his
creditors. Tom Brown, before he died in 1704, had alternated
his days between the tavern and the Marshalsea debtors'
prison. John Tutchin, irate editor of *The Observator,* had
been beaten up on the streets of the city in 1707 and died
shortly thereafter. William Pittis had disappeared from the
scene and William King was to die within the year in penury
and ill health. Of Ward's more widely known colleagues and
rivals engaged in the profession in 1700 only Defoe remained
active as a journalist, and his subsistence was fortified both
by political patronage and trade. Ward himself in his early
years had been sharply aware of the proximity of Grubstreet
to a debtor's prison.

By 1712, too, Ward must have been fully cognizant of the
vagaries of his reading public. For over a decade his success
had been directly dependent upon popular taste and appetite, an appetite easily satiated, and stimulated again only by
the recurring discovery of the startling and new. In his own
experience the popularity of the trip had waned and given
way to the character, and it in turn he had already exploited
from almost every conceivable angle. His failures, as well as
his successes, with his periodical ventures must also have
shown him the impermanence of his public. In the field of

periodical literature there had recently sprung up rather powerful rivals whose popularity clearly demonstrated a change in taste on the part of the reading public.

Moreover, the popular writer was distinctly without status in society. Ward himself had earlier referred to his own activity as the "Scandalous Profession" and to his catering to public taste as the prostitution of his talent.[1] To the puritanic tradesman and merchant in the city the writer was frequently a penurious and unprincipled vagabond, given to licentious and dissolute behavior. They believed him a potent factor in the corruption of youth and in the distraction of apprentices and journeymen. They recognized only too well that he maintained himself by leveling an almost constant attack upon the tradesman's thrift and industry, upon his religion and politics. To the gentleman reader, the Grubstreet wit to be sure was entertaining and amusing, but again a man without dignity or standing; willing to tolerate and support the man of polite letters and to associate with him, he still had a contempt for one who earned his living by his pen and was *ipso facto* no more than a hackwriter and a scribbler. Even to the party man, whose cause he frequently served, he was at best a hireling, employed without any personal association and without approval of his character.

Where the success of the pamphleteer was directly dependent upon the success of his own political party, his existence was still precarious. With his own party in the ascendancy, his readers would be in the majority and his public assured. Then the greater the furor generated by the political issue, the greater the writer's opportunity. But the party was always subject to defeat and the author likely to step beyond bounds. The loss of readers would inevitably follow and perhaps even the pillory or imprisonment. Ward's own experience had taught him the consequence of political reverses, and though the Tories were now at the height of their power, future events were to justify his elimination of his dependence upon the political success of the party.

For some months after Ward opened the alehouse he continued his writing. During the winter of 1712–13 he was busy with the successive numbers of *The Poetical Entertainer*.

The same year saw the publication of the first two volumes of *The History of the Grand Rebellion* digested into verse. In the autumn of 1713 with the death of Queen Anne and the dispersal of the Tory government the derisive, triumphant strain of *The Poetical Entertainer* gave way to melancholy. In *The Field Spy, or Walking Observator* (1713) he sadly laments the new turn in political affairs. Faction is once more arrayed against faction. Rumors of sedition and treason are abroad. In the city knaves are thriving in trade and the "falsely pious" are elevated to office. The poor are struggling against poverty and contentious law is ever on the side of the rich.

Indeed, the poem everywhere reflects the mood of depression which followed the shift in national affairs. The halcyon days of the Tory pamphleteers were over. Everywhere about him on the morning stroll through the outlying districts to the north of the city lay the evidence that trade alone could assure one a steady livelihood. Sadler's Music House and New Tunbridge Wells, the bowling green, the archery field, and the tavern were all of them indicative.

> What Ways, thought I, do humane Race devise,
> To gratify their Ease and Avarice!

And why not he? There were other commodities more easily marketed than those of the pen. They were further removed from the danger of the pillory and the debtors' prison.

Even so it was with a momentary feeling of chagrin that Ward reconciled himself to the life of a taverner. From the time of his earliest writings vintners and their unscrupulous practices had been a favorite subject of attack. *Sot's Paradise* had been the first among many. In *The London Spy* he had characterized the keeping of an alehouse as the last resort of a broken tradesman, allowed by the parish to set himself up in business chiefly to avoid the necessity of granting charity. In *A Journey to Hell* he had included vintners in the catalogue of rogues, at home among the apothecaries, the quacks, the pettifoggers, and the hypocritical, dissenting clergy. In "Morning Observations Upon a Topping Tavern over a Pint of Canary," a poem appearing in the third number of *The Diverting Muse* (1707), he had come near to being decently civil, but even there he had been able to say only that he had seen

> How fawning Sweet'ners get Estates by Wine,
> Whilst gen'rous Souls in Circumstance decline,
> Nay, whilst more Merit and Industry too,
> Shall the same wealthy Ends in vain pursue;
> Which shows that Fortune cares not to impart
> Her Smiles to Men of Honesty or Art.

It is on a note of defiance that a year after the opening of the alehouse he wrote *The Hudibrastick Brewer, or a Preposterous Union between Malt and Meter*. He recognizes, he says, that he is

> Apollo's first degen'rate Son,
> That e'er left Bacchus and his Tun,
> To make dull, heavy Ale agree
> With more aspiring Poetry.

But at that he is not the first in these uncertain times to "truckle to necessity." Defoe has long since demonstrated that the poet can deal in stockings as well as rhymes; nor ought ale to present any more difficulties to the versifier than a tile and brick yard. Steele aspired high and finally received as his reward a seat in the "awful legislative throng," but he received it only to lose it with the derisive laughter of his opponents ringing in his ears.

> Therefore, I think, since Poets may not,
> And Brewers do remain in Senate,
> Ned's in the right on't more for Brewing,
> Than Dick for Scribbling to his Ruin;
> For tho' one never hopes to thrive
> Into a Representative,
> Yet he's more bless'd whose Fortune falls
> Below St. Stephen's Chappel-Walls
> Than he that climbs, and is from thence
> Spew'd out for want of Pence or Sense.

As for Swift:

> His Cassock Friend had Wit to play
> His Cards a much securer Way,
> He wisely kept within his Tedder,
> And follow'd his successful Leader;

Drug'd Day and Night with Pen and Paper,
Like cunning Statesman's Under-Strapper,
And knew as well as any Man,
Which Side his Bread was butter'd on;
Thus whilst one Irish Author lost
His Credit, Int'rest, and His Post . . .
The other wisely got, we see,
A good fat Irish Deanery.

Many a man has done things he wasn't bred to. Let the Whigs remember Cromwell and cease shouting derision. The Tories are welcome to come drink his "salubrious" ale, brewed with an invocation to the nine muses.

How immediately profitable the alehouse proved to be we do not know. As the political fortunes of the day lent occasion Ward continued his writing. In 1714, upon the death of the queen, he published *The Mourning Prophet, or Drooping Faction Reviv'd by the Death of Queen Anne,* lamenting the change of political fortune involved. He had time, too, for the anonymous attack upon Marlborough, *The Republican Procession, or the Tumultuous Cavalcade,* already referred to. The death of Lord Wharton, newly created marquis, and that of Bishop Burnet, both in the same year, gave him occasion for two derisive poems, entitled *The Lord Whig-love's Elegy, to Which Is Added a Pious Epitaph upon the Late Bishop of Addlebury* (1715), the latter certainly one of Ward's most effective political efforts, frequently assigned to both Swift and Brown.[2]

In *St. Paul's Church, or the Protestant Ambulators* (1716) he took one more trip to the cathedral, lashing out at the throng of "whetters," mongrel politicians, scribblers, beaux, and wenches who repaired thither each for his own, and no one for the right, purpose. In 1717 when Dr. Hoadly, bishop of Bangor and leader of the lower house of convocation, became involved in a church war with Dr. Snape, elected by the House of Commons to preach before that body on the day set aside for the celebration of the restoration of Charles II, Ward contributed a burlesque fable entitled *The Tory Quaker, or Aminidab's New Vision in the Fields;*[3] while the alarming portents of murrain, fire, eclipse, and storm

which followed the death of the queen are described in
*The British Wonders, or a Poetical Description of the
Several Prodigies and Most Remarkable Accidents that Have
Happened in Britain since the Death of Queen Anne*
(1717).

It was owing to malt rather than meter that Ward in 1717
was able to leave the alehouse in Clerkenwell for the more
affluent Bacchus Tavern in Moorfields. Here he was to play
the merry host for the next thirteen years. Certainly he seems
to have prospered. Men of his political sympathies, we are
told, made his house their "constant Resort." Tradesmen
flocked in. Others, attracted by the unique phenomenon of a
scribbling taverner, came in to enjoy the wit and humor of
the host, whose own gilt-embossed volumes adorned the
shelf above the bar. Even Pope, we are told, sat in the
Bacchus and complimented the host by consuming his
liquor. "Of late Years," wrote Giles Jacob[4] of Ward in 1723,

he has kept a publick House in the City (but in a genteel way) and with
his Wit, Humour, and good Liquor has afforded his Guests a pleasurable
Entertainment; especially the High-Church Party, which is compos'd of
Men of his Principles, and to whom he is very much oblig'd for their constant Resort.

Ward was in his third year in the new tavern before time
permitted him once more to take up "his long neglected
Muse." First of the items he then offered his readers was a
poetical description of his own tavern under the engaging
title of *The Delights of the Bottle, or the Compleat Vintner,*
a valuable poem not only for its accounts of the Bacchus, but
for the general picture it presents of tavern life.

If the erstwhile journalist possessed both a conscience and
a good memory, he must have had more than one occasion
during the composition of the poem to remember his earlier
attacks upon vintners. But the world had changed with his
moving behind the bar. Forgotten now were the morning
headaches after nights of hard drinking. Forgotten, too, were
the evils of diluted wines and excessive prices. Now he only
remembered that one could neither celebrate friendship, sign
a contract, end a quarrel, subscribe allegiance to a cause, or
plight one's troth without the glass going around.

> Give me the gen'rous Soul that dares
> To drown in Wine all worldly Cares,
> The Jolly Heart who freely spends
> His Surplus with his Bottle Friends

he cries, and the invitation is, of course, to come to the Bacchus.

The sign, he tells us, is an enormous bunch of grapes, held by the tiny hand of a little punch-gut Bacchus astride a tun no bigger than a gallon. Inside the house all is spacious, cleanly, and in order. A neat well-dressed matron moves behind the bar, a dozen drawers awaiting the nod of her head. In the glass "safe" lie choice cuts of fish, flesh, and fowl, browned to a delicacy by the charcoal fire. In the kitchen among the shelves of gleaming pewter, the dangling saucepans, and burnished kettles, the cook all in white wields her knife, long as a backsword.

> In short, here's ev'rything to please
> All Pallats, Humours, and Degrees,
> Pickles and Spices from abroad,
> To season our domestick Food,
> And Foreign Wines of ev'ry Sort
> From costly French to common Port,
> Clean Rooms, where nothing can offend us,
> Brisk nimble Drawers to attend us.

And everywhere, upstairs or downstairs, as the occasion demands,

> A Jolly Master to redress
> What e'er disturbs our Happiness.

And the trade streams in. It is then that the jolly master needs must assert himself. He must flatter the whole world— the rich and the proud, the surly and knavish, the learned and dull, the wit and the prodigal, the fool and the sharper, the gamester and bully. It is galling sometimes for one who in his own day was himself the subject of the flattery, and Ward devotes the final canto to a portrayal of "tavern Tormentors." Worst of all are the "Bubble Upstarts," the newly-rich speculators in the South Sea bubble,

> Who growing proud and richer far,
> In fancy, than they really are . . .
> Huff, strut, and wrangle where they Dine,
> Reproach the Cook, dispraise the Wine,
> Dispute the Bill without a cause,
> And chatter worse than Pyes or Daws.

There are "Stingy Wranglers" who quarrel over every bill and always leave in a huff; "Dinner Spungers" who buy their wine but beg their bread; and "hungry Blades" who somehow or other manage to have the "safe" opened on the pretense of wanting a sample and end by cutting away half the joint. There are "Cook Teasers,"

> Who in some Kitchen-Box sit watching,
> To gratify themselves by snatching;
> If a fine Turkey's on the Spit,
> By stealth they seize the choicest Bit,
> Drink to the Cook, and whilst they give her
> A Glass, one sneaks away the Liver.

The "Pan Soppers" are those who soak their hard-baked crusts in the drippings of the roast and so, over three pennies' worth of wine, consume a pound of bread and tallow. The "Plate Twirlers" pivot the pewter on an up-ended knife until a hole is worn quite through the plate. There are "Table Whitlers" who deface the tavern property; "Spoon Pinchers" who carry off the silver and so subject the servants to blame without just cause; "Drawers biters" who collect from the crowd, confuse the drawer in changing the money, and, pocketing a share of the just dues, toss the waiter a sixpence as a blind. There are the young blades just come to town from country schools, who with money in their pockets and hell in their eyes meet at a tavern to roar out the night with "black-ey'd Susan" or Leveridge's *Philosophers.*[5]

> Thus is the Vintner plagu'd all Night,
> Till Morning dims the Candle-light,
> Unwilling to enjoy his Bed,
> For fear some Mischief should succeed
> That might intail an evil Fame
> Upon his Conduct and his Name;
> For none, tho' in a loftier Station,
> Have more regard to Reputation.

But when the guests are men of manners and sense, it is quite another matter.

> Then Manliness, deserving Praise,
> Appears in all he does or says,
> The best of Wines he sends or brings
> And treats his noble Friends like Kings,
> Enters the Room with comely Grace,
> And puts on such a Cherub's Face,
> So plump, so smiling, and as pleasant,
> As that the God of Wine was present;
> And if, when ask'd, domestick Care
> Will suff'r 'im to assume a Chair,   •
> Such Guests will in his Carriage see
> The utmost Affability.

One remembers that according to Giles Jacob it was in a "genteel way" that Ward managed the Bacchus.

II

In 1722 Ward was in his fifth year as proprietor of the Bacchus Tavern. In the interim between 1717 and that date he had written little.[6] In the summer of that year, however, an anonymous pamphlet, *The Parish Guttlers, or the Humours of a Select Vestry* appeared on the bookstalls and was hawked about the streets of London. Without doubt its pages contained the most bitter and outspoken attack on the system of the closed or select vestry and its attendant evils that appeared in the literature of the early eighteenth century. The nature of the attack, with its individualized portraits of the members of the vestry, made it a hazardous undertaking. Neither the author's name nor that of the printer appears on the title-page; nor is the parish under attack directly identified. If Ward was indeed the author—and the evidence seems more than convincing—it establishes the erstwhile pamphleteer and later tavern keeper as still a potent force in the satiric literature of the day.

The Parish Guttlers was first attributed to Ward by W. T. Lowndes,[7] and both external and internal evidence support the ascription. The intimate knowledge of parish affairs manifested by the author and the bitterness of the personal attacks upon members of the vestry would indicate that the author himself was a resident of the parish in question. As proprietor of the Bacchus Tavern, "against the middle of Middle-Moorfields," Ward was a resident of the parish of St. Botolph's, without Bishopsgate. The author of *The Parish Guttlers* describes the location of the parish under attack as follows:

> Without that Gate that bears the Title
> Of Rev'rend—leading to the Spittle,
> There lies an ancient ill-pav'd, hobbling
> Out Parish, fam'd of late for squabbling,
> Which has more Courts and Allies in it,
> Than I could name by this day sennit.

The "Rev'rend" gate at once suggests Bishopsgate, which led to St. Mary's Hospital, and the parish described as lying just outside the gate would then have to be St. Botolph's, without, as an examination of the ancient boundaries of the parish in *New Remarks of London, Collected by the Company of Parish Clerks* (London, 1732) indicates.[8] One additional factor serves to identify the parish as St. Botolph's. Following the lines already quoted, the text continues with a description of the vestry:

> This ancient, Parish partly nam'd
> Before, for present Discord fam'd
> Is wisely govern'd by the Mast'ry
> Of those that call themselves a Vestry,
> Their Number, by their own Accounts,
> To about Twenty six amounts.

According to *New Remarks of London* the parish of St. Botolph's had a closed vestry of twenty-seven, "with the Rector and two Church-Wardens for the time being." This was in 1732, ten years after the publication of *The Parish Guttlers*. The approximate agreement in number is extraordinarily striking in view of the great divergence in the number of members on the select vestries of the various metropolitan parishes. No two according to Maitland[9] had the same number. Those nearest St. Botolph's were St. Stephen's, Walbrook, with twenty-four, and All-Hallows, Barking, with thirty-one, neither of which could possibly have been the subject of the poem.

The internal evidence supporting Ward's authorship is, as we shall see, indubitable. In its emphasis upon both the serious and the comical and in its concern with the casual and impertinent as well as significant detail, the poem everywhere demonstrates Ward's most characteristic manner. The hudibrastic measure is distinctly like that of *Hudibras Redivivus* or *Vulgus Britannicus*. The detailed nature of the characters, particularly the emphasis upon the appearance and profession of the individual, suggests at once the citizen-portraits of *The London Terraefilius*. The author's admission that the poem was written by "fits and starts," presumably as his other duties permitted, coincides with what we know of Ward's activities as proprietor of the Bacchus.

The parish vestry and its system of parochial administration was, of course, a traditional subject for satire. The vestry levied and collected the church-rate; administered the charity for the parish; built and administered the almshouses; fixed the poor-rate; apprenticed the orphans; and supervised the workhouses for the able-bodied. With so much authority entrusted to a few men, many times without sufficient control or representation from the parish at large, evils were bound to creep in.[10]

A common charge of the parishioners, for instance, was that the church-rate was too high. Individual members of the parish, moreover, were certain that they had been discriminated against in the apportionment. The poor believed themselves treated in a niggardly fashion. To a sensitive open-minded individual the conditions in the workhouses and almshouses were appalling. Moreover, the responsibility of the parish to support the orphans and illegitimate children born within its precinct gave rise on the part of the warden and vestrymen to a certain paternalism over the morals of the parish resented by the young and the wayward. To enact parish business it was necessary for the vestrymen to meet, and they customarily did so at the tavern or alehouse with

THE DEVIL TAVERN ON FLEET STREET

From an engraving by J. H. Le Keux

the cost of the entertainment debited against parish funds.

These were charges Ward had already leveled at vestry-men in the third part of *A Journey to Hell* in 1705. The central point of attack in *The Parish Guttlers* is that the vestry is a select one. In the open vestry a majority of the parishioners, if they chose, could assume a more or less active role in parish affairs through their right to retire or elect the members of the vestry. In the closed or select vestry the en-tire control lay in the hands of a few members who held their office without any regard or provision for parish representa-tion. In case of a vacancy new members were either ap-pointed by the bishop or elected by the remaining vestrymen by the process of co-opt.

The authority for the system was in many cases lost. In the case of St. Botolph's, without Bishopsgate, the authority lay in a special bishop's *faculty,* or formal instruction, at the time of the creation of the parish. Parliament itself in various church building or local acts enacted in the late seventeenth and early eighteenth centuries authorized the formation of select vestries after the pattern of the mother parish or, in lieu of that, after the pattern in St. Martin's-in-the-Fields. But whatever the source for the authority of the closed vestry, its essential features remained the same.

Over its members the parish at large exercised no control whatever. The expenditures might be niggardly or lavish; the church-rate excessively high or low. There was no public accounting or auditing of records.[11] For a wealthy parish-ioner, not himself a member of the vestry, who might object to an excessively high apportionment, there was no appeal. For the destitute there was no recourse beyond an appeal to the vestry itself. Year after year a handful of men appointed from among their own number the officers of the parish— the warden or wardens, the overseers of the poor, the con-stables, the surveyors of streets and highways.

Though members of a select vestry were frequently honest and public-spirited men, there is plenty of evidence to indi-cate that the opposite was also frequently true. Members elected by co-opt were often unworthy of the distinction and authority placed upon them. Such a member might be elected merely for his complaisance or for his willingness to connive at the betrayal of trust exercised by the majority—a case of rogue succeeding rogue, as Defoe put it upon one occasion.[12] Certainly if a majority of the members were willing there was nothing to hinder them in systematically exploiting their office. Levying what rates they pleased upon others, their own were frequently scandalously lower than those of their neighbors. In more than one case on record their own rates were not collected at all. Parish funds were apt to find their way into private coffers, if not by outright theft, then by a partiality of administration that cleaned, paved, and lighted the streets of the vestry members while neglecting those of their neighbors. Even more vicious was the practice which grew up of "sharing supplies," by which members parcelled out to themselves the contracts for supplying the materials needed for the construction of buildings or the maintenance of almshouses. Elaborate building programs were on occasion embarked upon for no other reason than to enrich individual members at the expense of the parish. Even the poor relief became in time subject to a "toll" by its administrators. But what the common man remarked upon more often were the "glass coaches" in which members drove out to inspect the pauper children, the "venison dinners," and the "Gargantuan repasts" to which they treated themselves upon any occasion of business.

Strange as it may seem, the system of the closed vestry had not been a frequent subject of attack by the satirists of the late seventeenth and early eighteenth centuries. Writers were content for the most part to satirize the general vice rather than particular offenders. Defoe in 1714 had contributed a scathing denunciation of the system, but his attack had been not without political color and at any rate had been directed less at malfeasance in office than at the power of entrenched Tories in certain localities to influence the electors.[13] It had been this same aspect, rather than the inherent evils, that had been the basis for an assault upon the select vestry in the House of Commons in 1710. In that year the house had ordered a bill to be prepared for the regulation and suppression of select vestries at the petition of a number of parishes, among which interestingly enough was that of St. Botolph's, where, to quote from the petition itself: [14]

twenty-seven persons have for several years past, under the name of a Select Vestry, assembled themselves, and by an arbitrary power raise money upon the inhabitants . . . and clandestinely apply part of it among themselves, as they think fit; and take upon themselves to choose into and dispose of the parish offices without any regard to order or common justice, by which means they influence the electors for Parliament as experience has shown; and in time may tend to the utter subversion of the petitioners' liberty, and is a notorious oppression and grievance upon them.

The Whig majority, however, at the moment the bill was ordered, was already embroiled in the controversy over the prosecution of Sacheverell, and since its primary aim had been the discomfiture of the Tories, the bill was repeatedly postponed until the dissolution of parliament. With the defeat of the Whigs in the next election the bill was forgotten. In 1717, however, with the Whigs again triumphant in the house, a new bill was ordered for the regulation of all closed vestries in the metropolitan area. Because of its political bias the bill suffered defeat in the House of Lords, where the archbishop of Canterbury himself led the attack. Thereafter for a period of twenty years the select vestry exercised its power without occasioning further parliamentary discussion.

The Parish Guttlers reiterates the general charges associated with the system. Twenty-six men legislate for the entire parish. They levy what rates they wish irrespective of the wishes of the taxpayer. The vestry itself is controlled by a small number of its own members who wheedle or bribe the others into acquiescence. They appropriate parish funds to their own advantage. A churchwarden marries off his daughter with a huge dowry to which the parish has unwittingly contributed. The constable and his watch accept hush money from thieves and prostitutes and so make their offices worth hundreds of pounds a year. On all occasions of business the vestry dines royally, and members have been known to send home to their own families choice viands from such a repast instead of distributing them to the parish poor at the tavern, as custom and decency require.

From the general statement Ward comes rather reluctantly to particulars. He relates the squabble referred to in the opening lines of the poem. A goldsmith of the parish thought himself taxed unjustly and reprimanded members of the vestry publicly in his shop. Disturbed by the oratorical powers of the goldsmith, members of the vestry sent for him at their next meeting and forthwith elected him one of themselves. This served to change the attitude of the goldsmith, who then went about the parish saying,

> Ah Neighbor, what I said
> Before I knew them, I confess,
> Was but a wrong illnatur'd Guess . . .
> I find 'em, as I hope to thrive,
> The worthy'st Gentlemen alive;
> I did not think there could have been
> A Set of such wise honest Men.

After relating this story Ward in a series of verse-portraits presents the character and behavior of member after member of the select vestry. One is amazed at the audacity of the delineations. It is inconceivable that anyone could have had the slightest difficulty in identifying them. The first portrait, for instance, is that of a pewterer whose culinary articles, tavern pots, and nipperkins supply the entire parish. He is an elderly gentleman who recently married his own servant. He is lame and hobbles as he walks. He thinks himself something of a comic actor and recently at a public meeting came dressed in an old beggar-woman's vest and accompanying rags, imitating one of those destitute wretches he should have helped,

> Which none but an unthinking Fool,
> Would turn to Sport and Ridicule.

The second portrait is of a bookseller, a huge fat fellow with a stentorian voice, another member of the common council. He recently imprisoned a porter and later sent him to Bridewell for hawking papers adorned "with his own character." When he was churchwarden and overseer of the poor, he used to joke with them in their necessities,

> Ask 'em what Comfort they could have,
> Or bus'ness on this side the Grave,
> Swearing he'd give 'em Alms to buy
> Their Coffins, if they wou'd but die.

A third member of the vestry is a "gunsmith" who mis-
treated the poor in still another fashion:

> For if Powdero chanc'd to meet
> A Pensioner in Lane or Street
> Without a Badge, he'd stop their Pay
> A Week, and make 'em Fast and Pray.
> Whilst he himself, without remorse,
> Would to the Tavern have recourse,
> And there misspending what was theirs,
> Deserve their Curses not their Pray'rs.

Against a fourth member Ward has a special grievance,
and a full portrait takes the author somewhat longer. He is
one of the parish jobbers and supplies coffins for the poor
who are buried at parish expense. Recently, Ward attests, he
refused burial ground to the corpse of a poor porter whose
brother had provided "a good Elm Coffin," until the widow
sent back her brother-in-law's gift and accepted a "Slit-deal"
one of his own.

> For which he did vouchsafe to charge
> A Price extravagantly large,
> Having the Parish Purse in hand,
> To satisfy his own Demand;
> Which was no sooner made than paid,
> And thus to propogate his Trade,
> Wrong'd both the Living and the Dead.

That is merely the beginning of the charge. He is also an
upholsterer, who sells beds to the parish which are appraised
by his own servant, and so pays himself three times the actual
cost of the beds. Moreover, under the guise of assuming a
moral and religious concern for the welfare of the parish, he
has contributed to the delinquency of young women. Among
them had been the niece of his own wife, who, having gotten with child, he married off to a young man of the neighborhood. Upon the birth of the infant the young woman
committed suicide, and the uncle, having supplied the coffin,
rode behind in his single coach, while the young husband
trudged along on foot.

The moral improprieties, however, do not make the upholsterer one whit more kind to the poor.

For if a Poor old Parish-Dutches,
Applies for Alms upon her Crutches,
Or fruitful Dame o'erstock'd with Bearns,
Who starve on what her Husband earns,
Moves him with all due condescension,
To grant her a small weekly Pension,
Perhaps, thro' his great tenderness
To such poor Wretches in distress,
Out of the Parish Stock he grants
Three Farthings to relieve her Wants
Of five or six, so very poor
The Children beg from Door to Door;
And if they use one Harsh Expression,
Or mutter at the small Donation,
By aid of his robust Adherents,
To th' Workhouse he commits the Parents,
Where they're confin'd, like Whore and Robber,
To hard unprofitable Labour:
And if their Children are two little
To be apply'd to Block and Beetle,
He takes due care to send 'em down
To Enfield, or to Hartford Town,
Where, in a little time, in course,
They're choak'd with Filth, or starv'd at Nurse:
This in his Ward'nship has he done,
By more poor Families than one.
And when these Wretches, on their due
Submission to this Vestry Jew,
From their Confinement are enlarg'd,
They are not totally discharg'd,
Till on their Knees, in open Street,
They fall at Mr. Church-Ward'n's Feet,
And for their Fault, before his Shop,
Ask Pardon of this Parish Pope.

The modern reader would fain believe there was little to
add to the picture of depravity and brutality after that, but
the portraits continue to follow. There is "crafty G[eorge],"
the under warden,

Who by the W[ind]mil o'er his Door
Discovers how he grinds the Poor.

He has the contract to supply the parish poor with bread,
and in exchange for the tickets issued to them by the church-
warden, he provides them with light and frequently sour

loaves. There is a flour merchant who still withholds a five-year debt to the almshouses; a land-tax gatherer; a silk merchant who in fear of his life goes armed with a pistol; a "Count Tallard" whose byword is "Bona fide"; a Scotch cotton-wear seller who has been elected only recently,

> And ever since he swears the Clan
> Are truly honest to a Man.

Ward admits that there are three honest men in the vestry. Their characters are also given, though with less detail. The first of the three is one who never joins his fellow members in their designs to exploit the parish, but on the contrary is forward in rebuking them and in revealing their deceits to the general public. A second, whose motto is "Weave Truth with Trust," has often proposed that at all tavern feasts each member of the vestry pay for his own food and wine. The third, younger and braver than the rest, upon discovering their deceits and frauds, immediately resigned from the vestry. As for the rest, through their venality and peculation, they,

> Have brought the Parish Stock of late
> At least Two Thousand Pounds in Debt:
> And when they pass their vile Accounts,
> Shut out the Best Inhabitants,
> Because their Frauds so naked are,
> Their Books will no Inspection bear.
> Yet some of these are call'd upon
> The Court of Conscience, tho' they've none,
> Where their Grave Wisdoms sit to do
> That Justice which they never knew . . .
> Should all their num'rous Faults be told,
> No Volume would their Knav'ries hold.
> But this small Version, tho' 'twas wrote
> By fits and starts, with little Thought,
> Shows what each Parish must expect,
> From gutt'ling Vestries call'd *Select*.

Certainly none of Ward's readers acquainted with the parish could have mistaken the portraits. The charges are pointed and direct. It would be equally difficult to believe that none of them recognized as the author of the attack the genial host of the Bacchus, a writer whose ability in satire and burlesque was widely known and whose earlier writings were still sold in his own tavern. It is equally clear that no writer or bookseller would have dared to publish so caustic an attack under his own label,[15] and that no friend or crony of Ward's would have voluntarily divulged the secret of its author.[16]

As for the fairness of the picture itself, one cannot be too dogmatic. Ward loved to deride his enemies in damning colors. No character he ever drew suffered from too much leniency when the pen was ready in his hands. One can see him at work, writing the poem by "fits and starts" as his tavern duties allowed, poetizing his ideas as he heard a new story told on the upholsterer or hitting upon a new turn of phrase as the pewterer passed by the door. It is well to remember, however, that if every single count in the charge were allowed as fundamentally true the picture would be drawn in no blacker colors than those which recent investigations have agreed upon as substantially accurate for any of a half dozen of London parishes. St. Botolph's was one of the first of the metropolitan parishes to petition the House of Commons for relief from the tyrannical oppression of the closed vestry. Within a few years after the publication of *The Parish Gutlers* a new storm against the system broke out in the parish and gradually spread throughout the city. It was a matter of a full century, however, before the inhabitants of St. Botolph's succeeded in throwing off the yoke.[17]

To the student of Ward it is an interesting and salutary fact to know that the aging taverner employed his pen on at least one occasion in a direct, personal attack upon the social evils of the day. Here certainly he was less concerned with the ready penny than he was with the evil he characterized.

XI

No Mean Talent

Nor can there be a clearer Evidence of his unimitable Manner in this
way of Writing, than that this very Design was afterwards continued
by one who hath been thought to have no mean Talent of Humour,
and whose Writings have on that Score been very well receiv'd.

A Character of Mr. Thomas Brown and His Writings (1705)

AFTER MOVING to the Bacchus Tavern, Ward's journalistic
endeavor became increasingly intermittent and desul-
tory. Except for the attack on the select vestry of St.
Botolph's, only a few of his writings are significant for the
knowledge they provide either of the man or the times.
Much of what he wrote was in imitation of his earlier successes. In 1721 he offered his customers a long rambling poem
in two parts, entitled *The Merry Travellers, or a Trip upon
Ten Toes from Moorfields to Bromley,* a burlesque account
of a trip he and a friend by the name of Will, who kept a
tavern and billiard hall at the sign of the Lamb and Crown
in Long Alley, had taken to Bromley earlier in the summer.
In characteristic manner he records his observations and
experiences: the Quaker maids in full skirts without hoops
or laces in the shops along Gracechurch Street, the lobster
stalls on Fishstreet Hill, the tottering wooden houses of
London Bridge, the broom men, butchers, and cutlers of
Southwark's market district, the tavern incidents and adventures along the way, and a rather detailed description of
the country house of his host and the rural sports of rabbit
and deer hunting, which the latter provided for his guests.
In 1725, having attended a fashionable masquerade in Horse-
fodder Market, he wrote *The Amorous Bugbears, or the
Humours of a Masquerade,* an account of the evening's activi-

ties in dancing, gaming, and amorous intrigue sufficiently in the spirit of his earlier prose to be labeled "a Supplement to the London Spy." Adaptation, too, again interested him for a moment, as he turned an early Spanish tale into Hudibrastic doggerel under the title of *News from Madrid: The Spanish Beauty or the Tragi-comical Revenge* (1726), a diverting yarn of appropriate taste for the habitués of the Bacchus. None of the items has much interest for the modern reader. In 1724, however, under the title of *The Dancing Devils, or the Roaring Dragon* Ward reported for his readers an experience at the Lincoln's Inn Theater; a rare eye-witness account of the extremities to which the popular vogue for pantomime had given rise, and which merits attention.

For a writer concerned with the contemporary world, Ward has on the whole remarkably little to say about the legitimate theater. In the tenth part of *The London Spy* he tells us that he and his friend decided to see a play but found the playhouse closed, since most of the actors at the moment had "Translated themselves to Bartholomew-Fair," where it was as reputable for them "to Play the Fool . . . for Fifteen or Twenty Shillings a Day, as 'twas to please Fools in the Playhouse at so much per Week."

Adjourning to the fair themselves, the travelers took in a rope-dancing act and a droll and then turned to one of the more reputable booths where the very players who had deserted Drury Lane were now holding forth. "Having heard much of a Comedians Fame," Ward writes,

who had Manfully run the hazard of losing that Reputation in the Fair, which he had got in the Playhouse; and having never seen him in his proper Element, we thought the time might not be very ill spent if we took sight of another Best Show in the Fair, (for so they all stil'd themselves) that we might judge of his Performances.

The actor to whom Ward refers was William Pinkethman, who will presently be interesting to us in another connection. Of him Gildon wrote in 1702, he "is the Flower of Bar-

tholomew-Fair and the Idol of the Rabble. A fellow that
over-does everything, and spoils many a Part with his own
stuff." [1]

The play presented in the booth, according to the account
in *The London Spy,* was a truncated version of *Fryar Bacon,
or The Country Justice,* in which the spectacle of the brazen
head and the humorous exploits of a miller and his son con-
tended for the interest and plaudits of the crowd. An old
English court scene was followed by one showing Friar
Bacon in his study with the brazen head. With magical wand
and incantation the friar consulted the devil in an effort to
further the projects he had already announced. This was followed by a comical interlude between the miller and his son,
Ralph, the latter role played by Pinkethman, who by his
gesture and grimace "render'd the Character Diverting." A
scene in the office of a country justice concluded the production with a finale of dancing and singing.

These were the chief of their Characters jumbled Confusedly together,
with a Flying Shoulder of Mutton, Dancing and Singing of Devils, and
such like pieces of Conjuration by the Diabolical Fryar Bacon; with whose
Magical Pranks the Mob was wonderfully pleased, as well as greatly
astonished.

Ward's account of the performance is interesting at the
moment, for as we turn to his later characterization of the
drama, it is Bartholomew Fair which has moved to the playhouse, rather than the playhouse to Bartholomew Fair.

Even though the theater is seldom mentioned by Ward he
himself was not entirely divorced from dramatic and thea-
trical activity. [2] In 1704, though he had already belittled
Pinkethman's ability as an actor, he had joined the procession of wits who were writing the epilogues and prologues
for which Pinkethman was becoming famous. His own contributions had been "A Prologue, spoken by Mr. Pinkeman,
suppos'd to be Pres'd, and haul'd in before the Curtain, by
a couple of Press-Constables," and "an Epilogue, Spoken by
Mr. Pinkeman, upon the back of an Elephant." [3] The latter,
indeed, might have been an event in a theater already ex-
hausted in the search for innovation, had it actually been car-

ried out, but the assurance of a bricklayer that the structure
of the building would be endangered prohibited the show.[4]
In 1705, moreover, Ward, as we have already seen, had tried
his hand at a Bartholomew droll, entitled *Honesty in Distress
but Relieved by No Party, a Tragedy, as it is Basely Acted by
Her Majesty's Subjects upon God's Stage the World,* though
evidence of its actual production is wanting. In 1708 he had
written *Wine and Wisdom, or The Tipling Philosophers,* a
poem, "Set and Sung by Mr. Leveridge at the theater in
Lincoln's Inn Fields," and the fourth number of *The Poetical
Entertainer* (1712–1713) had contained a "Hymn sung before Her Majesty by the Charity-Children, at Kensington."

It was not, however, until 1724 that Ward provided his
readers with an account of an actual night at the theater. For
some eight years, John Rich, the manager of the playhouse
in Lincoln's Inn Fields, had been engaged in an increasingly
bitter rivalry with the managers of Drury Lane.[5] In an effort
to draw crowds from the rival theater the managers had
resorted to stage buffoonery that ten years earlier would have
surprised even the devotees of the Bartholomew Fair drolls.
Dancers and singers along with painters and carpenters had
supplanted the actors in importance. Shakespeare and Congreve had given way to Harlequin and Scaramouche. Pantomime, dumb show, and stage spectacle delighted and
amused an undiscriminating audience.

In 1718 John Thurmond, the dancing master at Lincoln's
Inn Fields, left the employ of Rich to become the manager
of the playhouse in Drury Lane. This intensified the rivalry.
By 1723 the afterpiece frequently preëmpted the major role
in the evening's performance. In that year Thurmond produced a pantomime—using the word in the sense then current of "Dancing, Gesture, [and] Action, intermix'd with
Trick and show"[6]—entitled *Harlequin Doctor Faustus, with
a Masque of the Deities.* Rich responded, first with *The Comical History of Doctor Faustus,* then with the more extended
Necromancer, or Harlequin Doctor Faustus, one of the most
elaborate pantomimes ever staged.

It was a performance of the latter that Ward attended late
in the same year. Disgusted by the inanities to which the old

story had been subjected and the extremities to which the rivalry had driven the managers, he wrote his burlesque account of the "Dumb Farce," "Lately acted at Both Houses." In spite of the reference to both theaters the account is confined to a description of *The Necromancer, or Harlequin Doctor Faustus* as it was produced at Lincoln's Inn Fields. That Ward is substantially correct, both in the outline of scenes and in the details of the spectacular display, is clear if one compares *The Dancing Devils* to another contemporary account written by one Thomas Merrivale,[7] who describes himself as "late of Trinity College, Oxon."

Merrivale was one of Rich's admirers, and his account is lavish in its praise. Ward's is satiric. Between encomium or burlesque, the latter obviously is the better choice. To have read Merrivale, however, is to exempt Ward from any charge of exaggeration or fanciful falsifying of the account. Any spectator in the theater must have seen the show unfold substantially as Ward presents it.

The curtain rises to display Dr. Faustus sitting in his study. About him are a group of dancers and singers, representing good and evil angels, half of their number clad in white, the other half in sable. Alternately the two groups contend in "harmonious Lays" for the soul of Faustus. Suddenly a large white sheet of paper flutters from an upper corner of the stage, landing miraculously between the finger and thumb of the Harlequin Faustus. It is, of course, the contract offered to Faustus by the devil. In a moment the devil himself arrives on the stage, where, after indulging his proclivity to song, he then proceeds to tempt Faustus by producing out of the air a table laden with golden crowns and scepters. This failing, the table vanishes and another bit of hocus-pocus produces Helen to stand beside Faustus on the stage. She sings sweetly to allure the doctor, and he, capitulating to the devil, signs the contract in his own blood. Turning then to embrace his prize Faustus finds her sinking slowly to the floor and an ugly hag, lean and frightful as "Belzebub's own sister" rising up in her place. The devil, giving out three piercing laughs, sinks back into hell. Faustus, somewhat stupefied, turns to an enormous folio which he strikes with his wand, the book flying open immediately. Henceforth, the audience is to know, the doctor will devote himself to magic.

The succeeding scenes are given over to the minor trickery of disappearing tables and exploding wines, and to music and dancing. Scene four, however, is the big one of the evening: the stage displays a huge windmill; presently Joan, the miller's wife, descends and "by chance" performs a dance for the audience.

> By chance, we say, because we know
> There's not one Motive in the Show.

In a moment she is joined by her husband who dances with her. Faustus comes in and asks the miller to deliver a letter. The latter, unable to read the superscription, delays and Faustus knocks him down. Whereupon the miller rises and hits the doctor with his mealy cap.

> This pretty Jest, in which does shine,
> So much Contrivance and Design,
> Does such a Laugh and Clap command,
> From e'ery Mouth and e'ery Hand,
> As if our brightest Wits had been
> Projectors of the wondrous Scene;
> Tho' some ill-natur'd carping Fools,
> Unskill'd in new Dramatick Rules,
> Suspect the Author stole the whole
> From some old Merry-Andrew's Droll.

Faustus runs upstairs after Joan and appears at a window above kissing her. The husband dashes upstairs after them, but as he appears in one window, Faustus and Joan are at another. Faustus climbs out of the window and runs along the cornice with the husband, Ralph, in pursuit. Then the doctor climbs high up into the wings of the mill, daring Ralph to follow. With Ralph in the "shrouds," the doctor jumps free, and by the wave of the wand, sets the wings turning. Poor Ralph hangs on tightly in fear,

> With Heels now pointing tow'rds the Skies,
> Which then again, in half the round,
> Are turn'd near Neighbours to the Ground.

But even that is not enough for Faustus.

> A Sack of Grain, which had before
> Been planted near the Miller's Door,
> In order, as we may suppose,
> For grinding, when the Wind arose,
> Now takes a sudden strange Figary,
> And skips and dances like a Fairy.

Faustus allows the sails to come to rest and while he disappears off stage, Ralph is assisted in his descent by his man, Collin. In a trice Faustus is back disguised as Punch doing a dance. Ralph and Collin recognize him, draw their knives, and cut off his head. Punch, however, dances equally well without a head, so they seize his arms and severing them from the body toss them upon the stage. Punch keeps on dancing. In desperation they try to seize him again, but Faustus scuttles out of his disguise whole-limbed, leaving his "mangl'd case behind."

> Excessive Claps, profusely loud,
> Were now most lavishly bestow'd.
> No Wonder, for what Tongue could hiss
> At such a grand Device as this?
> Not only worthy of the Smiles
> Of those that rule the British Isles,
> But e'ery Mortal that delights,
> In Raree-Shows and pritty Sights.

As the act ends a chariot in which Faustus and Joan are riding appears aloft, drawn by a flying mare with Ralph and Collin astraddle.

In the grand finale of the show a huge dragon, monstrous as a "Trojan Horse or Greenland Whale," with glaring eyes and wings like a man of war, descends onto the stage. Devils pour out of the dragon's mouth and dance across the stage, rolling their eyes at the doctor to terrify the crowd. A clock strikes the hour. Faustus, aghast, is seized upon by the devils, and, mounted upon the back of one of them, is carried to the dragon, who swallows him with a gulp and bellows in glee. Thunder rolls off stage. The devils climb aboard, and the dragon, gaping wide its angry mouth to display a roaring fire within, begins to ascend. A few remaining devils cling to the legs and wings. Scaramouche, the doctor's servant, neglected in the general melee,

> Catch'd hold o' th' Dragons Duggs and there
> He held and hung 'twixt Earth and Air.

As the huge form disappears above the proscenium arch scholars off stage sing a doleful melody,

> By which we do suppose they mean
> To hide the screeks of the Machine.

To the crowd in the upper galleries it was no doubt an evening to be remembered.

But *The Necromancer* was only one of the many outrageously extravagant productions of a theater devoted to the staging of spectacles in which buildings were consumed in roaring flames, earthquakes rumbled, and volcanoes erupted.[8] One recalls Pope's lines deriding the pantomimic rivalry:

> Hell rises, Heav'n descends, and dance on Earth,
> Gods, imps, and monsters, music, rage, and mirth,
> A fire, a jig, a battle, and a ball,
> Till one wide Conflagration swallows all.[9]

Some days after Ward's attendance at the Lincoln's Inn Fields Theater,

One James Field who represented the Miller's Man fell from the upper stage in a flying machine by the breaking of wires: he fractured his skull and died miserably: three others were hurt, but recovered. Some of the audience swooned, and the whole was in great confusion upon the sad accident.[10]

But the death of James Field, one takes it, served no more efficaciously to curb the extravagance than did the burlesque satire of Ned Ward, for the pantomime continued to flourish throughout the century.

II

In 1728 when Pope published the first edition of *The Dunciad*, Ward was sixty-two years of age. Up to that time he had, on the whole, lived amiably with his confreres. He

St. Dunstan's, Fleet Street

From a painting by Samuel Scott

had earlier, of course, relentlessly attacked Tutchin and Defoe, but they had been political opponents and scribblers for a rival faction. John Dunton, who had on more than one occasion praised him, had in 1705 launched a vituperative attack against him in *The Whipping Post, or a Satyr upon Every Body,* but that had been because he had mistaken Ward as the author of *The Wandering Spy, or the Way of the World Inquired Into.*[11] Booksellers, according to Ward, had been among his best friends, and at least one of them paused long enough to comment upon the "Notable, Learned, Ingenious, well-Read, and well-Bred Gentleman he [Ward] has always shew'd himself" to be.[12] Tom Brown, William King, and William Pittis had been among Ward's most intimate associates. Tom Brown, for instance, had written his own imitation of *The London Spy* entitled *Amusements Serious and Comical Calculated for the Meridian of London* (1699), and following Ward's attack upon the astrologer Partridge in the summer of 1699, both men had shared in the responsibility of carrying forward the jest into a weekly periodical. William King and Pittis, along with Dr. Joseph Brown, had written complimentary sonnets to Ward when in 1711 he had completed his adaptation of *Don Quixote.* Pittis had earlier been praised by Ward in *The Dissenting Hypocrite,* and to the memory of the former, after his miserable death in 1712, Ward intoned a solemn eulogy "Upon the Late Learned and Ingenious Dr. William King."[13]

For the most part, however, there had been few references among his contemporaries to Ward, and few references in Ward's own writings to his contemporaries. If in the former case this is not difficult to understand, since after all writers whose literary reputations were distinctly superior to Ward's might have most effectively met the sudden popularity of a Grubstreet wit by ignoring him, it is only fair to insist that the paucity of reference in Ward to his contemporaries is a reflection of the hardihood and complacence of his own genius. Mediocre as he must have frequently recognized his own talent to be, it was still a thoroughly independent one. For him it had been enough that publishers and booksellers had been willing to market his wares. As for his fellows, let them write as they please, and leave him alone. "As for my part," he had written in 1706,[14]

> I have always that respect for the Sons of the Muses, as never to interrupt them in their peaceable Enjoyments: and I am of this Opinion, that I have not far'd the worse for it. Nor am I at all partial to the Failings of other Authors, thro' fear of having my own expos'd, tho I am sensible they are many; but out of a Moral Duty of using others as I would be us'd myself.

To Ward's credit it needs to be recorded that he had not been among "the little rogues" who had been attacking Pope for years and so moved the latter to reply.[15] Indeed, if Ward heard the rumors circulating in the city early in 1728 about the forthcoming "Progress of Dulness," he may well have remained unperturbed. After all he had never given offense to Pope. He could flatter himself that Pope was numbered among the patrons of the Bacchus, that the great poet's verse had once appeared in *The Poetical Entertainer*.[16] What he may not have understood was that in Pope's projected satire on the low taste and vulgarity of the age he, himself, if indeed he merited any notice whatever, was one of the host of popular writers and Grubstreet wits against whom the poet would direct his ire.

When Pope in March of 1718 published the *Peri Bathous, or the Art of Sinking in Poetry,* Ward found himself listed among the frogs and referred to as a poetical John Taylor.[17] In the first edition of the *Dunciad* he escaped with a reference in which he is taunted with being read chiefly in the colonies.

> Adieu my children! better thus expire
> Un-stall'd, unsold; thus glorious mount in fire
> Fair without spot; than greas'd by grocer's hands,
> Or shipp'd with W—— to ape and monkey lands,
> Or wafting ginger, round the streets to go,
> And visit alehouse where ye first did grow.

and the line

> Another Durfey, W——! shall sing in thee.[18]

Ward felt called upon to reply. In December he issued *Durgen, or a Plain Satyr upon a Pompous Satyrist* "amicably

Inscrib'd, by the Author, to those Worthy and Ingenious
Gentlemen misrepresented in a late invective poem call'd
the *Dunciad.*" *Durgen* has always been dismissed by students of Pope as only another one of the scurrilous attacks on
the poet which justified Pope's original attack. But in fairness to Ward it is necessary to say that as attacks go—or as
they went in the eighteenth century—it was, save for the
cruelty of the epithet, mild enough. In the "Author to the
Reader" Ward protests that "he never till now, ever wrote
a line that could give . . . the minutest Provocation" to
Pope. Even if a man loves peace he can be provoked into a
quarrel. Throughout the poem the tone is not one of enmity
but rather of aggrieved admiration. Why should Pope whose
"sweet pen . . . the world admires" attack his friends,
especially

> Some, whom his pointed Vengeance might have spar'd
> Poets, who much esteem'd the mighty Bard,
> And scorn'd to write the least ill-natur'd Scroll,
> That could offend his great majestic Soul.

Ward says very little in direct reply to Pope's references
to him, but proceeds with a general admonition. Why attack
those who admire you? Why attack poverty? Has not poverty been characteristic of all great poets? Why attack, too,
a man like John Ward of Hackney for an unfortunate experience in the pillory, especially with the unwarranted in-
sinuation that eggs were thrown at him by the mob? His
parting advice to Pope was to look to himself:

> Durgen, take care, for this may be the Fate
> Of first-rate Poets, tho' at present Great . . .
> One day's mistake, if publish'd when its pen'd,
> May lose more Credit than seven Years have gain'd.

Pope, however, had only begun his sport. His victims had
replied and he was ready with the retort. In 1729 he brought
out *The Dunciad Variorum with the Prolegomena of Scrib-
lerus,* adding to the original text a series of notes and appendices in which he found additional opportunity to tor-
ment his enemies. He allowed the original lines on Ward to
stand but now spelled out the name.[19] In a footnote on the

passage, ostensibly to identify Ward, he quoted the account from Giles Jacob's *Poetical Register.* "Of late years," Jacob had written in a passage which it may be well to quote again,

he has kept a publick House in the City (but in a genteel way) and with his Wit, Humour, and good Liquor has afforded his Guests a pleasurable Entertainment; especially the High-Church Party, which is compos'd of Men of his Principles, and to whom he is very much oblig'd for their constant Resort.

Maliciously Pope inserted the word "(ale)" after Jacob's phrase "good Liquor." It was an ingenious trick thus to quote a complimentary account and by the insertion of a single word to annihilate the compliment. Pope, too, reasserted his original charge by adding "Great numbers of his works are yearly sold into the Plantations," and in a later edition concluded by saying, "He wrote a wretched thing against our Author, call'd *Durgen.*" [20]

Even that was not enough. In reply to Ward's accusation that he was inhuman in his attack on John Ward of Hackney, Pope appended to book III, line 26, a footnote paraphrase of Ward's lines on the subject in *Durgen,* and concluded, "But it is evident this verse cou'd not be meant of him (Ward of Hackney); it being notorious, that no Eggs were thrown at that Gentleman: Perhaps therefore it might be intended of Mr. Edward Ward the Poet." Once more Pope had turned the argument and used Ward's past to plague him.

In other notes and appendices Pope continued his jibes. In a note to the verse referring to John Taylor, the water poet who had kept a tavern, Pope could not forego the insertion of the phrase "like Mr. Ward." [21] In Appendix II, "A List of Books, Papers, and Verses, in which our Author was abused, etc." he identified *Durgen* as having been written by "Edw. Ward, with a little of James Moore." [22] In the "Index of Things (Including Authors) to be Found in the Notes" under the word alehouse he included a reference to Ward as the proprietor of one; under the letter W he noted "Ward, Edw., a Poet and Ale-house-keeper in Moorfields."

It was this continuous and repeated reference to the alehouse that nettled Ward most. The distinction between alehouse and tavern was an important one, and Ward had been
anxious that it be kept in mind. When he had moved to the
Bacchus it had been a step up in the world. He would have
been happy now to have his earlier induction into trade
forgotten. At any rate the accusation that he kept an alehouse was untrue, and Pope was aware of its falsity. In his
retort, *Apollo's Maggot in his Cups, or the Whimsical Creation of a Little Satyrical Poet* (1729), Ward replied to the
distorted quotation from Jacob by protesting he had never
kept a public house in the city and had never lived there
in his life.[23] Moreover, since he had moved to Moorfields he
had sold no ale nor any kind of malt liquor. To Pope's
reference to him in *The Index* under the letter W, Ward
replied,

> He might as well have said in his Index: Ward Edward, a Tavern-
> keeper in Moorfields, but then he had told the Truth, and lost the satis-
> faction of imposing a Falsity upon his Readers . . . Suppose, Ward should
> say, in an Index under the letter P, that Pope Alexander keeps a House
> of Intrigue at Twickenham, in order to curry favour with Quality, and
> that's the Reason why so many Gentlemen and Ladies are his constant
> Subscribers. All this is as true, as that Ward keeps an Ale-house in Moor-
> fields, tho' he lives there. But that which makes the insincerity of Pope
> the more provoking, is, his reporting things contrary to his own Knowl-
> edge and Conscience, for Pope has drank Wine at Ward's House, and
> knows it to be a Tavern.

To Pope's charge that his works were exported to the plantations, he replied, "And as for Ward's Works, which he
never was proud of, they have had as great a sale in England,
as ever they had Abroad, without much expensive Advertising or the recommendation of Flatterers."[24] To the substitu-
tion of himself for John Ward of Hackney, poor Ward had
no reply—the shoe fitted well enough—except to repeat at
greater length his charge that the original attack on his name-
sake had been "a very sinful breach of Christian Charity, as
well as a shameful deviation from all the Principles of
Humanity."

And so perhaps it had been. Later readers have forgiven

Pope his inhumanity. From a distance of two hundred years
the feelings of one John Ward of Hackney fade into insig-
nificance. The feelings of one Edward Ward, tavern keeper
in Moorfields, fade as well. And yet no one who follows the
quarrel through the writings of both men can be oblivious
of the fact that from Ward's point of view he was in the
right on the matter. Pope mischievously, if not maliciously,
distorted the truth. Ward had replied twice with vindictive
attacks upon Pope. Certainly if we are to forgive Pope's in-
difference to ordinary civility for the sake of his poetry, we
ought also to forgive Ward for defending himself in his own
medium—even though the latter happens to be particularly
puerile verse.

III

The attack upon Pope was among the very last of Ward's
efforts. Sometime between August 1729 and October 1730
he gave up the Bacchus Tavern in Moorfields. In September
of that year Humphrey Parsons, being one of the two senior
aldermen eligible for election to the position, was unan-
imously chosen lord mayor of London. For the occasion of
his installation on November 9 of that year, Ward composed
a complimentary address to his friend and fellow Tory who
had also been a tavern keeper in his day.[25] The preface he
signed, "From the British Coffee-House in Fullwood's Rents,
near Gray's Inn; where this poem and any other of the same
Author's Writings, may be had Bound or Single."

Why Ward gave up the Bacchus Tavern after his thirteen-
year sojourn we do not know, but there was something appropriate in his return to the neighborhood of Gray's Inn,
the scene of his earlier residence. Was the British Coffee-
House one more step up in the world? Did it help still further to retrieve the dignity that had been compromised when
the gentleman had turned tradesman? Unfortunately for us
Ward did not live to sketch the coffee-house as he had the
Bacchus Tavern.

He died on the night of June 22, 1731, something less

than two years after his return to Gray's Inn.[26] On the twenty-seventh he was buried in the churchyard at St. Pancras.[27] Six years earlier in the middle of the summer he had suffered a "dangerous fit of illness." It was then he had recorded his last wishes.[28] He desired to be buried not in noisy Cripplegate, but in peaceful, quiet St. Pancras. He requested a simple funeral with one coach to convey his wife and children. His goods and chattels were to pay his honest debts, the residue to go to his wife and children. The residue was probably not very large.

> My Blessing unto each I give,
> Let that suffice instead of Wealth:
> May Grace attend 'em whilst they live,
> And Virtue long preserve their Health.

Unfortunately much of the last chapter, as much of the first, remains unknown.

The years softened Ward, though his pen never became chaste. To the end he retained the pert, impudent style. If the metaphors and similes tumbled onto his pages less readily, quantities of them still appeared, indecent as ever. At the same time a certain soberness crept in, as is apparent in the autobiographical references to the wanton abandonment of his earlier years. In his later writings he is no longer the young dandy come to town, the would-be wit, the tavern habitué whose twin gods are Bacchus and Venus. There are fewer nights spent in hard drinking, fewer amorous excursions to Horn Fair and Hampton, fewer assignations in Hyde Park and the playhouse.

The life of the Grubstreet wit, of course, has never been circumspect. At the turn of the century and during the early years of Queen Anne's reign, it seems to have been particularly dissolute. "He liv'd but too fast, and too quickly he dy'd" runs an anonymous epitaph on Richard Ames.[29] Tom Brown's death was lamented by his contemporaries as a signal instance of a brilliant wit succumbing to indolence and disease. William Pittis earned for himself the sobriquet of "Drunken Pittis." His acquaintances testified that he could "guzzle more at a sitting than would keep a family a month." [30] He, too, was acquainted with the debtor's prison. And William King, who was by all odds the most respectable of the group, was reputed to have sat in a tavern composing verses three hours after he was too drunk to speak. [31] Even before Ward himself became a vintner, he spent the greater portion of his life in a tavern. In the morning he sat scribbling over his glass of claret; in the afternoon he joined his convivial friends with the pipe and bottle; at midnight, if one is to believe his contemporaries, he went reeling home to his garret. Drunkenness, too, we are told was only one of his vices. John Dunton, in one of his bad moments, assuming that Ward was the enemy who was deriding him in the weekly numbers of *The Wandering Spy,* burst out fiercely:

I know, at present W——— is a harden'd impudent Rake; for Peregrimes Maid is but one of his Breeding Whores, etc. and his *Wandering Spy* (tho' writ to Debauch the Town) is the Chastest Paper he ever Publish'd . . . Silk Gowns and Red Petticoats are all alike to him, he playing at Women, just as he does at Cards . . . His Whore in Little Britain Besieg'd his Door with a Child from Sunday Noon to Sunday Night; but came too late for Admittance, his other Strumpet having been there with a Bastard before her. [32]

We know too much about Dunton to take his words seriously. There were probably fewer bastards and less disease involved than his attack seeks to imply, but that Ward in his early life was open to attack is evident from his own writings. It is in this respect more than in any other that his writings changed with the years. Sometime during that middle period of his life he had married, [33] and had settled down to the business of being a vintner. He had given up the fopperies of youth for a steady livelihood. Then the years had come on. Gradually the rake and libertine had become the proprietor, the husband and father.

To the end he retained some share of his popularity. "On Tuesday Night," wrote the editor of *The Country Journal or the Craftsman,* died "Mr. Edward Ward, famous for his poetical Performances," a sentiment echoed by *The Gentleman's Magazine,* which characterized him as "celebrated for his Writings." [34]

Nor was his fame completely interred with his bones.

In seeking to annihilate the dunces Pope inadvertently assured them of immortality. In Ward's case that is not quite the full story; he himself had given his age something to remember him by. The popular writer supplies the demand of his market; he does not create it. John Dunton, whatever his record as bookseller and editor, was nevertheless keenly aware of the tendencies of his own time, and he succeeded at the turn of the century, as no one else did, in exploiting the popular market. "For alas," he writes in advertising one of his own works,[35]

we have many Moral and Divine Discourses that tell us the general notions of humane Nature, with the Precepts of Morality, and that inform us what Man should do, but none that I know of that so lively, so naturally and so particularly describe what is in Man, and what is ordinarily done by Men of all sorts, and what secret Intrigues are carried on by Mortals of all degrees, contrary to the outward appearance they mutually impose upon one another as this ingenious author.

For the readers of popular literature it was enough that the writer should focus upon their own world, that they were to be both instructed and amused by a portrayal of their own antics and behavior. It may even have been with them a matter of conscious pride that they themselves were the subject of discussion, an acknowledgment as it were, of their own arrival in the realm of literature. Ward was a writer whose inclination and talent fell in with the popular demand. Time and again he indicated how little he felt himself bound either by tradition or by the rules for correct writing. He prays to be delivered from the proud poet, the snarling critic, and the pedantic blockhead who seeks to instruct him in writing.[36] "The most implacable Enemies" of the poets, he writes, are those who "seek to raise a Reputation to themselves, by raking into the little Slips and Failings of other Men's Writings, in hopes, by piling up their Rubbish, to build a Monument of Praise to themselves."[37] As for himself, he will neither justify his errors by reference to "the venerable Authority of some Ancient Bard" nor be content to rest for support upon "the Applause of Fools or Flatterers." He will "no more thank the World for its Praise, than Blame it for its bad Opinion."[38]

If readers were to be interested by a portrayal of themselves, that was a task Ward was eminently fitted to perform. "I'll engage a Man cannot go Twenty Yards in any Street in London, but he will meet some Original or other, whose likeness he will find so well preserved, that he may know them by their Pictures," Ward said of his own writings,[39] and the reader may well have been impressed with his veracity. His description of buildings and institutions, his account of life in the taverns and coffee-houses, at the watering places and fairs were based upon observation. The festival at Mob's Hole, the ludicrous trial between Parker and Partridge, the most extravagant incident of contemporary behavior in all of his writings—that of an Irishman eating a live cock, feathers, entrails, and all—were occurrences many of his readers had witnessed.[40] In his writings it was the familiar that became strangely accented. The cheating vintner, the reforming constable, or the brawling sailor could see his own portrait, expressed in language energetic in imagery and colloquialism, piquant to the hearty middle class palate as a French sauce. The qualities that Dunton as a bookseller had found worthy of praise in Ward as a young writer, one recalls, were his concern with the contemporary scene, his rapidity of composition, and his ability for timely and ingenious innovation,[41] factors obviously central in the contemporary appraisal of a popular talent.

As a satirist, on the other hand, Ward is not to be taken too seriously. No writer of the day would have had the temerity to demonstrate an interest in the contemporary scene purely for its own sake. "To scourge the vice and to expose the villainy of the age" was his expressed creed, and only under its guise could the indulgence of the popular taste escape the wrath of the moralists. Ward was, indeed, more forthright on the matter than most of his colleagues and on occasion made no pretense at any moral purpose whatsoever. Even for him, however, such frankness is the exception rather than the rule.

In *The London Spy* he expresses his purpose as that of exposing "the Vanities and Vices of the Town" in order that the innocent may see by reflection what he himself shall gain by observation and intelligence, though certainly not by practice and experience. The series of characters in *The London Terraefilius* he presents to the reader because "Stubborn Folly and Habitual Vice must be corrected with Severity." In *The Modern World Disrob'd* he who reads will find "Satyr, without Spite; Novelty, without Fiction, Pleasantry, without Levity; and an abundance of Truth, without personal Reflection." "Family Misconducts, or the private failings of Mankind," he writes in the preface to *The Fourth Volume of the Writings,*

I am ready to acknowledge ought not to be jested with, nor will they indeed admit of personal Reflections, without breach of Charity; but Publick Miscarriages I think very justly deserve Publick Chastisement; Nor is there any better way to bring Great Men to a due sense of their open Errors, than by scourging of 'em into it, after such a manner as may be suitable to their quality, for tho' many are beneath Satyr, yet no man but a King, whose Character is sacred, ought to think himself above it.

In spite of the protest to the contrary Ward and many of his contemporaries were interested more in the sale of their material than they were in the trenchancy of their satire. They sought to divert and amuse rather than to reform and correct. The exposition of villainy and the expunging of vice was a convenient and fashionable label, under the cover of which one might indulge in the obscene and the salacious. Even the oft-repeated protest that they were satirizing the vice rather than any particular individual was in itself no more than an additional attempt to pique the reader into a purchase of the pamphlet.

The assumption of the satiric role, however, led occasionally to the performance of the satirist's function. Ward's description of Bedlam, for instance, must have amused his readers, but it is difficult to believe that it did not also move them to disgust and anger. So, too, many an incident in which he portrays the inhuman treatment of debtors, the indecent flogging of women, the conditions of the compters, the corruption of parish administration, the government's neglect of crippled and maimed soldiers are on the whole too poignantly done to suggest mere interest in the description of fact. Indeed, Ward suggests throughout many of his writings, in spite of the affected cynicism and brutality of his style, a genuine sympathy for the common man, especially the mean and oppressed.

More often, however, Ward was merely writing in the accustomed tenor of the age. His prejudices and loyalties were the prejudices and loyalties of his readers. His writing is not so much a criticism of society as it is an expression of that society's traditional attitudes and behavior. The objects of his most continual derision—the dandified beaux, the stupid constables, the mountebanks and the astrologers, the pettifogging lawyers, and the cheating tradesmen—had after all been the legitimate prey of satirists for centuries.

Certainly the most serious charge that one can bring against Ward is not that he was a man "of low extraction," or that he was given to the depiction of low life, but rather that he was a man of low taste. *Le style c'est l'homme,* and Ward's was of the traditional alehouse variety.

" 'Sblood," says the prince of alehouse jesters, "I am as melancholy as a gib-cat or a lugg'd bear."

"Or an old Lion; or a lover's lute," the prince replies.

"Yea, or the drone of a Lincolnshire bagpipe," answers Falstaff.

"What say'st thou to a hare, or the melancholy of Moorditch?" replies Hal, outwitting even the jester in the use of the "unsavoury simile." It had been Falstaff's contemporaries, the Deloneys, the Dekkers, the Greenes, and the John Taylors, who had first established the style in the popular literature of pamphlet and broadside. In Ward's own day it had been men like Sir Roger L'Estrange, Tom D'Urfey, and Tom Brown who had given expression to their own impertinent jocularity and cynical insolence by a facile and energetic use of the colloquial in language and image. It was Ward's own distinction—if distinction it was—that he became its chief exponent in the days of Queen Anne.

Even for Ward the style is not always enviable. Too often the forward progress of the narrative is impeded by the attempt at witty innuendo and unsavory simile. The pace is monotonously regular, and the language indecently vulgar. On the other hand the style is graphic. Ward's portraits are drawn in bold and hard lines. No feature of a man's appearance or his conduct is described without drawing upon a more or less apt analogy. In the metaphors and similes, as well as in the diction itself, the slang of the street and the coffee-houses, the billingsgate of the fishmarket and brothel are all brought to bear. It is the language of the men whom he knew; it is at the same time something more. Ward consciously sought the facetious phrase; he coined his own compounds and epithets. It was a satisfying experience to him when after publication he heard his own phrases quoted in the taverns and music halls.[42]

The alehouse style was his forte. We need no more evidence of his success than the compliment paid him by Dr. James Drake, the biographer of Tom Brown. Characterizing the latter's ability in unsavory simile and humorous conceit, Dr. Drake concludes with a reference to Ward:

Nor can there be a clearer Evidence of his unimitable Manner in this way of Writing, than that this very Design was afterwards continued by one who hath been thought to have no mean Talent of Humour, and whose Writings have on that Score been very well receiv'd.[43]

In the final appraisal the inadvertent compliment given to Ward by Dr. Drake, couched, as it is, obliquely and in understatement, will do as well as any. Certainly judged by his own readers in his own day, he was a man of no mean talent. He was not the first writer who struggled to eke out a livelihood by the exercise of his pen, but he was certainly among those who, in an age when the quest was hazardous, succeeded in doing so. For a full decade, before the arrival of Addison and Steele, he was the foremost figure in the popular literature concerned with the contemporary scene. It is true that few of his own innovations achieved a permanent character. The rapidity and haste of his writing precluded any attempt at the refinement and finish of his art. He did not possess the inclination or the ability to deal with the problems of his own day in a sympathetic and kindly manner. He had neither the seriousness of purpose nor the sense of direction of the artist.

The truly great literary journalist is one whose character

and insight, whose understanding and perception impinge upon the mind of the reader. To have written for the market, to have given the readers what they wanted, in no age is per se a high achievement—even though, to be sure, "writings have on that Score been very well receiv'd."

To the end Ward's was an impudent, self-satisfied air. He had not asked much of life; and life had given him what he had asked for. That his talent was a superficial one, essentially casual and shallow, he must have had an inkling of at times, but for the most part he was proud of his achievement. A sharp eye and a bold tongue had succeeded in diverting a host of readers. He would have asked for no better epitaph than that which Juliet's nurse gave to her husband: "God be with his soul! 'A was a merry man."

Notes

A List of Libraries, with Their Symbols

The Bodleian	BL
The British Museum	BM
The Huntington Library	CSH
Yale University Library	CtY
Library of Congress	DLC
Newberry Library	ICN
Private Library of Dr. George Sherburn	ICS
Boston Public Library	MB
Boston Athenaeum Library	MBA
Harvard University Library	MH
Massachusetts Historical Society	MHi
New York Public Library	NN
Columbia University Library	NNC
University of Texas Library	TxU
Private Library of Professor R. H. Griffith	TxUG
University of Virginia Library	VaU

A List of Abbreviations

British Museum Catalogue	BMC
Dictionary of National Biography	DNB
Modern Language Notes	MLN
Modern Philology	MP
Notes and Queries	N&Q
Philological Quarterly	PQ
Publications of Modern Language Association	PMLA
Studies in Philology	SP
Wrenn Library Catalogue	WLC

CHAPTER I

1. (4 vols.; London, 1753), IV, 293–294.
2. (2 vols.; London, 1723), II, 295.
3. See page 9.
4. "The Epistle Dedicatory" to the *Third Volume of Writings* (1706).
5. See Chapter X.
6. "London in 1699: Scenes from Ned Ward" in the issue for October. See also note 11, Chapter III.
7. See Chapter XI.
8. Oldys's notes on Ward appear in the *Biographia Dramatica*. See note 9.
9. D. E. Baker, I. Read, and S. Jones (3 vols.; London, 1812), I (Pt. II), 736.
10. (5 vols.; London, 1819), V, 18–19.
11. See L. B. Wright, *Middle-Class Culture in Elizabethan England* (Chapel Hill: The University of North Carolina Press, 1935).
12. *Twice Round the Clock* (London: Haulston and Wright, 1859), p. 13.
13. The events recounted here as well as the quotations are taken from *The Poet's Ramble after Riches* (2nd ed.; London, 1699).
14. See the account in *Biographia Dramatica*.
15. See *The London Spy* (London: The Casanova Society, 1924), pp. 2–3, 407–422.
16. *The Poet's Ramble after Riches* did not have any ready sale until after the success of *A Trip to Jamaica* in 1698 assured it of a market. The first edition (1691) had been printed by J. Millet in September. A second edition was entered in the *Stationers' Register* for June 1692 by G. Conyers. In November of the next year Conyers entered it again under the title, *A Country-Scuffle over a Pot of Ale,* adding by way of inducement that it might serve as a "Second Part to the Counter-Scuffle," a popular seller of the day.
17. See Wright, *Middle-Class Culture,* Chapter XIII.
18. For an account of *The Ladies Mercury* see Bertha Monica Stearns, "The First English Periodical for Women," *MP,* XXVIII (1930), 45–59.
19. Ward himself did not include *Female Policy Detected* in any of his later collected writings. Ironically enough the avowed piety of the author and the nature of the material made it a popular work frequently reprinted throughout the eighteenth and nineteenth centuries not only in England but America as well.
20. Two other items have at times been assigned to Ward during this period: *The Miracles Perform'd by Money* (1692) and *A Dialogue between Claret and Darby-Ale* (1692). Aitken in his article for the *DNB* accepts both of them. The former is assigned to Ward in the catalogues of MH, CSH, and TxU; the latter in the catalogue of CSH, but to Richard Ames in the catalogue of MH. *A Dialogue between Claret and Darby-Ale* is definitely not Ward's, but may with certainty be assigned to Ames. *The Bacchanalian Sessions, or the Contention of Liquors, with a Farewell to the Wine. By the Author of the Search after Claret, etc. To which is Added, a Satyrical Poem on One Who had Injur'd his Memory. By a Friend* (London: E. Hawkins, 1693) is inscribed "To the Memory

of Mr. Richard Ames." It includes, as the title-page indicates, two poems. *The Bacchanalian Sessions, or the Contention of Liquors,* it is quite clear, is a post-humously published poem of Ames, to which the friend has added *A Satyrical Poem on One Who had Injur'd his Memory.* The conclusion of the second poem is followed by a list of books "written by the Author of this Poem," a phrase obviously referring to Ames, and not to the *friend.* Among the works listed is *A Dialogue between Claret and Darby-Ale, a Poem.* The case for *The Miracles Perform'd by Money* is less definite. But I have been unable to find any ground for its ascription to Ward. Against its attribution to him is the fact that he never claimed it later. It was not reprinted, as was *The Poet's Ramble after Riches,* in the days of his popularity. It was not included in any of the collected writings. To one who is familiar with Ward's zeal in collecting and preserving his own contributions, the evidence is more than convincing.

CHAPTER II

1. *A Trip to Jamaica* and *a Trip to New-England* have both been reprinted within recent years and are generally available. The former was reprinted in 1905 by The Society for Colonial Reprints (Providence, Rhode Island); both appear in *Five Travel Scripts* (The Facsimile Text Society, New York, 1933), series 1, vol. VII. References are to the latter edition.

2. Compare the account in *N&Q,* 4th series, XI (1873), 143.

3. I have checked the early newspapers for a notice regarding the ship *Andalucia* without any success. Unfortunately the records being compiled by George Sherwood, *American Colonists in English Records* (London, 1933), are as yet very incomplete.

4. C. N. Greenough, "John Dunton's Letters from New England," reprinted from *Publications of the Colonial Society of Massachusetts* (Cambridge: J. Wilson and Son, 1912), vol. XV.

5. Included in *A Trip to Jamaica.*

6. For some of the details in the description of the storm, as well as for the quotation, I have relied on *The Wars of the Elements* (1708).

7. The list of birds also comes from Blome.

8. For a general historical account of the island see W. J. Gardner, *A History of Jamaica* (New York: D. Appleton & Co., 1909); for a more detailed account of Port Royal see Frank Cundall, *Historic Jamaica* (London, 1915), pp. 45–80.

9. The name *Prudent Sarah* seems to have been a fairly common one at the time. A manuscript list of early shipping records in possession of the Massachusetts State Historical Society, for instance, records the clearance from Boston of the ship *Prudent Sarah* of Boston, 100 tons, for London, in 1688; and of the sloop *Prudent Sarah* of Salisbury, 25 tons, for London, in 1715. Frederick W. Cook, secretary of the Commonwealth of Massachusetts, informs me that the state archives contain reference to a *Prudent Sarah,* of London, Benjamin Gillam, master, as having registered in Boston, September 29, 1698.

10. Josselyn had made the first journey in 1638, the second one in 1663. The reference here is to *An Account of Two Voyages to New-England* (2nd ed., London: G. Widdowes, 1675).

11. George Parker Winship in the "Introduction" to *A Trip to New-England* (Society for Colonial Reprints: Providence, 1905), pp. ix–xxviii, finds in the sermons of Increase and Cotton Mather general substantiation for Ward and speaks of his "considerable talent for observation and keenness of insight." An earlier writer, N. B. Shurtleff in *A Topographical and Historical Description of Boston*

(Boston, 1871), pp. 51–60, takes Ward seriously enough to identify the four ministers referred to as the Reverend Benjamin Wadsworth of the First Church, the Reverend Cotton Mather of the Second Church (Old North), the Reverend Samuel Willard of the Third Church (Old South), and the Reverend Samuel Myles of the Episcopal Church (King's Chapel), though he adds that none of them was entitled to be called a dunce or clown.

12. T. N. Hatfield, *The True Secret History of Mr. John Dunton*, an unpublished thesis in the Harvard University Library (1926) indicates that Dunton borrowed his material from *A Brief Character of Ireland* (London, 1692).

13. *A Trip to North Wales*, *A Trip to Holland*, and *A Trip to Ireland* are reprinted in *Five Travel Scripts*.

14. Reprinted in Shea's *Early Southern Tracts*, No. 2 (New York, 1865).

15. Aitken accepts *A Trip to Ireland*. *A Trip to North Wales* is assigned to Ward in the catalogue of MH; *Journey to Scotland* in the catalogue of CtY; *A Trip to Holland* in the catalogue of NNC.

CHAPTER III

1. The reprint of *The London Spy* by The Casanova Society (London, 1924) is an excellent copy, but not generally available. The more widely known edition by A. L. Hayward (London: Cassell and Company, 1927) is, on the other hand, inadequate. Hayward has taken many liberties with the text. Quotations here are from the former.

2. Begun in Paris by Giovanni Paolo Marana, the single volume of letters published in 1684 had grown to four volumes by 1688. In 1687 William Bradshaw began their translation into English, some twenty-five editions following before the turn of the century.

3. The motif is similar to that of Thomas D'Urfey's in *Collin's Walk through London and Westminster* (London, 1690). It is possible that Ward drew upon the poem, since many of the sights at which D'Urfey's country man gaped are also described by Ward. It seems more likely, however, that the similarities owe themselves to the fact that both men are writing of London.

4. Part I originally appeared without a preface. When the eighteen parts were reprinted in the first collected edition (1700), the preface to Part II, with the exception of the final paragraph, was used as a preface for the entire volume. This rearrangement is followed in all later editions.

5. See *The London Spy*, Appendix A.

6. Compare the description of the traffic jam caused by the long procession of coaches at the funeral of Dryden in Part VI of Volume II.

7. According to a street lighting act enacted in the reign of William and Mary, the streets were lighted in the winter from dark until midnight. See Dorothy George, *London Life in the Eighteenth Century* (London, 1925), p. 101.

8. For other descriptions of the coffee-house in Ward's writings, see *The Weekly Comedy* (1699); *The Humours of a Coffee-House* (1707); and a poem, "The Humours of a Coffee-House," which appears in *The Diverting Muse*, No. 2, 41–56.

9. The first reference is obviously to Dryden, the second to Wycherley, the fifth to Tom Brown, the sixth to Congreve, the seventh to D'Urfey, and the eighth to Sir Richard Blackmore.

10. Quoted from the issue for April 20–22, 1699.

11. It is this description of the festivity at the King's Head, and the use of the name "Ned" in Ward's complimentary verses to the vintner, that gave rise to the

suggestion on the part of an anonymous writer in *The Gentleman's Magazine and Historical Review* that Ward was himself the proprietor of the tavern. See Chapter I, note 6. Unfortunately the suggestion was widely accepted without further investigation. George Aitken, in his article for the *DNB* for instance, assumes Ward may have been the proprietor, though he refers to Oldys as having listed Ward's successive residences as Gray's Inn, Clerkenwell, Moorfields, and Fulwood's Rents. Recent editors and writers have followed Aitken. See, for instance, Geoffrey Callender, *The Wooden World by Edward Ward* (The Society for Nautical Research, Occasional Publications, xi; London, 1929), foreword; Straus, *The London Spy*, preface; and Hayward, *The London Spy*, foreword, p. ix. Even more recently R. J. Allen, "Ned Ward and The Weekly Comedy," reprinted from Harvard Studies in Philology and Literature, XVII (1935), 1–13, has assumed the King's Head was a coffee-house as well as a tavern. There is no evidence whatever that Ward either owned or operated an alehouse, a tavern, or a coffee-house before 1712. Had Giles Jacob in 1723 been referring to a period as early as 1699, he would not have written "of late years he has kept a public House in the City." For Ward's ventures into trade, see Chapter X.

12. Edmund Malone, *The Critical and Miscellaneous Prose Works of John Dryden* (3 vols.; London, 1800), I, 336–379. Malone accepts the general outline of Ward's account as accurate except for the unique role Ward assigns to Lord Jefferies. Apparently both Montague and Dorset, as well as Jefferies, were responsible for the funeral arrangements. See Hugh Macdonald, *John Dryden: A Bibliography of Early Editions and of Drydeniana* (Oxford: Clarendon Press, 1939), p. 292, n.2. Also James M. Osborn, *John Dryden: Some Biographical Facts and Problems* (New York: Columbia University Press, 1940), p. 138.

13. Parker's almanac was entitled *Mercurius Anglicanus;* Partridge's bore the title *Merlinus Liberatus*. For an interesting account of Partridge, whose real name was Hewson, and the numerous controversies in which he engaged, see W. A. Eddy, "The Wits *vs.* John Partridge, Astrologer," *SP*, XXIX (1932), 29–40. The quarrel between Partridge and Parker seems to have begun in 1696 when the latter's *Mercurius Anglicanus* carried uncomplimentary references to Partridge. It resulted in a pamphlet war the following year when Partridge published a scurrilous attack on Parker, entitled *Flagitious Mercurius Flagellatus, or the Whipper Whipped*. The quotation in the case of Parker is from the *Mercurius Anglicanus* for 1698; in the case of Partridge the reference is to the *Merlinus Liberatus* for 1699. For another instance of Ward's attack on Partridge, see Chapter IV, also Chapter IV, note 24.

14. May 7–9, 1700.

15. *The Cambridge History of English Literature*, IX, 294.

CHAPTER IV

1. *London in the Eighteenth Century* (London, 1902), p. 585.

2. Besant, p. 584, gives the number of men allowed to beg at one time as eight. The begging at the gate began at five in the morning, on the Blackfriars' side of the prison at seven. The average takings for a day were twenty-four shillings at the gate, and eight shillings at the window opening into Blackfriars.

3. The steward, newly elected each month, had as his chief duties the administration of charity, the division of the profit from the boxes, the distribution of the daily allowance of food to the poor, the provision of mops, brooms, and pails for cleaning purposes. As compensation he received one shilling a day from the charitable contributions.

4. According to Besant there were six beds in the Lower Ward. The fees were as follows: threepence for a bed and twopence for a blanket per night; eightpence per month for sheets, a penny a week for lamp and candles.

5. See *Labour in Vain, or What Signifies Little or Nothing* (1700), reprinted in the *Harleian Miscellany* (1745), VI, 346–359.

6. See Chapter I.

7. Compare, for instance, Richard Ames, *Islington-Wells, or the Three-penny-Academy* (London, 1691); *A Rod for Tunbridge Beaus, Bundl'd up at the Request of the Tunbridge Ladies* (London, 1701).

8. Quoted from D. Lyson, *The Environs of London,* (1796), IV, 325. Besant, p. 471, derives a less probable explanation for the name from the fact that October 18 was St. Luke's day. "Everybody who went there," he writes, "carried a horn, not knowing in the least why. The reason was that in pictures representing St. Luke a horned ox's head was always placed at the corner."

9. According to Lyson, *Environs of London,* IV, 379, the pensions had increased by the end of the century to eighteen pounds per annum for single men, twenty-eight for married ones. Ward would imply that there was a good deal of maladministration. He charges that most men pay in more than their allowance would amount to if they were to become pensioners for fifty years, that though many legacies are left it, the allowances are never increased, that an East India captain left them 1300 pounds with no apparent advantage other "than a Statue of the Benefactor set up in the Garden."

10. Compare the account of May Fair by Charles Knight, *London* (London: n.d.), I, 313.

11. *Reasons Formerly published for the Punctual Limiting of Bartholomew Fair to those Three Days to which it is determined by the Royal Grant of it to the City of London. . . . Humbly Addressed to the present Right Honourable the Lord Mayor, to the Worshipful Court of Aldermen, and to the Common Council of the said City* (London, 1711). Excerpts from the account are quoted by Henry Morley, *Memoirs of Bartholomew Fair* (London: Chapman and Hall, 1859), pp. 379–382.

12. The fair had, of course, been the subject of satire for over a century. The accounts most nearly contemporary with Ward's are *A Walk to Smithfield, or a True Description of the Humours of Bartholomew Fair* (London, 1701) and *The City Revels, or the Humours of Bartholomew Fair* (London, 1690).

13. Many of the contemporary handbills are quoted by Morley. See also Thomas Frost, *The Old Showmen and the Old London Fairs* (London, 1874).

14. See *The Original Weekly Journal* for September 28, 1717.

15. For the account of Sturbridge Fair I have drawn upon "The History and Antiquities of Barnwell Abbey, and of Sturbridge Fair" (*Bibliothica Topographica,* No. XXXIII; London: J. Nichols, 1786).

16. For a description of this palace built by Howard, Earl of Suffolk, see Evelyn's *Diary and Correspondence,* ed. William Bray (4 vols.; London, 1854), I, 305. Pepys records a visit to Audley End which took place on February 27, 1660.

17. According to the account in "The History and Antiquities of Barnwell Abbey, and of Sturbridge Fair" (Appendix III, pp. 82–83) the vice-chancellor's court had oversight of all weights and measures, and the responsibility of licensing all booths devoted to entertainment or the exhibition of beasts, as well.

18. See "The History and Antiquities of Barnwell Abbey," Appendix III, p. 84.

19. In 1710 a quarrel broke out between Little St. Andrew's, Barnwell, and the Corporation of Cambridge over the right to appoint a preacher for the fair,

since the collections amounted to considerable money. The bishop's court, however, decided the case in favor of Little St. Andrew's. "The History and Antiquities of Barnwell Abbey," Appendix III, pp. 79–80.

20. For the early history of Bath see Richard Warner, *The History of Bath* (London, 1801). See also John Wood, *An Essay Towards the Description of Bath, etc.* (Bath: Thomas Boddely, 1742).

21. The road into the city was in extremely bad condition in 1700. It was rebuilt in 1704. See Warner, *The History of Bath*, p. 367. Ward's account checks remarkably well throughout with the accounts of both Wood and Warner.

22. In 1700 there were four public baths in the city administered under the supervision of the corporation. King's Bath, a large rectangular enclosure, was the oldest and most famous. Connected with it and filled with water from the same well was the smaller, twenty-five foot square, Queen's Bath, so-called in honor of the visit of the queen of James I. At the other end of the city was the Cross Bath, named for its triangular shape. This was the most popular one for public amusement as Ward indicates. Hot Bath was named for the extreme heat of the water, one hundred and seventeen degrees Fahrenheit. An overflow of the latter free to the poor was known as Leppers' Bath.

23. *The Flying Post* for March 9–11, 1699 contains the following item: "Yesterday the Tiger was baited which was very diverting to the Spectators; he kill'd one Dog, but there was care taken to prevent his doing any further hurt."

24. For an account of Brown's role in the attack on Partridge, see W. A. Eddy, "Tom Brown and Partridge the Astrologer," *MP*, XXVIII (1930), 163–168; also Benjamin Boyce, *Tom Brown of Facetious Memory* (Cambridge: Harvard University Press, 1939), pp. 130–133. For an account of *The Infallible Astrologer*, see W. A. Eddy, "Ned Ward and Lilliput," *N&Q*, XXVIII (1930), 148–149. Both Brown and Ward varied the title of the publication. The fifth number (under Brown's authorship) was entitled *The Infallible Astrologer: or, Physick Rectified;* the sixteenth number (under Ward's authorship) was called *The Astrological Observor: or, Mr. Silvester Partridge's Merry Inteligence;* the seventeenth and eighteenth, *The Jesting Astrologer: or, The Merry Observator.* The issues by both Ward and Brown were reprinted in *A Legacy for the Ladies* (1705).

25. Part I.

26. *The Visions of Don Francisco de Quevedo Villegas . . . Made English by R. L.* (London, 1667). For the general popularity of the *Visions,* see Benjamin Boyce, "News from Hell," *PMLA,* LVIII (June, 1943), 402–437.

27. February 1702.

28. *The Life and Errors of John Dunton* (London: J. Nichols, Son, and Bentley, 1818), p. 355.

CHAPTER V

1. For the general historical account I am indebted to G. H. Clark, *The Later Stuarts, 1660–1714* (Oxford, 1934) and to the eighteenth-century historians: G. Burnet, *History of My Own Time* (2 vols.; London, 1734); Abel Boyer, *History of the Reign of Queen Anne* (London, 1722); Paul Chamberlen, *An Impartial History of the Life and Reign of Queen Anne* (London, 1738); John Oldmixon, *The History of England during the Reign of the Royal House of Stuarts* (London, 1729).

2. Allen, "Ned Ward and The Weekly Comedy," suggests as the reasons for its suppression a political ballad in Number II, the attack on the election of sheriffs in Number VIII, and its general obscenity. When one considers the general

level of the periodical literature of the day, the charge of obscenity does not seem valid. It is doubtful, too, that the political ballad would have been considered sufficiently offensive.

3. *The Kentish Fable* has apparently been lost. See bibliography, Appendix A. The title itself is plainly indicative of Ward's support of the Tory position. To his unquestioning allegiance to the Tories it is interesting to contrast the more heroic behavior of Defoe in behalf of the Whigs. See James Sutherland, *Defoe* (J. B. Lippincott Company: New York, 1938), pp. 69–76.

4. Among the doubtful items ascribed to Ward in the printed catalogue for the Wrenn Library, University of Texas, are the following: *Protestant Divisions, or Party against Party, with a view of the old Buildings at London and Westminster* (1702); *The Character of a Sneaker* (1704); *A Step to the Lobby* (1704); and *A Whip for the Whigs* (1705). An obvious reason for rejecting them is Ward's failure to include them in his collected writings and the absence of any external evidence that warrants the ascription. In the case of *A Whip for the Whigs* there is evidence against Ward's authorship in an autobiographical reference within the poem inapplicable to Ward.

5. See *The Observator* for September 27, 1704; also for September 30, 1704.

6. "The Preface."

7. For Ward's relation to Butler and a discussion of the Hudibrastic tradition in the early eighteenth century, see E. A. Richards, *Hudibras in the Burlesque Tradition* (Columbia Studies in English and Comparative Literature, No. CXXVII; New York, 1937), pp. 57–58; 164–166. See also R. P. Bond, *English Burlesque Poetry* (Harvard Studies in English, vol. VI; Cambridge, 1932), pp. 145–154.

8. See *The Review* for November 24 and 27, 1705. For an account of the controversial pamphlets, see Walter Wilson, *Memoirs of the Life and Times of Daniel De Foe* (3 vols.; London, 1830), II, 397–404.

9. C. E. Doble, *Remarks and Collections of Thomas Hearne* (Oxford, 1885). Under the date of February 7 Hearn wrote, "One Ward is taken into Custody for publishing a Burlesque poem call'd Hudibras Redivivus in which he lays on some sort of People in a little too lively Colours."

10. *A Brief Historical Relation of State Affairs, from September 1678 to April 1714* (Oxford, 1857), VI, 36.

11. Little information seems available concerning Brown. Oldmixon, *History of England*, III, 380, identifies him as a "Doctor of Physick, one of Oxford's libellers." The attack on the lord keeper was entitled *The Country Parsons Advice to that Judicious Lawyer, and Worthy Minister of State, the Lord-Keeper*. Brown also accompanied Ward to the pillory in November for a second offense, *A Letter to the Right Honourable Mr. Secretary Harley occassion'd by his late Commitment to New Gate*.

12. Pageants accompanying the procession were discontinued in 1703. A revival of the custom in 1708 was suspended on account of the death of Prince George, the husband of Queen Anne. See F. W. Fairhold, *Lord Mayors' Pageants* (London, 1893), p. 121.

13. The completed project, an adaptation in verse of Clarendon's *History*, ran to three volumes. See Appendix A.

14. Ward revised the lines to read:

> Good Deeds become an English Heart;
> Fine Words are full of Fraud and Art.

15. Witnesses at the trial of the three prisoners taken by the troops estimated the number in the mob variously at figures ranging from 500 to 2000. See

A Complete Collection of State Trials, ed. T. B. Howell (21 vols.; London, 1816), XV, 522–702.

16. *A Complete Collection of State Trials*, XV, 522–702.

17. The five numbers of *The Poetical Entertainer* appear in Ward's *A Collection of Historical and State Poems, Satyrs, Songs, and Epigrams* (1717). Ward was responsible for the periodical and wrote most of the material, though he accepted a number of contributions from other authors. Pope himself appears to have been among the contributors. See George Sherburn, *The Early Career of Alexander Pope* (Oxford, 1934), p. 124.

18. See the account of Marlborough's return in William Cox, *Memoirs of John Duke of Marlborough, with his Official Correspondence* (6 vols.; London, 1820), VI, 306–307; Winston Churchill, *Marlborough, his Life and Times* (6 vols.; New York: Scribner's, 1938), VI, 594–638.

19. As late as 1874 James Hogg characterizes the poem as "a piece of great cleverness" marked by its "sterling rough humour." *The Jacobite Relics of Scotland*, p. 258; 271–278.

CHAPTER VI

1. From the Dedicatory Epistle of the fourth edition, 1704. The quotations in the text are from the fifth edition, 1705, and the eighth edition, 1713.

2. ii, 108–116. Later writers who have accepted the ascription include Leigh Hunt, *The Town; its Memorable Characters and Events* (London, 1859), pp. 371–374; John Timbs, *Clubs and Club Life in London* (London: Chatto and Windus, 1886), pp. 21–29; George Aitken in his article on Ward for the *DNB*; R. J. Allen, *The Clubs of Augustan London* (Cambridge: Harvard University Press, 1933), pp. 56–59.

3. The "Author of the following Lines" is given in the "Preface" as Benjamin Bridgewater.

4. Charles Leslie had already charged the dissenters with the existence of the club as early as 1702. See *The New Association* (London, 1702), p. 12. See also *Cassandra* (London, 1704), p. 47.

5. The early editions of *The Secret History* carried the simple notation that copies were "printed and Sold by the Booksellers of London and Westminster." In 1706 B. Bragge, however, seems to have acquired the publishing rights and the sixth and seventh editions were published under his name. The eighth edition was printed and sold by J. Morphew and the ninth was printed by S. Briscoe and sold by Thomas Bickerton. Wilson finds an additional factor pointing to Ward's authorship in the fact that the eighth edition (1713) made use of cuts which Morphew had earlier used in the publication of *Vulgus Britannicus*.

6. The second edition of *Vulgus Britannicus* (1710) had carried the familiar caption "by the Author of the London Spy."

7. References to the club among the minor writers and political journalists are widespread and numerous. Even men like Swift and Arbuthnot found the Calves-Head Club an effective political weapon. Compare "Tolands Invitation to Dismal," *The Poems of Jonathan Swift*, ed. H. Williams (Oxford, 1937), I, 161–166; "The History of John Bull," *The Life and Works of John Arbuthnot*, ed. G. Aitken (Oxford, 1892), 193–290.

8. See also Allen, *Clubs of Augustan London*, pp. 58–59.

9. "Ludlow the Regecide to the Calves-Head Club," in *Letters from the Dead to the Living*, 5th ed. (London, 1708), pp. 472–478.

10. Compare the account in "The Preface."

11. See Allen, *Clubs of Augustan London*, pp. 58–61.

12. The same anthem also appears in *The Calves-Head Club. A Sermon Preached at Maggot-Hall, in Good-Old-Cause-Lane On the 30th of January 1704 in Memoration of the Calves-Head Club* (London, 1704).

13. This is Allen's conclusion. An examination of the three versions, as well as a study of the remaining anthems, leads me to concur.

14. For an account of the riot see Joseph Spence, *Observations and Characters of Books and Men* (London, 1820), pp. 391–397. See also *N&Q*, 1st series, VIII (1853), 315.

CHAPTER VII

1. The pamphlet literature of the day, of course, rarely merited patronage. Only six of Ward's writings carry dedicatory epistles. *The Third Volume of Writings* is dedicated to "An Anonimous Worthy Gentleman, a Loyal Subject, a Good Patriot, and a True Churchman." *The Wars of the Elements* (1708) is delicated to his "Generous friend, T—— S——, Esquire." *Nuptial Dialogues and Debates* (1710) addresses an "Epistle Dedicatory, To the Worthy Gentlemen of the County and Corporation of Leicester." And *The Life and Adventures of that Renown'd Knight, Don Quixote de la Mancha* (1711) and *The History of the Grand Rebellion . . . Digested into Verse* (1713–15) were humbly inscribed "to the Worshipful John Cass, Esq.; Alderman of the City of London."

2. "The Preface," *The Fourth Volume of the Writings of the Author of the London Spy* (London: G. Sawbridge, 1709).

3. "The Preface," *The Third Volume consisting of Poems on Divers Subjects* (1706).

4. "The Bookseller to the Reader."

5. See the "Introduction," Richard Aldington, *A Book of Characters* (London: G. Routledge and Sons). For a bibliography of seventeenth-century English characters see E. C. Baldwin, "The Relation of the Seventeenth Century Character to the Periodical Essay," *PMLA*, XIX (1904), 75–114. See also Gwendolen Murphy, *A Bibliography of English Character-Books, 1608–1700* (*Supplement to the Bibliographical Society's Transactions*, No. 4; Oxford, 1925).

6. D. Lupton, *London and the Country Carbonadoed into Several Characters* (London, 1632).

7. Aldington lists no characters between 1689 and 1700. Baldwin's bibliography would also indicate that character writing suffered a lapse of popularity in the last decade of the century.

8. *The Moral Characters of Theophrastus Made English from the Greek, with a Prefatory Discourse concerning Theophrastus, from the French of Mons, De La Bruyere* (London, 1698). Another edition of *The Moral Characters*, translated by Eustace Budgell, appeared in 1714; an edition by Henry Galley in 1725.

9. The reference is to L'Estrange's *Observator* (1681) and to Dunton's *Athenian Mercury* (1691–96). A third periodical in dialogue form was *Heraclitus Ridens* (1681).

10. Dialogue xxx was issued as a separate poem under the title, *The Forgiving Husband and the Adulterous Wife, or a Seasonable Present to the Unhappy Pair in Fenchurch-Street* (1708).

11. A second edition followed in 1711; a third in 1723; a fourth in 1759.

12. Compare the general point of view in Defoe's *Family Instructor* (1715).

13. In 1707 upon completing the last number of Volume II of *Hudibras Redivivus*, Ward began a new periodical along the lines of the earlier *Weekly*

Comedy entitled *The Humours of a Coffee-House: A Comedy.* Though he increased the number of characters over those in the earlier periodical, it was essentially a repetition of the earlier venture with somewhat more emphasis upon the events of the day, indicative of the need Ward must have felt for broader scope. *The Humours of a Coffee-House* was, however, only one of three periodical ventures Ward was engaged with at the moment. In the same month he issued the first number of a poetical miscellany, *The Diverting Muse, or the Universal Medley;* two weeks later he launched *The London Terraefilius.* After seven numbers of *The Humours of a Coffee-House,* therefore, he relinquished the authorship to Oldisworth, who continued it under a slightly modified title. See Allen, "Ned Ward and The Weekly Comedy."

14. Both G. S. McCue, "A Seventeenth-Century Gulliver," *MLN,* L (1935), 32–34, and F. S. Rockwell, "A Possible Source for *Gulliver's Travels,*" *N&Q,* CLXIX (1935), 131–133, assume Swift's indebtedness to Ward. The assumption is based upon the general similarity of the idea as well as upon Swift's reference to the year 1699 as the year in which Gulliver set out upon his travels. It is not unreasonable to suppose that Swift read *The Weekly Comedy,* since he indicates elsewhere that he was familiar with Ward's works. See *The Prose Works,* ed. Temple Scott (12 vols.; London, 1897–1908), XI, 221. The use of the year 1699, however, seems to me in spite of McCue's mathematics a mere coincidence. Quotations from *The Weekly Comedy* are from Volume II of the *Writings,* fifth edition, 1717.

15. Pontack's, or Pontac's, was the famous French restaurant in Ab-Church-Lane. Evelyn refers to having dined there on November 30, 1694. See also Timbs, *Clubs and Club Life in London,* p. 58.

CHAPTER VIII

1. The second edition was issued in 1702.

2. Ward has given us a picture of the inside of such a flogging house in *The London Spy,* vol. I, part II.

3. See "A Complete Collection of Genteel and Ingenious Conversation," *The Prose Works of Jonathan Swift,* XI, 197–301.

4. Compare the conclusion on the same subject by Williams Matthew, "The Character-Writings of Edward Ward," *Neophilologus,* XXI (1936), 116–134.

5. The most recent edition of *The Wooden World* is that reprinted by The Society for Nautical Research, Occasional Publications, No. XI (London, 1929), from which the quotations in the text are taken.

6. *The Wooden World* was published anonymously. The second edition (1708), however, carries an advertisement exclusively of Ward's writings.

7. This was widely practiced as the following advertisement in *The London Gazette* for March 5–8, 1704 will indicate.

> The Counterfeiting of Powers to receive Seaman's Wages being grown so frequent a Practice, it is thought fit to give Publick Notice, as a Caution against such evil Practices, that William Browne, of the Parish of St. Botolphs-Aldgate, formerly a Waterman and now a Common Receiver, was on Friday last, at the Sessions in the Old Bailey, convicted of procuring a false Letter of Attorney to be forged, whereby to receive the Wages of one John White deceased, and was sentenced to stand in the Pillory, and fined Forty Marks for the same.

8. Ward gives a graphic picture of a Wapping music house in *The London Spy*, vol. II, part IV.

9. See Appendix A, *The Wooden World*.

10. The quotations are from the 1709 edition.

11. *The London Spy*, vol. I, part VIII.

CHAPTER IX

1. See Besant, *London in the Eighteenth Century*, pp. 319–320. See also Allen, *Clubs of Augustan London*, p. 186. It is possible that the misapprehension concerning Ward's purpose arose from the statement on the title-page of J. Collier's edition of *The Secret History of Clubs* (London, 1745) which reads: "A Compleat and Humorous Account of all the Remarkable Clubs and Societies in the Cities of London and Westminster . . . Compiled from the original Papers of a Gent. who frequented these Places upwards of twenty years." Allen assumes that all of the clubs depicted by Ward are fictitious with the exception of the Kit-Cat and Beefsteak Clubs, which "seem to have been introduced at the end of the book as an afterthought, largely to lend an air of actuality to the whole performance." This is an overstatement of the case. Quotations in the text are from *The History of the London Clubs* (1709), and from *Satyrical Reflections upon Clubs* (1710).

2. That the word club was frequently used in the broader sense in the eighteenth century, much as it is today, is apparent to any one familiar with the writings of the time. For a special discussion of the subject, see Allen, *Clubs of Augustan London*, pp. 100–101.

3. Vol. I, part v.

4. *The Female Tatler, by Mrs. Crackenthorpe, the Lady that Knows Everything*, No. V.

5. In *The History of the London Clubs, or the Citizens Pastime*, part I, the name is given as Sir Harry Flunt.

6. The suggestion was not original with Ward. See *The Wandering Spy, or the Way of the World Inquired Into*, No. XII (August 1705), 18–25.

7. Compare in the case of Addison, Nos. 9, 17, and 73 of *The Spectator*; in the case of Steele, Nos. 30, 43, 78, and 474. See also *The Guardian*, Nos. 91, 92, 108, and 121.

8. Timbs, *Clubs and Club Life*, p. 146, accepts the existence of the club.

9. See Thornton Shirley Graves, "Some Pre-Mohock Clansmen," *SP*, XX (1923), 395–421.

10. See *The Spectator*, Nos. 324, 332, 335, and 347. See also Allen, *Clubs of Augustan London*, pp. 105–118; Louis C. Jones, *The Clubs of the Georgian Rakes*, pp. 18–22.

11. For a description of the Hell-Fire Club, see Allen, *Clubs of Augustan London*, pp. 119–124. Allen does not see any connection between the two clubs, but quotes Oldmixon as saying that the Hell-Fire Club was an offshoot of the Scourers and Mohocks, a remark indicative of the confusion which existed in the public mind regarding these mysterious clubs at the time. Jones, *Clubs of the Georgian Rakes*, pp. 33–47, cites a story by Ward about the dissolution of the earlier club as evidence that there was no connection between the two. Ward's account of the dissolution of "The Atheistical Club" seems, however, little more than a tavern yarn. Certainly the existence of the earlier society depicted by Ward, as well as the depiction itself, lent credence in the public mind to the charge against the Hell-Fire Club in 1721.

12. Quoted by Allen, *Clubs of Augustan London*, p. 102. Allen does not connect the poem with Ward's account.

13. For an account of Briton, see Knight, *London*, VI, 184–186.

14. For an account of the early meetings of The Royal Society as a club, see Timbs, *Clubs and Club Life*, pp. 56–69.

15. Both Allen and Timbs seem to feel that Ward deliberately misinformed his readers about the origin of the Kit-Cat Club. What misinformation there was does not seem to have been deliberate on Ward's part, however. There is plenty of evidence that the important role he assigned to Tonson in the formation of the club was a matter of contemporary speculation and gossip. Ward seems to have been guilty only of repeating what was currently assumed. The facts about the origin of the club are unknown even today.

16. "The Kit-Cats," *A Collection of Poems on Various Subjects* (1718), pp. 105–106. "The Kit-Cats" originally appeared in 1708.

17. For the opposite view, that Ward meant to deride the Beefstake Club even as he had the Kit-Cats, see Allen, *Clubs of Augustan London*, pp. 140–141. In this case it seems to me the tone is one of good-natured raillery.

18. See an advertisement in *The Spectator* for December 28, 1711.

CHAPTER X

1. See Chapter I.

2. Included in Brown's *Remains* (London, 1721), p. 144, and assigned to Swift with an appropriate anecdote by Mrs. Arthur Colville, *Duchess Sarah* (London, 1904), pp. 259–60. See also *The Poems of Jonathan Swift*, III, 1148–9. Ward's authorship rests upon the fact that it was included in *A Collection of Historical and State Poems, Satyrs, Songs, and Epigrams* (1717), a volume he himself supervised. Since the text of the poem varies, it may be well to quote Ward's version:

> Here Scotus Lyes, of late as Wise
>   And Learn'd as Tom Aquinas;
> Lawn Sleevs he wore, yet was no more
>   A Christian than Socinus.
>
> Oaths Pro and Con he swallow'd down,
>   Lov'd Gold like any Layman;
> Wrote, Preach'd, and Pray'd, but yet betray'd
>   God's Holy-Church for Mammon.
>
> Of e'ery Vice he had a Spice;
>   Altho a Rev'rend Prelate,
> Yet liv'd and dy'd, if not bely'd,
>   A true Dissenting Zealot.
>
> If such a Soul to Heav'n hath stole,
>   And 'scap'd Old Satan's Clutches,
> We'll then presume there may be room
>   For M—— and his D——.

3. The title had been used earlier in the controversy which arose over the prosecution of Dr. Sacheverell. Compare, for instance, *Aminadab, or the Quaker's Vision* (London, 1710), and *Aminadab Explained, or an Answer to the Quaker's Vision, paragraph by paragraph* (London, 1710).

4. II, 295.

5. This was Ward's own composition, set to music by Leveridge. See Appendix A, *The Tipling Philosophers.*

6. In 1717, the year in which he became the proprietor of the Bacchus, Ward published volume five of the *Miscellanies,* a collection of earlier political pieces; *The British Wonders;* and *The Tory Quaker.* His next publication was *The Delights of the Bottle* in 1720. In 1721 he published *The Mery Travellers* and *The Northern Cuckold,* both of them relatively insignificant poems. See Chapter XI.

7. *Bibliographers' Manual* (1865), V, 2835–7.

8. Pp. 151–154.

9. W. Maitland, *The History and Survey of London from its Foundation to the Present Time,* 3rd ed. (2 vols.; London: T. Osborne, 1760), 1050–1191.

10. For materials relating to the organization of the parish and the administration of parish affairs I am indebted to Sidney and Beatrice Webb, *English Local Government from the Revolution to the Municipal Corporation Act: the Parish and the County* (London: Longmans, Green, and Co., 1906). See also Dorothy George, *London Life in the Eighteenth Century,* Chapter V.

11. In some cases the administration of the vestry was subject to examination by the justices of peace; in other cases the justices were themselves subject to the authority of the vestry. See Sidney and Beatrice Webb, *English Local Government,* p. 230.

12. *Parochial Tyranny, or the Housekeeper's Complaint against the Insupportable Exactions and Partial Assessments of Select Vestries.* See Sidney and Beatrice Webb, *English Local Government,* p. 252.

13. Sidney and Beatrice Webb, *English Local Government.* Defoe charged not only that members of the closed vestry made scot and lot men of whom they chose, but also that they discriminated against dissenters in filling parish offices and exercised an undue influence over the voters by virtue of their parochial office. Webb refers to two other attacks on the closed vestry. The first was entitled *An Historical Account of the Constitution of the Vestry of the Parish of St. Dunstan's-in-the-West* (London, 1714); the second, *The Art of being Honest for a little Time, or the Method of Making Parish Rates to Chastise Inhabitants Demonstrated, in the Assessments made for Scavengers of St. Dunstans-in-the-West, London, for the year 1713 and 1712.* See p. 252n. All of these attacks were of a political nature.

14. Quoted by Sidney and Beatrice Webb, *English Local Government,* p. 251. The original appears in *House of Commons Journals,* XVI (1710), 315.

15. No publisher's name appears on the title-page. See Appendix A, *The Parish Guttlers.*

16. Because of its local reference the poem would, of course, have been limited in its appeal. Apparently only one edition was published.

17. The closed vestries were not generally abolished until the Hobhouse Act of 1831.

CHAPTER XI

1. Charles Gildon, *A Comparison Between Two Stages* (London, 1702), p. 199.

2. See Chapter VII.

3. Reprinted in *The Third Volume consisting of Poems on Divers Subjects.* See *The Writings* (1706). Both prologue and epilogue are advertised in *The Daily Courant* for April 27, 1704.

4. An account of the affair is given by John Genest, *Some Account of the English Stage from the Restoration in 1660 to 1830* (10 vols.; Bath, 1832), II, 315. See also M. Wilson Disher, *Clowns and Pantomimes* (London, 1925), pp. 239–240.

5. For an account of the rivalry between the two theaters see Disher, *Clowns and Pantomimes*, pp. 229–246. See also John Weaver, *The History of Mimes and Pantomimes* (London: J. Roberts and A. Dod, 1728); Cyril W. Beaumont, *The History of Harlequin* (London, 1926), pp. 84–113; E. L. Avery, "Dancing and Pantomime on the English Stage 1700–1737," *SP*, XXXI (1934), 417–452; M. P. Wells, "Some Notes on the Early Eighteenth-Century Pantomime," *SP*, XXXII (1935), 589–607.

6. See Weaver, *History of Mimes and Pantomimes*, p. 1.

7. Thomas Merrivale, *The Necromancer, or Harlequin Doctor Faustus* (London: J. Roberts, 1724). For an earlier satire on the subject of pantomimes, see *The British Stage, or the Exploits of Harlequin* (London, 1724). The British Museum contains a copy of Rich's production, *A Dramatick Entertainment, call'd the Necromancer, or Harlequin Doctor Faustus*, 9th ed. (London, 1731). *The Vocal Parts of an Entertainment, call'd the Necromancer, or Harlequin Doctor Faustus as perform'd at the Theatre Royal in Lincoln's Inn Fields* (London: A. Dodd, 1723), MH, contains parts for the earlier pantomime, *The Comical History of Doctor Faustus*.

8. In John Thurmond's rival production at Drury Lane one of the "sights" was the setting afire of a barn by a wave of the doctor's wand. See a description of the pantomime in *Harlequin Doctor Faustus: with the Masque of the Deities* (London, 1724). In *The Rape of Proserpine*, one of Rich's productions, "an earthquake is felt, and part of a Building falls . . . Mount Ætna emits Flames." See *The Dunciad*, ed. James Sutherland (London: Methuen and Co., 1943), p. 176n.

9. *The Dunciad*, III, 233–236.

10. Quoted by Disher, *Clowns and Pantomimes*, p. 246. For another account of the accident, see Wells, "Eighteenth Century Pantomime," p. 606n.

11. *The Wandering Spy, or the Way of the World Inquired Into* has been attributed to Ward by T. F. M. Newton, "William Pittis and Queen Anne Journalism," *MP*, XXXIII (1936), 169–186, 279–302. Compare, however, Ward's own statement in *The Observator*, June 9–13, 1705:

> Whereas sometime since an Advertisement was Published by the Author of the London-Spy That in a short time there would be publish'd a Monthly six Penny Book Intituled The Wandering-Spy: This is to give Notice, that a late Paultrey Weekly-Paper Midwived into the World by Mrs. Maltus, under that Title, is not written by the afore-mentioned Author, and that the Publick in a little time will be sufficiently convinc'd, he is in no way concern'd in that Ridiculous Paper.

I have not been able to locate the original advertisement to which Ward refers, but it is worth notice that it apparently called for a monthly and the paper as it appears was a weekly, that it was published by Mrs. Maltus, never elsewhere a publisher of Ward's. It is on the basis of this statement of Ward's, as well as on the basis of the consideration of the spirit of *The Wandering Spy*, which is not Wardian, that I reject the ascription. Dunton was not at all sure of Ward's authorship when he published his reply, *The Whipping Post, or a Satyr on Everybody* (London: B. Bragg, 1706) as an examination of the text, p. 34, will show. Newton's ascription of *The Wandering Spy* to Ward grows out of a confusion of that item with a somewhat similar title of a genuine Ward item not published, however, until 1722—*The Mery Travellers, or the Wandering Spy,* part II. The evidence Ward expected to present that he was not the author of the earlier *Wandering Spy* was undoubtedly *Hudibras Redivivus,* which made its first appearance within a month.

12. J. How in "Bookseller to the Reader," *The Second Volume of the Writings of the Author of the London Spy.* How's praise of Ward was not entirely gratuitous. The publisher of the first six numbers of *The London Spy* was J. Nutt. Beginning with the seventh number, however, Nutt's printer, J. How, set up as bookseller and took over *The London Spy* for the remaining numbers. See Appendix A, *The London Spy.* Thereafter for a period of five years How was Ward's favorite publisher. There is evidence to show, as a matter of fact, that How rose to prosperity and prominence as a bookseller through the success of Ward's writings. Compare the account of How in *The Life and Errors of John Dunton,* p. 220. See also H. R. Plomer, *A Dictionary of the Printers and Booksellers* (Oxford, 1922), pp. 162–163.

13. *The Poetical Entertainer,* No. IV, 17–23.

14. "The Preface," *The Third Volume consisting of Poems on Divers Subjects.*

15. *The Dunciad,* intro. x-xv.

16. See Chapter V, note 17. Pope, of course, may have been offended at Ward's publication of the offensive epigram against Addison in 1713, at a time when Pope was seeking Addison's support for his translation of the *Iliad.* No evidence of any ill will between Pope and Ward exists, however, before 1728 and the *Peri Bathous.*

17. *The Works of Alexander Pope,* ed. Elwin and Courthope (London, 1871–86), X, 362, 390.

18. I, 97–202; III, 138. The more widely known reference to Ward is a later revision of these lines, which appears in the 1743 edition (I, 233–234).

> Not sail with Ward, to Ape-and-Monkey Climes,
> Where vile Mundungus trucks for viler rhymes.

19. At the same time Pope included another reference to Ward in the text of the poem (III, 162).

> Sense, speech, and measure, living tongues and dead,
> Let all give way—and Durgen may be read.

20. "The Second Edition, with some Additional Notes." See *Dunciad,* p. 87n. In the same edition under *Errata* Pope included a note on Ward's protest against the misuse of Jacob's account: "The said Ward declares . . . that 'He selleth Port: neither is his Publick House in the City, but in Moor-fields.'" At the same time, however, Pope elsewhere repeatedly used the word alehouse in connection with Ward.

21. II, 323.

22. In *Apollo's Maggot in his Cups*—"Postscript," 35–36, Ward writes: "Another of Alexander Pope's false suggestions, for Mr. James Moor had not the least Finger in the Poem call'd the Durgen, etc. nor did the Author think the subject worthy of such Assistance."

23. "Postscript," 29–31.

24. Pope's charge that Ward's works sold freely in the colonies is substantiated by a reference to Ward in Cotton Mather's *Manducto ad Ministerium* (Boston, 1726), p. 43. "How much do I wish," writes Mather, "that such

Pestilences, [plays] and indeed all those worse than Egyptian Toads (the Spawns of a Butler, and a Brown, and a Ward, and a Company whose name is legion!) might never crawl into your chamber."

25. *To The Right Honourable Sir Humphrey Parsons, Lord Mayor of the City of London, a Congratulatory Poem upon his Lordship's Accession to the Chair* (London: J. Wilford, 1730).

26. See *The Country Journal*, June 26, 1731; also *The Gentleman's Magazine*, June 1731.

27. Lyson, *Environs of London*, III, 371.

28. The poetical will was printed in *Applebee's Weekly Journal*, September 28, 1731.

29. *The Bacchanalian Sessions, or the Contention of Liquors, with a Farewell to the Wine. . . . To which is Added a Satyrical Poem on One Who had Injur'd his Memory.*

30. This was Dunton's remark. See Newton, "William Pittis and Queen Anne Journalism," p. 283.

31. *Works of Pope*, X, 207.

32. See note 11. For the quotation, see *The Whipping Post*, p. 30, and *The Living Elegy*, p. 16.

33. I have been unable to find any record of Ward's marriage, but there are references to his wife in *The Delights of the Bottle*, as well as in the poetical will.

34. *Gentleman's Magazine*, June 1731.

35. In *The Compleat Library, or News for the Ingenious*, July 1692, p. 205.

36. "A new Litany, very proper to be Read by a Merry Society over a Glass of Good Liquor," *The Diverting Muse*, No. V, 197–203.

37. "The Preface," *The Third Volume consisting of Poems on Divers Subjects.*

38. "The Preface," *The Poet's Ramble after Riches.*

39. "The Preface," *The London Terraefilius.*

40. Ward's account of the incident is in the mouth of Whim, one of the characters in *The Weekly Comedy*. See the issue for May 10–17, 1699. The eating of the cock was one of the events of the summer in 1699. See *The Flying Post* for July 20:

The Man that eat the live Cock at Islington, and another since, on the 15 of June last, at Standup-Dicks at Newington Butts, near the Burrough of Southwark, is to eat another there on Tuesday next, being St. James's Day, with Feathers, Bones, and Garbage. And Person may see it performed, paying but 2d. for their Admittance.

41. See Chapter IV.

42. See "the Beau Apprentice," in *The Reformer, exposing the Vices of the Age* (1700).

43. *A Legacy for the Ladies, or Characters of the Women of the Age. . . . To which is prefixt, "The Character of Mr. Tho. Brown, and his writings"* (London, 1705), p. ix.

Appendices

Appendix A

A Bibliography of the Writings of Edward Ward

A bibliography of Ward's writings can be determined with a fair degree of certainty. Invaluable for such a purpose are the advertisements of Ward items published by J. How, which appear on the backs of the title-pages of the original folio editions of *The London Spy*. They account for all the items with the exception of *Female Policy Detected* (1695) up to the end of May 1700. Next in importance are *A Collection of the Writings, Hitherto Extant, of Mr. Edward Ward* published by J. How in 1700, 1701, and 1702. A further help are the collected items published as the "Second," "Third," and "Fourth" volumes of the writings "By the Author of the London Spy" during the years 1703–09; *A Collection of Historical and State Poems, Satyrs, Songs, and Epigrams* (1717); and the volumes of *Miscellanies* published in 1717–18, accounting for all items—with the exception of those of strong political bias—to the middle of the year 1717. It may be remarked that since the collected editions were published during Ward's own lifetime under his own surveillance, there can be little question concerning any item so included.

During the later years the nature of Ward's materials only rarely demanded anonymity and nearly all of the items convincingly Ward's on the basis of internal evidence also bear his name either on the title-page or in the preface. It seems reasonable, therefore, to proceed with caution in accepting items assigned to Ward on the basis merely of a similarity in form or subject matter. All such items are here relegated to the list of "Doubtful Attributions" with the exception of such political writings as demanded anonymity and where the case for Ward's authorship seems unquestionably certain.

It has seemed desirable to record in so far as possible the original issue and all subsequent editions of each item. The record is based upon an examination of existing copies in American and British libraries, and upon newspaper and other advertisements. The basis upon which each item is accepted as Ward's is presented in a note in all cases where his name or an identifying caption does not appear on the title-page or where the item itself does not appear in a contemporary collection of Ward's works. It has seemed advantageous to list the items alphabetically rather than chronologically, for the convenience of students of the period who are more apt to be interested in an individual item and the question of its authenticity than in a chronological record.

Libraries are listed under the system used by Crane and Kaye, "A Census of British Newspapers and Periodicals, 1620–1800," *SP*, XXIV (1927), 1–205.

Adam and Eve Stript of Their Furbelows
> See *The Modern World Disrob'd.*

Aesop at Paris
> 1701—Aesop at Paris, His Life and Letters.
>> Issued in May: *The History of the Works of the Learned*, May 1701. Listed as a Ward item on the verso of the title-page, *The Revels of the Gods* (1701). I have been unable to locate a copy.

All Men Mad
> 1704—/All Men Mad:/Or,/England/A/Great Bedlam./A/Poem./[—]/London,/Printed in the Year, MDCCIV./
>> Quarto; 1—28; A—C⁴, D².
>> Issued in September: *The History of the Works of the Learned*, September 1704. Reprinted in *The Third Volume of the Writings* (1706). See *The Observator*, 27–30, September 1704, for a discussion of the poem. [BM; CtY; MH]

The Amorous Bugbears
> 1725—/The/Amorous Bugbears:/Or, The Humours of a/Masquerade./Intended as a/Supplement to the London-Spy./[Band of ornaments]/By E. W./[Band of ornaments]/[Quotation]/[Band of ornaments]/London:/Printed: And Sold by A. Bettesworth, J. Bately/in Pater-noster-Row, and J. Brotherton at the/Bible in Cornhil, 1725./
>> Octavo; [i—ii], 1—62; A—H⁴. [BM; TxU]

Apollo's Maggot
> 1729—/Apollo's Maggot in his Cups:/Or, The/Whimsical Creation/Of A/Little Satyrical Poet./[Band of printers' ornaments]/A Lyric Ode./[Band of printers' ornaments]/[Quotation]/[Band of printers' ornaments]/Merrily Dedicated to Dicky Dickson,/the Witty, but deform'd Governour of/Scarborough-Spaw./[Band of printers' ornaments]/London/Printed: and Sold by T. Warner at the Black-/Boy in Pater-Noster-Row, and the Booksellers of/London and Westminster. MDCCXXIX. Price 1 s./
>> Octavo; [i—xiv], 1—48; A—G⁴, H³.
>> Issued in August: *The Monthly Chronicle*, August 1729. "The Postscript" identifies this as Ward's. [CtY; ICS; TxU]

The Author's Lamentation in the Time of Adversity
> See *The Poet's Ramble after Riches.*

The Barbacue-Feast
> 1706—The Barbacue-Feast; or The Three Pigs of Peckham, broil'd under an Apple-Tree; Where the Cooks were Numberless; the Company Masterless; the Meat carv'd with Hatchets; and Punch drunk by Pail-fulls. By the Author of the Trip to Jamaica. Sold by B. Bragge, in Pater-Noster-Row. Price 6 d.
>> Issued in November: *The Observator*, 9–13 November 1706. I have been unable to locate a copy.

The Batchelor's Estimate
> [1725]—The Batchelor's Estimate of the Expences of a Married Life. In a letter to a friend . . . To which is added the lady's answer. A. More: London, [1725.]

Folio.

This is the date suggested by *BMC*. See, however, *Female Policy Detected* [1720].

For attribution to Ward see *Female Policy Detected* [1720]. [MH]

1729—Third edition. T. Payne: London, 1729.

Folio. [BM]

[1729]—/The/Batchelor's Estimate/Of The/Expenses/Of A/Married Life,/In a Letter to a Friend./Being an/Answer/To A/Proposal/Of Marrying a Lady with/2000 L. Fortune./[—]/[Quotation]/[—]/The Fourth Edition./

Twelve pages; margins are clipped too close for pagination and signatures. [MH]

[1730]—Another edition.

Duodecimo. [MH]

Battle without Bloodshed

1701—Battle without Bloodshed, Or, Martial Discipline Buffoon'd by the City Train-Bands. J. How: London, 1701.

Folio.

Issued in August: *The History of the Works of the Learned,* August 1701. Adv.: *The Observator,* 8–11 July 1702. Reprinted in *The Second Volume of the Writings* (1703). [BM]

Bribery and Simony

1703—/Bribery and Simony;/Or, A/Satyr/Against the/Corrupt Use/Of/Money./[—]/By the Author of the London Spy./[—]/[Ornament]/[—]/London,/Printed for C. C. and Sold by John Nutt near/Stationers-Hall, 1703./

Folio; 1—16; A—D².

Issued in November: *The History of the Works of the Learned,* November 1702; apparently reissued with a new title-page in 1703. Reprinted in *The Third Volume of the Writings* (1706). See also *Honesty in Distress* [1725]. [CSH; CtY; TxU]

British Wonders

1717—/British Wonders:/Or,/A Poetical Description of the several/Prodigies/And Most/Remarkable Accidents/That have happen'd in Britain since/the Death of/Queen Anne./[—]/[Ornament]/[—]/London:/Printed and Sold by John Morphew near Stationer's-/Hall MDCCXVII./

Octavo; [i—ii], 1—38; A—E⁴. Title-page boxed in double rule.

Adv.: *The Daily Courant,* 20 April 1717. Included in *A Collection of Historical and State Poems* (1717). [BM; CSH; CtY; ICN; MH]

1717—[Another edition.]

Octavo; 1—62; A²⁻⁴, B—H⁴ (title-page missing).

See note under *A Collection of Historical and State Poems* (1717).

The Charms of Liberty

See *The Satyrical Works of Titus Petronius Arbiter.*

The Cock-Pit Combat

1699—/The Cock-Pit Combat:/Or, The/Baiting/Of The/Tiger,/on Thursday March 9, 1698./

Broadside. Bottom of p. 2: "London, Printed in the Year 1699."

Reprinted in *The Second Volume of the Writings* (1703). [BM; NNC]

A Collection of the Best English Poetry

1717—/A/Collection/of the Best/English Poetry,/By/Several Hands./(Viz.)/[List of authors, separated by single rule.]/[—]/In Two Vol's Octavo./

[—]/London:/Printed, and Sold by T. Warner, at the Black Boy in Pater-Noster-Row, 1717./(Price 10s.)/

This is a collection with individual title-pages, pagination, and signatures, and contains three poems by Ward: *The Rambling Fuddle-Caps,* H. Hills (1709); *The Libertine's Choice,* H. Hills (1709); *The Forgiving Husband and the Adulteress Wife,* H. Hills (n.d.). [NN]

A Collection of Historical and State Poems, Satyrs, Songs, and Epigrams
See *Miscellanies,* vol. V.

A Collection of Miscellaneous Poems

1709—A Collection of Miscellaneous Poems. In Twelve Parts. Consisting of All Sorts of Poetry, as Odes, Songs, Satyres, Epistles, Elegies, Epigrams, Pastorals, Dialogues, Prologues, Epilogues, etc. chiefly compos'd by the best Hands, viz. Dr. Garth, Dr. Baynard, Dr. King, Dr. Brown, Capt. Phillips, Capt. Steele, Mr. Rowe, Mr. Smith, Mr. Den, Mr. Gildon, Mr. Pittis, Mr. Ward, Mr. Dyke, Mr. Green, Mr. Hawke, and several other Authors of Eminency. Sold by B. Bragge in Pater-Noster-Row and J. Woodward in Threadneedle Street, near the Royal Exchange.

Adv.: *The Observator,* 21–24 September 1709. I have been unable to locate a copy.

A Collection of the Writings, Hitherto Extant

1700—/A/Collection/Of The/Writings,/Hitherto Extant,/Of/Mr. Edward Ward,/viz/[List in double column, separated by single rule]/[—]/London, Printed and Sold by John How, in the Ram-/Head-Inn-Yard in Fenchurch-Street, MDCC./

Title-page boxed in double rule. This is a collection of remainders with individual title-pages, pagination, and signatures.

The items included in this volume are as follows: *The Poet's Ramble after Riches; Sot's Paradise; Ecclesia et Factio; Modern Religion and Ancient Loyalty; A Walk to Islington; A Trip to Jamaica; A Trip to New-England; A Frolick to Horn-Fair; The Dancing-School; The First and Second Volumes of the London-Spy: In Eighteen Parts.* [NNC]

1701—/A/Collection/Of The/Writings,/Hitherto Extant,/Of/Mr. Edward Ward,/viz./[List in double column, separated by single rule]/[—]/London, Printed and Sold by John How, in the Ram-/Head-Inn-Yard in Fanchurch-street, 1701./

Title-page boxed in double rule. This is a collection of remainders with individual title-pages, pagination, and signatures.

The items in this volume are identical with the above, plus the following additions: *The Insinuating Bawd and the Repenting Harlot; A Step to Stir-Bitch-Fair; A Step to the Bath.* [MHi]

1702—A Collection of the Writings, Hitherto Extant, of Mr. Edward Ward. Sold by E. Jaye at the Golden Candlestick in Cheapside.

Listed in the *Term Catalogues,* May 1702. The items in this volume are identical with the 1700 edition, plus the following additions: *The Insinuating Bawd and the Repenting Harlot; The Revels of the Gods; A Step to Stir-Bitch-Fair.*

A Comical View of London and Westminster

1705—/A/Legacy for the Ladies./Or,/ Characters/Of The/Women of the Age./[—]/By the late Ingenious Mr. Thomas Brown./[—]With A/ Comical View of London and West/minster: Or, The Merry Quack;/ Where-/in Physick is Rectified for both the Beaus/and Ladies./In Two

Parts. The First/Part by Mr. Tho. Brown: The Second/Part by Mr. Edw. Ward, Author of The/London-Spy, etc./To which is prefixt,/The Character of Mr. Tho. Brown,/and his Writings, Written by Dr. Drake./[—]/ London, Printed by H. Meere, for S. Briscoe,/and Sold by J. Nutt, near Stationers-Hall, 1705./[—]/[adv.]/

Octavo; [i—xii], i—xvi, 1—192; A⁸, b⁶, B—N⁸. Title-page boxed in double rule.

A Comical View, pp. 109–192, has a separate title-page: /A Comical/View/Of The/Transactions that will happen in The/ Cities of London and Westminster./Or, The/Merry Quack;/Wherein/ Physick is Rectified for both the Beaus/and Ladies./[—]/In two Parts./ [—]/The First Part Written by the late Ingenious/Mr. Thomas Brown./ The Second Part Written by Mr. Edward/Ward, Author of the London Spy, etc./[—]/London, Printed for Sam. Briscoe, 1705./

For Ward's share in the production, see note 24, Chapter IV. [BM; MH]

A Compleat and Humorous Account of All the Remarkable Clubs and Societies
See under *The History of the London Clubs.*

The Contending Candidates
See *The Merry Travellers*, Part II

The Dancing Devils
1724—/The/Dancing Devils;/Or, The/Roaring Dragon./A Dumb Farce./As it was lately Acted at Both Houses, but/particularly at one, with un-accountable/Success/[—]/[Quotation]/[—]/[Quotation: Latin]/[—]/ London/Printed; and Sold by A. Bettesworth at/the Red-Lion, J. Bately at the Dove, in Pa-/ter-noster-Row; and J. Brotherton at the/Bible in Cornhil. MDCCXXIV./Price One Shilling./

Quarto; 1—70; A—H⁴, I⁸. Title-page boxed in double rule.

Assigned to Ward: David E. Baker, *Biographia Dramatica* (London, 1812). Undoubtedly Ward's on the basis of internal evidence. See Chapter XI. [BM; CtY; DLC; MH; NN; TxU]

The Dancing-School
1700—/The/Dancing-School./With the/Adventures/Of The/Easter Holy-Days./[—]/[Ornament]/[—]/London,/ Printed by J. How, in the Ram-Head-Inn-Yard, in Fanchurch-Street, 1700./

Folio; 1—16; A—D². Title-page boxed in double rule.

Issued in March: see the verso of the title-page, *The London Spy*, vol. II, pt. v, March 1700. Included in *A Collection of the Writings, Hitherto Extant* (1700). Reprinted in *The Second Volume of the Writings* (1703). An edition adv.: *The Observator*, 19–22 May 1703. [BM; MH; NNC; TxU]

The Delights of the Bottle
1720—/The Delights of the Bottle:/Or, The/Compleat Vintner./ With the Humours of/[List separated by rule]/[—]/A Merry Poem/[—]/To which is added,/A South-Sea Song upon the late Bubbles./[—]By the Author of the Cavalcade./[—][Quotation]/[—]/London./Printed for Sam. Briscoe at the Bell-Savage/on Ludgate-Hill. MDCCXX./

Octavo; 1—56; A—G⁴. Title-page boxed in double rule.

"By the Author of the Cavalcade" is a reference to *The Republican Procession or the Tumultuous Cavalcade* (1714). [DLC; NN (NN copy has pp. 55–56, G⁴, missing.)]

[Another copy. Identical with the above to:]/London./Printed by W. Downing in George-Court in/St. John's-Lane. MDCCXX./

Octavo; 1—56; A—G⁴. Title-page boxed in double rule. [BM; ICN; MH]

1720—[The second edition.]

Adv.: *The Weekly Journal or Saturday's Post*, 15 October, 1720.

1721—[The third edition. Identical with the above to:]/By the Author of the *Cavalcade*./[—]/The Third Edition./[—]/[Quotation]/[—]/London; Printed for Sam. Briscoe at the Bell-Sa-/vage on Ludgate-Hill. 1721./Price One Shilling./

Octavo; 1—56; A—G⁴. Title-page boxed in double rule.

Adv.: *The Post Boy*, 8 November 1720. See also *The Northern Cuckold* (1721). [NN]

1743—[Another edition.]

Octavo. [BM]

Die von ihren Feigen-Blättern entblösseten Adam und Eva

See *The Modern World Disrob'd*.

The Dissenting Hypocrite

1704—/In Imitation of Hudibras./The Dissenting Hypocrite,/Or,/Occasional Conformist;/With/Reflections/On Two of the Ring-Leaders, etc./Viz./ I. Their Works and Writings./II. Their Professions and Principles./ III. Their Qualifications and Parts./IV. Their Persons and Practices./[—]/ [Quotation: Latin]/[—]/London, Printed in the year, 1704./

Octavo; [i—xviii], 1—78; A⁴, a⁴, B—L⁴. Title-page boxed in double rule.

First attributed to Ward by Walter Wilson, *Memoirs of the Life and Times of DeFoe* (London, 1830). There is no external evidence of Ward's authorship, but it is his in style and spirit. [CtY; MH]

The Diverting Muse

1707—/The/Diverting Muse,/Or, The/Universal Medley./[—]/Written by a Society of Merry Gentlemen, for/the Entertainment of the Town./ [—]/The First Part/[—]/Consisting of/[Five titles]/[—]/London:/ Printed and Sold by B. Bragge, at the Raven in Pater-noster-row, 1707./ Octavo; 1—40; A—E⁴ (A² missigned A³).

Part I was issued in June: *The History of the Works of the Learned*, June 1707. A. E. Case, *A Bibliography of English Poetical Miscellanies, 1521–1750* (Oxford, 1935) lists only the first number. Altogether, however, there were six numbers. Parts III and IV were issued in September: *The History of the Works of the Learned*, September 1707. The six numbers with cancelled title-pages are included in *The Fourth Volume of the Writings* (1709). "The Wine-bibbers Wish" from Part I of *The Diverting Muse* was reprinted in T. Campbell, *British Poets* (London, 1819) under the title of "A Song." [BL; TxU]

The Diverting Works

1709—/The/Diverting/Works/of The/Famous/Miguel de Cervantes,/Author of the History of/Don Quixote./[—]/Now first Translated from the Spanish./[—]/With an Introduction by the Author of/The London-Spy./[—]/London,/Printed and Sold by J. Round, in Exchange-Alley in Cornhill;/E. Sawyer, at the Post-House; A. Collins, at the Black-Boy;/ And T. Atkinson, in the Temple Change, in Fleet-street; and/T. Baker, at the Bible and Rose in Ludgate-Street, 1709./

Octavo; [i—iv], i—xii, 1—232; A—P⁸, Q⁴.

A note in *BMC* identifies this as a translation from *Para Todos* of Juan Perez de Montalban. Ward contributed only the introduction. [BM; NN]

Durgen

1729—/Durgen./Or, A/Plain Satyr/Upon A/Pompous Satyrist./[Band of printers' ornaments]/[Quotation: Horace]/[Band of printers' ornaments]/Amicably Inscrib'd, by the Author, to those/Worthy and Ingenious Gentlemen misrepre-/sented in a late invective Poem, call'd,/ The Dunciad./[Band of printers' ornaments]/London:/Printed for T. Warner at the Black-Boy in Pater-/noster-Row. MDCCXXIX/Price 1 s./ Octavo; [i—viii], 1—56; A—H⁴.

Issued in December: *The Monthly Chronicle*, December 1728. Acknowledged by Ward as his own production in the "Postscript" to *Apollo's Maggot*. [BM; CtY; MH; TxU]

1742—/The/Cudgel,/Or, A/Crab-tree Lecture./To the Author of/The Dunciad./[—]/By Hercules Vinegar, Esq;/[—]/[Quotation]/[—]/London: /Printed for the Author, and sold at his House, the Crab-Tree,/ in Vinegar-yard, near Drury-Lane. (Price 1 s.)/[—]/MDCCXLII./ Octavo; [i]—4, 3—56; B²; B²⁻⁴; C—H⁴.

Identical with *Durgen* except for the omission of the Preface and the resetting of the title-page and the first and second pages of the poem. This has been erroneously ascribed to Henry Fielding by Knox Chandler, "Two Fielding Pamphlets," *PQ*, XVI (1937), 410–411. I am indebted to Professor George Sherburn for calling my attention to *The Cudgel* and for providing me with the copy from his own library.

The Dutch-Guards Farewel

1699—/The/Dutch-Guards/Farewel To/England. 1699./ Broadside. Reprinted in *The Second Volume of the Writings* (1703). [DLC]

Ecclesia et Factio

1698—/Ecclesia et Factio./[—]/A/Dialogue/Between/Bow-Steeple Dragon,/ And The/Exchange Grasshopper./[—]/London, Printed in the Year, 1698./ Folio; 1—16; A—D². Title-page boxed in double rule.

Issued in December: see the verso of the title-page, *The London Spy*, vol. I, pt. II, December 1698. Included in *A Collection of the Writings, Hitherto Extant* (1700). Reprinted in *The Second Volume of the Writings* (1703). [BM; CtY; CSH; DLC; MH; NNC; TxU]

1698—/Aesop/in Select/Fables./viz.[I. At Tunbridge. II. At Bathe. III. At Epsom. IV. At Whitehall. V. From Tunbridge. VI. At Amsterdam.]/ [—]/With A/Dialogue/Between/Bow-Steeple Dragon,/And the Exchange Grasshopper./[—]/London,/Printed and are to be Sold by most Booksellers/in London and Westminster, 1698./ Octavo; [i—iv], 1—104 (i.e., 110; numerous errors in pagination); [i—ii], 1—12; A—H⁸. Title-page boxed in double rule. [MH]

The English Nun

[1700]—The English Nun: Or, a Comical Description of a Nunnery. With the Lives and Intrigues of the Priests and Nuns. Price 6 d.

Listed as a Ward item on the verso of the title-page, *The Rambling Rakes* (1700) and *A Step to Stir-Bitch-Fair* (1700). I have been unable to locate a copy.

An Epitaph on the Late Bishop of Addlebury
   See *The Lord Whiglove's Elegy.*
Female Dialogues
   1704—/Female/Dialogues:/Or,/Ladies/Conversations./[—]/By the Author
     of the London-Spy./[—]/London,/Printed in the Year, 1704./
        Octavo; 1—40; A—E⁴. Title-page boxed in double rule. [CtY]
Female Policy Detected
   1695—Female Policy Detected; or, the Arts of a designing Woman Laid
     Open, etc., 1695.
     Duodecimo.
     For attribution to Ward, see [1720] edition below. [BM]
   1702—[Another edition.]
     Octavo. [BM]
   1704—[Another edition.]
     Duodecimo. [BM]
   1712—[Another edition.]B. Harris and Mrs. Bond: London, 1712.
     Adv.: *The Protestant Post Boy,* 4–6 March 1712.
   1716—[Another edition.]
     Duodecimo. [BM]
   [1720]—/Female/Policy/Detected:/Or,/The Arts of a Designing Woman/
     Laid Open/Treating/[Description of contents]/[—]/By E. W. Author of
     the London-Spy, and Trip/to Jamaica/[—]/To which is added, The
     Batchelor's Estimate of the Expences of a Married Life./[—]/London:/
     Printed for John Willis and Joseph Boddington/at the Angel and Bible
     in Tower-Street./
        Duodecimo; [i—iv], 1—140; A⁶, B—F¹², G⁶. Title-page boxed in
     double rule. [BM; MH]
   1749—[Another edition.] [MB]
   1755—[Another edition.] [CtY]
   1828—/Female Policy/Detected,/Or The/Arts of Designing Women/Laid
     Open/[—]/By Edward Ward,/Author of the London-Spy, etc./[—]/
     Together with/Nuptial Dialogues,/By the same Author/[Ornament]
     /Seekonk:/Sykes and Cyphax, Printers,/Nos. 47 and 73 Queen Street./
     1828./
        Duodecimo; 1—128 (i.e., 126; pp. 4 to end misnumbered).
     This edition was obviously prepared for American readers. It contains
     "The Epistle Dedicatory to the Apprentices of London" of the [1720]
     edition, adding the note: "But will serve with little variation for the
     young gentlemen of America, more especially to those who live in great
     cities." Curiously enough it is signed E. Ward, dated "London, Novem-
     ber 1828." It contains four dialogues from *Nuptial Dialogues and Debates*
     (1710): nos. XIII, XXV, and XXIX of vol. I; no. IX of vol. II. [MH]
   [1830]—/Female Policy/Detected:/Or The/Arts Of A/Designing Woman/
     Laid Open./[—]/By E. Ward,/Author of The London Spy, and/A
     Trip To Jamaica./[—]/Teaching:/[Description of contents]/[—]/Balti-
     more:/Printed For The Purchasers./
        1—86; [A], A⁴, B⁸, E⁵, D—F⁶, G⁷. [DLC]
   [1835]—[Another edition.] Glasgow.
     Duodecimo. [BM]
The Field-Spy
   1714—/The/Field-Spy:/Or, The/Walking Observator./A Poem./[—]/By the
     Author of the London-Spy./[—]/[Ornaments]/[—]/London Printed:

/And Sold by J. Woodward in Scalding-Ally,/overagainst Stocks-Market; and J. Morphew/near Stationers-Hall. MDCCXIV./Where may be had the Four Volumes of the London-Spy./

Octavo; [i—ii], 1—38; A—E⁴. Title-page boxed in double rule.

An advertisement for an earlier edition, published by J. Woodward and J. Morphew, appears in *The Evening Post*, 27–29 October 1713. The copy above probably represents the first impression with a new title-page. [BM; CtY; MH]

The Forgiving Husband and Adulteress Wife

[1709]—/The/Forgiving Husband,/And/Adulteress Wife:/Or, A Season-able/Present/To The/Unhappy Pair in Fanchurch-Street/[—]/[Quota-tion]/[—]/By the Author of the London Spy./[—]/London:/Printed and Sold by H. Hills, in Black-fryars,/near the Water-side./

1—12; A⁶.

The *BMC* suggests the date 1708. This seems doubtful, since the edition is a pirated one. *The Observator*, 9–12 February 1709, advertises an edition by J. Morphew. It is likely that this represents the earlier edition. The edition by Hills appears in *A Collection of the Best English Poetry* (1717). The poem appears as dialogue XXX in *Nuptial Dialogues and Debates*, vol. I (1710). [BM; CtY; ICN; MH; NN; TxU]

Fortune's Bounty

1705—Fortune's Bounty; Or an Everlasting Purse, for the greatest Cuckold in the Kingdom.

Issued in July: *The History of the Works of the Learned*, July 1705. Adv.: *The Daily Courant*, 14 July 1705. Reprinted in *The Third Volume of the Writings* (1706). *BMC* suggests the date 1700. [BM]

A Frolick to Horn-Fair

1699—A Frolick to Horn-Fair. With a Walk from Cuckold's-Point thro' Deptford and Greenwich. J. How: London, 1699.

Issued in October: see the verso of the title-page, *The London Spy*, vol. I, pt. XII, October 1699. Included in *A Collection of the Writings, Hitherto Extant* (1700).

1700—/A/Frolick/To/Horn-Fair./With a Walk from/Cuckold's-Point/Thro'/Deptford and Greenwich./[—]/[Ornament]/[—]/London, Printed and Sold by J. How, in the Ram-Head-/Inn-Yard in Fanchurch-Street, 1700./

Folio; 1—16; A—D². Title-page boxed in double rule.

The second edition, issued in November: *Term Catalogues*, November 1700. [BM; CSH; DLC; MH; NNC]

1702—[Another edition.] J. How: London, 1702.
Adv.: *The Observator*, 21–24 October 1702.

1704—[Another edition.] J. How: London, 1704.
Adv.: *The Observator*, 28 October 1704.

Helter Skelter

1704—/Helter Skelter:/Or,/The Devil upon Two Sticks:/A/Comedy,/ As it is spitefully Acted between/High-Church/and/Low-Church./In/Most Taverns about London./[—]/By the Author of, All Men Mad, etc./[—]/London:/Printed in the Year, MDCCIV./

Quarto; 1—28; A—C⁴, D².

Reprinted in *The Third Volume of the Writings* (1706). [BM; CtY; DLC]

[1704]—/Helter Skelter:/Or, the/Devil upon two Sticks:/In a Comical Dialogue between High Church and Low Church, relating to/the Times./ [—]/By the Author of, All Men Mad./[—]/
 Quarto; 1—4. Dropped head.
 Designated in *WLC* as in 1696 edition. This is not possible, since *All Men Mad* was not published until 1704. Indications are that it is a second edition. [TxU]

The History of the Grand Rebellion . . . Digested into Verse
 Volume I
  1713—/The/History/Of The/Grand Rebellion;/Containing,/The most Remarkable Transactions/from the beginning of the Reign of King/Charles I. to the Happy Restoration./Together/With the Impartial Characters of the most/Famous and Infamous Persons, for and against/the Monarchy. Digested into Verse./Illustrated with about a Hundred Heads, of the/Worthy Royalists and other Principal Actors; drawn/from the Original Paintings of Vandike, A. More,/Dobson, Cor. Johnson, and other Eminent Painters;/and Engrav'd by the best modern Artists; as appears/by their Names in the List annex'd to the First Volume./Useful for all that have, or shall buy the Lord Claren-/don, or other Historians of those Times./[—]/In Three Volumes./The Two First End with the Murder of King Charles I./The Third Ends with the Restoration of King Charles II./To which is added an Appendix of several Tracts,/referr'd to by the Lord Clarendon, Sir R. Baker, T. Hobbs of/ Malms. and other Authors, from whom this Work was taken./[—]/ Volume the First./[—]/London:/Printed for J. Morphew near Stationer's-Hall,/MDCCXIII./
   Octavo; [i—ii], i—x, [xi—xxvi], 1—208; A⁶, a⁸, B—O⁸. Title-page boxed in double rule.
   The dedicatory epistle to John Cass, Esq., is signed Edward Ward. [BM; CSH; CtY; MH (MH copy is identical with above save for pp. [xi—xxvi], a⁸, which are missing); NN]
 Volume II
  1713—[Identical with the above to:]/In Three Volumes/[—]/Volume the Second, which ends with the Mur-/der of King Charles the First./ The Third Ends with the Restoration of King Charles II./To which is added an Appendix of several Tracts,/referr'd to by the Lord Clarendon, Sir R. Baker, T. Hobbs of/Malms. and other Authors, from whom this Work was taken./[—]/Volume the Second./[—]/London:/Printed for J. Morphew near Stationer's-Hall,/MDCCXIII./
   Octavo; [i—ii], 207—452; A², P—Ff⁸, Gg². Title-page boxed in double rule. [BM; CtY; MH (MH copy has pp. [xi—xxvi], a⁸, attached to end of volume; see above); NN]
 Volume III
  1715—/The/Lord Clarendon's/History/Of The/Grand Rebellion/Compleated. /Containing,/I. The Heads of the Great Men on both Sides,/whose character he gives, (being 85 in Number)/Drawn from Original Paintings of Vandike, A. Moore,/Dobson, Cor. Johnson, and other Eminent Painters./And Engraven by Mr. Vertue, Mr. Vandegutch,/Mr. Sturt, etc./ II. The Tracts, Speeches, Letters, Memorials, etc./mention'd in the said History, are here at large, and referr'd to the Page therein. With his Lordship's Life./III. Three Maps, viz. 1. South Britain (with the Tract/

of King Charles the Second's miraculous Escape from Worcester). 2. North Britain. 3. Ireland./IV. Two Tables, one of the Heads, and who Painted/and Engrav'd them. The other, of all the Battles/that was fought; both referring to the Pages in the/aforesaid History./[—]/Useful for all that had the same Bound up before those/Heads, etc. were Engrav'd./[—]/London:/Printed for John Nicholson at the King's-Arms/in Little-Britain. MDCCXV./

Octavo; [i—iv], 453–862, [i—vi]; G^2, Hh—Fff^8, Ggg^7. Title-page boxed in double rule. [BM; CtY; MH; NN (NN copy has a slight variation in pagination and signatures: [i—viii], 453–862, [i—vi]; G^4, Hh—Fff^8, Ggg^7.)]

The History of the London Clubs

Part I

1709—/The/History of the London Clubs,/Or, The/Citizens Pastime/Particularly,/[List in double column]/With a Sermon Preach'd to a Gang of High-way-Men/[—]/Part I./[—]/By the Author of the London Spy./[—]/[Vignette]/[—]/London, Printed by J. Dutten, near Fleet-street./

Octavo; 1—8; A^4. [BM; MH]

1711—[Another edition.] J. Bagnall: London, 1711.

Duodecimo. [BM]

Part II

1709—/The Second Part,/Of The/London Clubs;/Containing,/[List in double column]/[—]/By the Author of the London Spy./[—]/[Vignette]/[—]/London, Printed by J. Dutten, near Fleet-/street, also the First Part./

Octavo; 1—8; [A^4].

The clubs included here and in Part I were incorporated in *The Secret History of Clubs* (1709). [BM; MH]

1709—/The/Secret History/Of/Clubs:/Particularly The/[List]/With Their/Originals:/And The/Characters/Of The/Most Noted Members thereof./[—]/[Quotation: Latin]/[—]/London/Printed, and Sold by the Booksellers, 1709./

Octavo; [i—xiv], 1—392 (i.e., 396; 289 to end misnumbered); A^7, B—Aa^8, Bb^7. [BM; CSH; CtY; DLC; MBA]

1710—/Satyrical Reflections/On/Clubs:/In XXIX Chapters./[List in double column separated by rule]/[—]/By the Author of the London-Spy./[—]/Vol. V./[—]/London, Printed for J. Phillips, at the/Black Bull in Cornhill, 1710./

Octavo; [i—xiv], 1—392 (i.e., 398; 289 to end misnumbered); A^7, B—Bb^8. Title-page boxed in double rule.

Volume V on the title-page refers to the fact that this was to be considered the *Fifth Volume of the Writings*. See note under *Writings*, Volume V. [MH]

1745—/A/Compleat/and/Humorous Account/Of all the Remarkable/Clubs and Societies/in The/Cities/Of/London and Westminster,/From the R——l-S——y down to the/Lumber-Troop, etc./Their Original with Characters of the most/noted Members, containing great Vari-/ety entertaining Discourses, Frolicks,/and Adventures of the principal Managers/and Members, a Work of great Use and/Curiosity./Compil'd from the original Papers of a Gent. who/frequented those Places upwards of

twenty Years./London:/Printed for the Author and Sold by Joseph Col-
lier/at Shakespear's Head in Ludgate-Street./[—]/MDCCXLV./<Price
Sew'd Two Shillings, Bound 2 s, 6 d.>/

> Duodecimo; [i—xiv], 1—332 (pp. 328–332 advs.), (i.e., 266; pp. 121
> to end misnumbered); A⁶, a¹, B—L¹², M⁶. [BM; CSH; CtY; MH;
> NN]

1756—/A/Compleat/and/Humorous Account/Of all the Remarkable/Clubs
and Societies/In The/Cities of London and Westminster,/From the
R——- S——y down to the/Lumber-Troop, etc./Their Original with
Characters of the most noted/Members, containing great Variety of enter-
tain-/ing Discourses; Frolicks, and Adventures of the/principal Managers
and Members, a Work of/great Use and Curiosity./Compil'd from the
original Papers of a Gentleman who/frequented those Places upwards of
Twenty Years./[—]/The Seventh Edition./[—]/London: Printed for
J. Wren, at the Bible and Crown, in Salis-/bury-Court, Fleet-street 1756.
/<Price Sew'd Two Shillings, Bound 2 s. 6 d.>/

> Duodecimo; [i—xiv], 1—328 (i.e., 262; 121 to end misnumbered);
> [A], A⁶, B—L¹², M⁴. [BM; MH]

1896—/The History Of The/London Clubs./Or, The/Citizens' Pastime,/
Particularly/[List in double column]/[—]/Part 1/[—]/By the Author
of the London Spy./[Vignette]/London, Printed by J. Dutten, near
Fleet Street, 1709./

> 1—31
> This is a reprint of *The History of the London Clubs* (1709), parts
> I-II. [BM; CtY; NNC; TxU]

Honesty in Distress

1705—/Honesty in Distress,/But/Reliev'd by no Party./A/Tragedy,/As is
basely Acted/By Her Majesty's Subjects/Upon/God's Stage the World./
[—]/[—]/London:/Printed and are to be Sold by B. Bragge at the/
Blue-Ball in Avy-Mary-Lane, 1705/[printing below this line cut off]

> Quarto; [i—iv], 1—24; [A]⁶, B—D⁴.
> Issued in January: *The History of the Works of the Learned*, Janu-
> ary 1705. Adv.: *The Daily Courant*, 9 January 1705. Reprinted in *The
> Third Volume of the Writings* (1706). [BM; CSH; CtY]

1708—[Another edition.] J. Morphew and T. Morris: London, 1708.

> Adv.: *The Daily Courant*, 24 January 1708, and *The Post-Man*, 12–14
> February 1708.

1708—/Honesty/in/Distress;/But/Reliev'd by No Party:/A/Tragedy,/As it
is Acted on the Stage, etc./[Lists of scenes and characters in two col-
umns]/[—]/London: Printed and sold by Hen. Hills, in Black-fry-/ars,
near the Water-side. 1708. Price 4 d./

> Octavo; 1—16; [A⁸].
> A pirated edition. [BM; DLC; ICN; MH; TxU]

1708—[Identical with the above to:]/London: Printed and sold by Hen.
Hills, in Black-/fryars, near the Water-side. 1708. Price 1 d./

> Octavo; 1—16; [A⁸].
> A pirated edition. [BM; TxU]

1710—/Honesty/in Distress;/But/Reliev'd by No Party:/A/Tragedy,/As it is
Acted on the Stage, etc./[Lists of scenes and characters in two columns]
/[—]/London: Printed for, and Sold by H. Hills, in Black-/Fryars near
the Waterside, 1710. Price 1 d./

> Octavo; 1—16; [A⁸].

A pirated edition. [BM; CtY; MH; TxU]

[1725]—[Another edition.] To which is added A Satyr, against the Corrupt Use of Money. Bury St. Edmunds.

Octavo. [BM]

Hudibras Redivivus

Volume I, Parts I-XII

1705—/Hudibras Redivivus:/Or, A/Burlesque Poem/On The/Times./[—]/Part the First./[—]/London,/Printed: and Sold by B. Bragge, in Ave-Mary-/Lane 1705. Price 6 d./

Quarto; [i—iv], 1—24; A², B—D⁴.

Parts I-XII of Volume I were issued at irregular intervals from 28 August 1705 to 27 July 1706. With minor exceptions in the case of Parts V and VII, title-pages are identical for all twelve parts. Pagination and signatures are uniformly 1—28; A—C⁴, D². Parts I-III were reprinted in a second edition. See below. Dates of issue where known are as follows: Part I. *The Daily Courant,* 28 August 1705; Part II. *The Daily Courant,* 3 October 1705; Part III. *The Daily Courant,* 8 November 1705; Part IV. *The Daily Courant,* 7 December 1705; Part V. *The Daily Courant,* 16 January 1706; Part VII. *The Daily Courant,* 12 March 1706; Part VIII. *The Daily Courant,* 8 April 1706; Part X. *The Daily Courant,* 15 June 1706; Part XI, *The Daily Courant,* 26 June 1706; Part XII. *The Daily Courant,* 27 July 1706. [CSH; TxU; MH]

1708—/Hudibras Redivivus:/Or, A/Burlesque Poem/On the Times./[—]/Part I. Vol. I./[—]/The Second Edition./[—]/To which is added,/An Apology, and some other Im/provements throughout the whole./[—]/London,/Printed: And sold by the Booksellers of London and/Westminster. 1708. Price Sixpence./N.B. The two volumes are now publish'd in twelve Parts each Volume, and/may be had at 12 s. compleat, or single Parts at 6 d. each Part./

Quarto; 1—28; A—C⁴, D². [BM; NNC]

1709—/Hudibras Redivivus/Or, A/Burlesque Poem/On The/Times./[—]/Part the Second./[—]/The Second Edition, corrected and augmented by the/Author./[—]/London,/Printed: And sold by the Booksellers of London and/Westminster. 1709. Price Six-pence./

Quarto; 1—28; A—C⁴, D². [NNC]

1709—[Part III. Title-page identical with the above save for "Part the Third."]

Quarto; 1—28; A—C⁴, D². [NNC]

Volume II, Parts I-XII

1706—/Hudibras Redivivus:/Or,/A Burlesque/Poem/On the various Humours of/Town and Country/[—]/Part the First/[—]/Vol. II./[—]/London,/Printed: and Sold by Benj. Bragge, at the Raven in/Pater-Noster-Row, against Ivy Lane, 1706./(Price Six-pence.)/

Quarto; 1—28; Aa—Cc⁴, Dd².

Parts I-XII of Volume II were issued at irregular intervals from 15 August 1706 to sometime in June 1707. Title-pages are identical for the twelve parts, pagination is uniformly 1—28, but signatures are continuous throughout: viz., Aa—Cc⁴, Dd²; Ee—Gg⁴, Hh²; Ii—Ll⁴, Mm²; Nn—Pp⁴, Qq²; Rr—Tt⁴, Uu²; Xx—Zz⁴, Aaa²; Bbb—Ddd⁴, Eee²; Fff—Hhh⁴, Iii²; Kkk—Mmm⁴, Nnn²; Ooo—Qqq⁴, Rrr²; Sss—Uuu⁴, Xxx²; Yyy—Aaaa⁴, Bbbb².

Dates of issue where known are as follows: Part I. *The Daily Courant,*

15 August 1706; Part II. *The Daily Courant,* 29 August 1706; Part III. *The Daily Courant,* 20 September 1706; Part IV. *The Daily Courant,* 3 October 1706; Part V. *The History of the Works of the Learned,* October 1706; Part VI. *The History of the Works of the Learned,* February 1707; Part VII. *The History of the Works of the Learned,* February 1707; Part X. *The History of the Works of the Learned,* April 1707. [MH; (Volumes I–II of *Hudibras Redivivus* variously made up from the parts above and labeled as the second to the fourth edition appear at BM; DLC; NNC.)]

[1710]—/Hudibras Redivivus:/Or, A/Burlesque Poem/On The/Times./[—] /In Twenty Four Parts./[—]/With/An Apology, and some other improvements/throughout the Whole./[—]/The Fourth Edition./[—]/ To which is now added,/The Rambling Fuddle-Caps: Or a Tavern Struggle for/a Kiss./[—]/By E. Ward, Gent. Author of the London Spy./ [—]/London:/Printed for John Wren, near Great Turn-Stile, High-Holborn./Price Bound in Calf, Six Shillings./

This is a copy of remainders issued with cancelled title-pages, the original "Preface" to Part I, the "Apology" originally issued with Part I of the second edition, and a frontispiece. [MH]

The Hudibrastick Brewer

1714—/The Hudibrastick/Brewer:/Or, A/Preposterous Union/Between/Malt and Meter./A/Satyr/upon the suppos'd/Author/Of the/Republican Procession;/Or, The/Tumultuous Cavalcade./[—]/London: Printed for John Morphew near/Stationers-Hall, 1714./(Price Six-pence.)/

Octavo; 1—36; A—D⁴, E².

Included in *A Collection of Historical and State Poems* (1717). [BM; CtY; DLC; ICN; MH; TxU]

1727—[Another edition.]

See *The Republican Procession* (1727).

A Hue and Cry after a Man-Midwife

1699—/A/Hue and Cry/After/A Man-Midwife,/who has lately Deliver'd the/ Land-Bank/of their/Money./

Broadside.

Bottom of p. 2: "London, Printed in the year 1699." Reprinted in *The Second Volume of the Writings* (1703). [BM; DLC; NNC]

[1699]—[Another edition.] London. [BM]

The Humours of a Coffee-House

1707—The Humours of a Coffee-House; A Comedy as it is Daily Acted by [List of characters]. London, Printed for the Benefit of Bohee, the Coffee-Man; and Sold at the Publishing Office, in Bearbinder-Lane, 1707.

Numbers I–VII were issued each Wednesday, 25 June to 6 August. See note 13, Chapter VII for the relation of this periodical to *The Weekly Comedy* (1699). See also *The Weekly Comedy* (1699) below. [BM; (Nos. I, II, and III are in CSH.)]

The Insinuating Bawd

[1699]—The Insinuating Bawd: And the Repenting Harlot. Written by a Whore at Tunbridge, and Dedicated to a Bawd at the Bath. J. How: London, 1699.

Folio. [BM; CSH]

1700—/The/Insinuating Bawd:/And The/Repenting Harlot./[—]/Written by a Whore at Tunbridge, and/Dedicated to a Bawd at the Bath./[—]/

[Ornament]/[—]/London/Printed, and are Sold by most Booksellers./
Folio; [i—iv], 1—12; A—D². Title-page boxed in double rule.

This edition is listed in the *Term Catalogues,* November 1700. Included in *A Collection of the Writings, Hitherto Extant* (1701). An edition adv.: *The Observator,* J. How, 26–29 August 1702. [CSH; MH; NNC]

1755—[Another edition.] To which is added, *Love. An Ode to a Lady.* By a Married Gentleman.

    Octavo. [BM]

1758—[Another edition.] To which is added, *The Six Nights Rambles,* by a Gentleman, etc.

    Duodecimo. [BM]

A Journey to Hell

Part 1

1700—/A/Journey to Hell:/Or, A/Visit paid to the Devil./A/Poem./[—]/
[Ornament]/[—]/London,/Printed, and are to be Sold by the Booksellers of/London and Westminster. 1700./

    Folio; 1—32; A—H². Title-page boxed in double rule. [BM; CSH; MH]

1700—[Identical with the above to:]/A/Poem./[—]/The Second Edition/
[—]/[Ornament]/[—]/London,/Printed and are to be Sold by the Booksellers of/London and Westminster. 1700./

    Folio; 1—32; A—H². Title-page boxed in double rule. [CSH; CtY; MH; NNC; TxU]

Part ii

1700—/A/Journey to H——:/Or, A/Visit paid to, etc./A/Poem./[—]/Part
ii/[—]/Both Parts by the Author of the London-Spy./[—]/[Ornament]/
[—]/London,/Printed and are to be Sold by the Booksellers of/London and Westminster. 1700./

    Folio; 1—24; A—G². Title-page boxed in double rule. [CSH; MH; NNC; TxU]

Part iii

1705—/A/Journey to H-ll:/Or, A/Visit paid to the D—l./A/Poem./[—]/
Part iii./[—]/By the Author of the First and Second Parts./[—]/
London:/Printed, and are to be Sold by the Booksellers of/London and Westminster. 1705./

    Folio; 1—16; A—D². Title-page boxed in double rule.

This is probably a late edition. *The Daily Courant,* 2 November 1704, carries an advertisement of Part iii (the earliest record I have found), but that leaves what seems to be an unreasonable lapse between Part iii and Parts i and ii. The three parts were reprinted in *The Third Volume of the Writings* (1706). [CSH; MH]

The Kentish Fable

1701—The Kentish Fable of the Lyon and the Foxes: Or, the Honesty of the Kentish petition Made Manifest, etc.

    Issued in June: *The History of the Works of the Learned,* June 1701. Listed as a Ward item on the verso of the title-page, *The Revels of the Gods* (1701). I have been unable to locate a copy.

Labour in Vain

1700—Labour in Vain: Or, What Signifies Little or Nothing, viz. I. The Poor Man's Petition at Court. II. Expectation of Benefit from a Covetous

Man in his Life-time. III. The Marriage of an Old Man to a Young Woman. IV. Endeavours to Regulate Men's Manners by Preaching or Writing. V. Being a Jacobite. VI. Confining an Insolvent Debtor. VII. Promise of Secrecy in a Conspiracy. VIII. An Inquiry after a Place. Quarto.

Listed as a Ward item on the verso of the title-page, *The Rambling Rakes* (1700), *A Step to Stir-Bitch-Fair* (1700), and *The Insinuating Bawd* (1700). Reprinted in *The Harleian Miscellany,* vol. VI (London, 1810). The edition is described as a quarto, pp. 32, with the colophon: "London, Printed and Sold by most Booksellers in London and Westminster." [BM]

Laugh and Be Fat

1700—Laugh and be Fat, or an Antidote against Melancholy; containing a variety of Comical Intreagues in Town and Country; with pleasant Humours, Frolicks, Fancies, Epigrams, Satyrs, and Divertisements. To which is added, Nine delightful Tales. Octavo. Printed for J. How in Ram-head Inn, Yard, in Fenchurch St.

Listed in the *Term Catalogues,* February 1700. Regularly included as a Ward item on the verso of the title-page, *The Insinuating Bawd* (1700), *The Rambling Rakes* (1700), *A Step to Stir-Bitch-Fair* (1700), *A Step to the Bath* (1700), and *The Revels of the Gods* (1701). *The Observator,* 10–13 April 1705, carries the following adv.: "Laugh and be Fat: Or, An Antidote against Melancholy, by the most ingenious Authors of the Age. J. How. 1 shilling." The relation between the two items is not clear. Ward may have been one of the contributors and so included the title as his own. On the other hand the title seems to have been a common one. Compare, for instance, *An Antidote Against Melancholy, Containing Above a Hundred Comical Intrigues in Town and Country, London, J. How, 1700,* a general title-page for the thirteen weekly numbers of *The English Lucian,* 17 January 1698, [DLC]. MH contains an edition of *Laugh and be Fat, Or, The Fire-side Companion. Being the best Collection of Funny Jokes, and Humorous Tales . . . The Tenth Edition, Dublin: P. Dugdale, 1783.* It is interesting that this contains a story about two busybody clergymen which Ward had told about two Boston elders in *A Trip to New England.* The scene of the story here is laid in Bristol. The *BMC* lists the following editions of *Laugh and Be Fat, or an Antidote against Melancholy:* 1733, the eleventh edition, duodecimo; 1741, the twelfth edition, duodecimo; 1761, the tenth edition, duodecimo.

A Legacy for the Ladies

See *A Comical View of London and Westminster.*

The Libertine's Choice

1704—The Libertine's Choice; or the Mistaken Happiness of a Fool in Fashion. B. Bragg: London, 1704.

Quarto.

Adv.: *The Observator,* 2–5 February 1704.

Reprinted in *The Third Volume of the Writings* (1706). [BM]

1709—/The/Libertine's Choice/Or,/The Mistaken Happiness/Of/The/Fool in Fashion/[—]/[Ornament]/[—]/London:/Printed and Sold by H. Hills, in Black-fryars near/the Water-side./1709./

Octavo; 1—16; A⁸.

This was a pirated edition. The poem appears in *A Collection of the Best English Poetry,* vol. I (1717). [BM; CtY; ICN; NN]

The Life and Noble Adventures of Don Quixote
　Volume I
　　1711—/The/Life/And/Noble Adventures/Of That/Renown'd Knight,/Don
　　Quixote/De la Mancha./[—]/Merrily translated into Hudibrastick Verse./
　　[—]/By Edward Ward./[—]/Vol. I./[—]/London:/Printed for T.
　　Norris at the Looking-Glass,/and A. Bettesworth at the Red-Lyon/on
　　London Bridge; J. Harding at the/upper-end of St. Martin's-Lane; and
　　Sold/by J. Woodward in Scalding-Alley, over-/against Stocks-Market.
　　MDCCXI./
　　　　Octavo; [i—xvi], 1—475 (i.e., 500; errors in pagination: 75–76 miss-
　　ing; 83 to end misnumbered; 161 to end misnumbered; 175 misnumbered
　　177; 181 misnumbered 185; 193–200 misnumbered 137–144; 441–448
　　misnumbered 437–444; 456 duplicated); [i—vi]; A^9, B—K^4, L^3, M—
　　Ooo^4, Ppp^5 (Lll$^{1-4}$ missigned Mmm$^{1-4}$; Z$^{1-4}$ missigned Y$^{1-4}$). Title-
　　page boxed in double rule. [BM; CtY; DLC; ICN; MH (MH copy is
　　identical in text but has pp. [i—xviii], A^{10}, at beginning and [i—iv]
　　at end); MHi; NN (NN copy omits [i—iv] at end; has cancelled title-
　　pages for Pts. 1 and 11)]
　Volume II
　　1712—[Identical with the above to:]/[—]/London:/Printed for T. Norris at
　　the Looking-Glass, and A./Bettesworth at the Red-Lyon on London-
　　Bridge;/J. Harding at the upper end of St. Martin's Lane;/J. Woodward
　　in Scalding-Alley, over against Stocks-/Market; E. Curl at the Dial, and
　　R. Gosling at the/Mitre in Fleet-street, MDCCXII. Price 5 s./Where also
　　may be had the First Volume./
　　　　Octavo; [i—vi], 1—477, [i—iii]; A^3, B—Hh^8. Title-page boxed in
　　double rule. [BM; DLC; ICN; MH; MHi; NN (NN copy has title-page
　　missing)]

The London Spy
　Volume I, Part 1
　　1698—/The/London/Spy./[—]/Part 1./[—]/By the Author of the Trip to
　　Jamaica./[—]/[Ornament]/[—]/London,/Printed for J. Nutt, near
　　Stationers-Hall, 1698./
　　　　Folio; 1—16; A—D^2. Title-page boxed in double rule. [MH; NNC]
　　[1699]—/The/London/Spy./[—]/For the Month of November, 1698/[—]/
　　Part 1./[—]/By the Author of the Trip to Jamaica./[—]/[Ornament]/
　　[—]/London,/Printed for J. Nutt, near Stationers-Hall, 1698./
　　　　Folio; 1—16 (p. 15 misnumbered 51); A—D^2. Title-page boxed in
　　double rule.
　　　　The second edition, issued in March 1699: advs. on the verso of the
　　title-page include *The London Spy*, pts. 1-v. [DLC]
　　1700—/The/London/Spy./[—]/For the Month of November, 1698./[—]/
　　Part 1./[—]/By the Author of the Trip to Jamaica./[—]/The Third
　　Edition/[—]/[Ornament]/[—]/London,/Printed and Sold by J. How,
　　in the Ram-Head-Inn-/Yard, in Fanchurch-street, 1700./
　　　　Folio; 1—16 (p. 15 misnumbered 51); A—D^2. Title-page boxed in
　　double rule.
　　　　Included in *A Collection of the Writings, Hitherto Extant* (1700).
　　[CtY; TxU]
　Part 11
　　1698—/The/London/Spy./Part 11./[—]/By the Author of the Trip to
　　Jamaica./[—]/[Ornament]/[—]/London,/Printed for J. Nutt, near
　　Stationers-Hall, 1698./
　　　　Folio; 1—16; A—D^2. Title-page boxed in double rule.

The first edition. Advs. on the verso of the title-page include *The London Spy*, pt. I. Included in *A Collection of the Writings, Hitherto Extant* (1700). [DLC; NNC]

[1698]—[The second edition.] I have been unable to locate a copy of this edition.

1701—/The/London/Spy./[—]/Part II./[—]/By the Author of the Trip to Jamaica./[—]/The Third Edition./[—]/[Ornament]/[—]/**London,/** Printed and Sold by J. How, in the Ram-Head-Inn-Yard/in Fanchurch-Street, 1701./

Folio; 1—16; A—D². Title-page boxed in double rule. [TxU]

Part III

1699—/The/London/Spy./[—]/For the Month of January, 1699./[—]/Part III./[—]/By the Author of the Trip to Jamaica./[—]/[Ornament]/ [—]/London,/Printed for J. Nutt, near Stationers-Hall, 1699./

Folio; 1—16; A—D². Title-page boxed in double rule.

The first edition. Advs. on the verso of the title-page include *The London Spy*, pts. I-II. [BM; NNC]

Included in *A Collection of the Writings, Hitherto Extant* (1701).

1699—/The/London/Spy./[—]/For the Month of January, 1699./[—]/Part III./[—]/By the Author of the Trip to Jamaica./[—]/[Ornament]/ [—]/London, Printed and Sold by J. How, in the Ram-Head-Inn-/Yard in Fanchurch-street, 1699./

Folio; 1—16; A—D². Title-page boxed in double rule.

Included in *A Collection of the Writings, Hitherto Extant* (1700). [DLC; TxU]

Part IV

1699—/The/London/Spy./[—]/For the Month of February, 1699./[—]/ Part IV./[—]/By the Author of the Trip to Jamaica./[—]/[Ornament]/ [—]/London,/Printed for J. Nutt, near Stationers-Hall, 1699./

Folio; 1—16; A—D². Title-page boxed in double rule.

The first edition. Advs. on the verso of the title-page include *The London Spy*, pts. I-III. Included in *A Collection of the Writings, Hitherto Extant* (1700). [NNC]

1699—/The/London/Spy./[—]/For the Month of February, 1699./[—] Part IV./[—]/By the Author of the Trip to Jamaica./[—]/[Ornament]/ [—]/London, Printed and Sold by J. How, in the Ram-Head-Inn/Yard in Fanchurch-street, 1699./

Folio; 1—16; A—D². Title-page boxed in double rule.

The second edition, issued in November. Advs. on the verso of the title-page include *The London Spy*, pts. I-XII. [ICS]

1701—/The/London/Spy./[—]/For the Month of February, 1699./[—]/ Part IV./[—]/By the Author of the Trip to Jamaica./[—]/[Ornament]/ [—]/London,/Printed and Sold by J. How, in the Ram-Head-Inn-Yard in/Fanchurch-street, 1701./

Folio; 1—16; A—D². Title-page boxed in double rule.

This is the third edition. The advs. on the verso of the title-page of this edition indicate that it is a reprint of the second edition above. [MHi]

Part V

1699—/The/London/Spy./[—]/For the Month of March, 1699./[—]/Part V./[—]/By the Author of the Trip to Jamaica./[—]/[Ornament]/ [—]/London,/Printed for J. Nutt, near Stationers-Hall, 1699./

Folio; 1—16; A—D². Title-page boxed in double rule.

The first edition. Advs. on the verso of the title-page include *The London Spy*, pts. I-IV. [NNC]

1699—/The/London/Spy./[—]/For the Month of March, 1699./[—]/Part v./[—]/By the Author of the Trip to Jamaica./[—]/[Ornament]/ [—]/London,/Printed and Sold by J. How, in the Ram-Head-Inn-Yard, in/Fanchurch-street, 1699./

Folio; 1—16; A—D². Title-page boxed in double rule.

The second edition, issued October 1699. Advs. on the verso of the title-page include *The London Spy*, pts. I-XI. Included in *A Collection of the Writings, Hitherto Extant* (1700). [TxU]

Part VI

1699—/The/London/Spy./[—]/For the Month of April, 1699./[—]/Part vI./[—]/By the Author of the Trip to Jamaica./[—]/[Ornament]/ [—]/London,/Printed for J. Nutt, near Stationers-Hall, 1699./

Folio; 1—16; A—D². Title-page boxed in double rule.

The first edition. Included in *A Collection of the Writings, Hitherto Extant* (1700), [NNC]

1699—/The/London/Spy./[—]/For the Month of April, 1699./[—]/Part vI./[—]/By the Author of the Trip to Jamaica./[—]/[Ornament]/ [—]/London,/Printed and Sold by J. How, in Ram-Head-Inn-Yard in/ Fanchurch-street, 1699./

Folio; 1—16; A—D². Title-page boxed in double rule.

The second edition. [DLC]

1701—/The/London/Spy./[—]/For the Month of April, 1699./[—]/Part vI./[—]/By the Author of the Trip to Jamaica./[—]/The Third Edition./[—]/[Ornament]/[—]/London,/Printed and Sold by J. How, in the Ram-Head-Inn-Yard/in Fanchurch-Street, 1701./

Folio; 1—16; A—D². Title-page boxed in double rule. [TxU]

Part VII

1699—/The/London/Spy./[—]/For the Month of May, 1699./[—]/Part vII./[—]/By the Author of the Trip to Jamaica./[—]/[Ornament]/ [—]/London,/Printed and Sold by J. How, in the Ram-Head-Inn-Yard in/Fanchurch-street, 1699./

Folio; 1—16; A—D². Title-page boxed in double rule.

The first edition. Advs. on the verso of the title-page include *The London Spy*, pts. I-VI. Included in *A Collection of the Writings, Hitherto Extant* (1700). [DLC; NNC]

1702—/The/London/Spy./[—]/For the Month of May, 1699./[—]/Part vII./[—]/The Second Edition./[—]/By the Author of the Trip to Jamaica./[—]/[Ornament]/[—]/London, Printed and Sold by J. How, in the Ram-Head-/Inn-Yard, in Fanchurch-street, 1702./

Folio; 1—16; A—D². Title-page boxed in double rule. [TxU]

Part VIII

1699—/The/London/Spy./[—]/For the Month of June, 1699./[—]/Part vIII./[—]/By the Author of the Trip to Jamaica./[—]/[Ornament]/ [—]/London,/Printed and Sold by J. How, in the Ram-Head-Inn-Yard in/Fanchurch-street, 1699./

Folio; 1—16; A—D². Title-page boxed in double rule.

The first edition. Advs. on the verso of the title-page include *The London Spy*, pts. I-VII. Included in *A Collection of the Writings, Hitherto Extant* (1700). [DLC; NNC]

Part IX

1699—/The/London/Spy./[—]/For the Month of July, 1699./[—]/Part
IX./[—]/By the Author of the Trip to Jamaica./[—]/[Ornament]/
[—]/London,/Printed and Sold by J. How, in the Ram-Head-Inn-Yard
in/Fanchurch-street, 1699./

　　　Folio; 1—16; A—D². Title-page boxed in double rule.

　　　The first edition. Advs. on the verso of the title-page include *The
London Spy*, pts. I-VIII. Included in *A Collection of the Writings, Hitherto
Extant* (1700). [NNC (NNC has two copies, one of which lacks
pp. 11–12, C²); TxU]

Part X

1699—/The/London/Spy./[—]/For the Month of August, 1699./[—]/
Part X./[—]/By the Author of the Trip to Jamaica./[—]/[Ornament]/
[—]/London,/Printed and Sold by J. How, in the Ram-Head-Inn-Yard
in/Fanchurch-street, 1699./

　　　Folio; 1—16; A—D². Title-page boxed in double rule.

　　　The first edition. Advs. on the verso of the title-page include *The
London Spy*, pts. I-IX. Included in *A Collection of the Writings, Hitherto
Extant* (1700). [NNC]

Part XI

1699—/The/London/Spy./[—]/For the Month of September, 1699./[—]/
Part XI./[—]/By the Author of the Trip to Jamaica./[—]/[Orna-
ment]/[—]/London,/Printed and Sold by J. How, in the Ram-Head-
Inn-Yard in/Fanchurch-street, 1699./

　　　Folio; 1—16; A—D². Title-page boxed in double rule.

　　　The first edition. Advs. on the verso of the title-page include *The
London Spy*, pts. I-X. Included in *A Collection of the Writings, Hitherto
Extant* (1700). [NNC]

Part XII

1699—/The/London/Spy./[—]/For the Month of October, 1699./[—]/Part
XII./[—]/By the Author of the Trip to Jamaica./[—]/[Ornament]/
[—]/London,/Printed and Sold by J. How, in the Ram-Head-Inn-Yard
in/Fanchurch-street, 1699./

　　　Folio; 1—16; A—D². Title-page boxed in double rule.

　　　The first edition. Advs. on the verso of the title-page include *The
London Spy*, pts. I-XI; pp. 15–16: "The Contents of the Twelve Parts of
the First Volume of The London-Spy." Included in *A Collection of the
Writings, Hitherto Extant* (1700). [NNC (NNC copy does not contain
pp. 15–16); TxU]

Volume II, Part I

1699—/The/London/Spy./[—]/For the Month of November, 1699./[—]/
The Second Volume./[—]/Part I./[—]/[Ornament]/[—]/London,
Printed and Sold by J. How, in the Ram-Head-Inn/Yard in Fanchurch-
street, 1699./

　　　Folio; 1—16; A—D². Title-page boxed in double rule.

　　　The first edition. Advs. on the verso of the title-page include *The
London Spy*, pts. I-XII. Included in *A Collection of the Writings, Hitherto
Extant* (1700). [NNC]

Part II

1699—/The/London/Spy./[—]/For the Month of December, 1699./[—]/
The Second Volume./[—]/Part II./[—]/[Ornament]/[—]/London,
Printed and Sold by J. How, in the Ram-Head-Inn-/Yard in Fanchurch-
street, 1699./

Folio; 1—16 (p. 12 is misnumbered 13); A—D². Title-page boxed in double rule.

The first edition. Advs. on the verso of the title-page include *The London Spy*, pts. I-XII; vol. II, pts. I-II. Included in *A Collection of the Writings, Hitherto Extant* (1700). [NNC]

1701—/The/London/Spy./[—]/For the Month of December, 1699./[—]/ The Second Volume./[—]/Part II./[—]/The Second Edition./[—]/ [Ornament]/[—]/London, Printed and Sold by J. How, in the Ram-Head-/Inn-Yard, in Fanchurch-street, 1701./

Folio; 1—16; A—D². Title-page boxed in double rule. [TxU]

Part III

1700—/The/London/Spy./[—]/For the Month of January, 1700./[—]/ The Second Volume./[—]/Part III./[—]/[Ornament]/[—]/London, Printed and Sold by J. How, in the Ram-Head-Inn-/Yard in Fanchurch-street, 1700./

Folio; 1—16; A—D². Title-page boxed in double rule.

The first edition. Advs. on the verso of the title-page include *The London Spy*, pts. I-XII; vol. II, pts. I-III. Included in *A Collection of the Writings, Hitherto Extant* (1700). [NNC; TxU]

Part IV

1700—/The/London/Spy./[—]/For the Month of February, 1700./[—]/ The Second Volume./[—]/Part IV./[—]/[Ornament]/[—]/London, Printed and Sold by J. How, in the Ram-Head-Inn-/Yard in Fanchurch-street, 1700./

Folio; 1—16; A—D². Title-page boxed in double rule.

The first edition. Advs. on the verso of the title-page include *The London Spy*, pts. I-XII; vol. II, pts. I-IV. Included in *A Collection of the Writings, Hitherto Extant* (1700). [NNC (lacks two leaves); ICS]

Part V

1700—/The/London/Spy./[—]/For the Month of March, 1700./[—]/ The Second Volume./[—]/Part V./[—]/[Ornament]/[—]/London, Printed and Sold by J. How, in the Ram-Head-Inn-/Yard in Fanchurch-street, 1700./

Folio; 1—16 (pp. 15 and 16 misnumbered 51 and 61); A—D². Title-page boxed in double rule.

The first edition. Advs. on the verso of the title-page include *The London Spy*, pts. I-XII; vol. II, pts. I-IV. Included in *A Collection of the Writings, Hitherto Extant* (1700). [NNC; TxU]

Part VI

1700—/The/London/Spy./[—]/For the Month of April, 1700./[—]/ The Second Volume./[—]/Part VI./[—]/[Ornament]/[—]/London, Printed and Sold by J. How, in the Ram-Head-Inn-/Yard in Fanchurch-street, 1700./

Folio; 1—16; A—D². Title-page boxed in double rule.

The first edition. Advs. on the verso of the title-page include *The London Spy*, pts. I-XII; vol. II, pts. I-V. Included in *A Collection of the Writings, Hitherto Extant* (1700). [NNC]

1703—/The/London-Spy./Compleat,/In Eighteen-Parts./[—]/By the Author of the Trip to Jamaica./[—]/London,/Printed and Sold by J. How, at the Se-/ven Stars in Talbot-Court in Grace-/Church-street, 1703./

Octavo; [i—iv], 1—438; [A²], B—Ee⁸. Title-page boxed in double rule.

Adv.: *The Observator*, 21–27 July 1703. "To the Reader" contains the first three paragraphs of the original preface to Part II for December 1698. [BM; MH (MH copy has pp. 189–192, N$^{6-8}$, missing; pp. 241 to end misnumbered); TxU]

1704—/The/London-Spy/Compleat,/In Eighteen Parts./[—]/The First Volume of the Authors Writings./[—]/The Second Edition much Enlarged and Corrected./[—]/London,/Printed and Sold by J. How, at/the Seven Stars in Talbot-Court, in Grace-Church-Street,/MDCCIV./

Octavo; [i—iv], 1—440; A—Dd^8, Ee^6. Title-page boxed in double rule.

Page 440 contains advs. of books sold by J. How. Adv.: *The Observator*, 24–28 June 1704. [DLC]

1706—/The/London-Spy/Compleat,/In Eighteen Parts./[—]/The First Volume of the Authors/Writings./[—]/The Third Edition./[—]/London,/Printed and Sold by J. How, at/the Seven Stars in Talbot-/Court, in Grace-Church-Street,/MDCCVI./

Octavo; [i—iv], 1—440, i—iv: advs.; A—Ee^8. Title-page boxed in double rule. [BM; MH]

1709—[The fourth edition.] J. How: London, 1709. [BM; CSH; ICN]

1718—/The London-Spy/Compleat,/In Eighteen Parts,/Being the/First Volume/Of The/ Writings/Of/Mr. Edward Ward./[—]/The Fifth Edition./[—]/London,/Printed for A. Bettesworth, at the Red-/Lion in Pater-Noster-Row, 1718./

Octavo; [i—iii], 1—439; A—Z^8, Aa—Dd^8, Ee^6. Title-page boxed in double rule.

See *Miscellanies,* vol. I. [CSH]

1924—/The/London-Spy/Compleat,/In Eighteen Parts/by/Ned Ward/[—]/With an Introduction by/Ralph Straus/[—]/London,/Published and Sold by The/Casanova Society, in Tooks/Court, in Cursitor Street,/MCMXXIV./

1927—The London Spy; the vanities and vices of the town exposed to view. . . . A. L. Hayward: London, 1927.

The London Terraefilius

Number I

1707—/The/London Terraefilius:/Or, The/Satyrical Reformer./Being/Drolling Reflections on the Vices and Vanities/Of/Both Sexes./[—]/To be Continu'd./[—]/By the Author of the London-Spy./[—]/Numb. I./[—]/London Printed for J. How, in Talbot Court, in/Grace Church-Street; and G. Sawbridge, in Little-/Britain; and Sold at the Publishing-Office,/in Bearbinder-Lane, 1707. Price 6d./

Octavo; 1—32; A—D^4. Title-page boxed in double rule.

Listed in the *Term Catalogues,* July 1707. [BM; CtY]

Number II

1707—[Identical with Number I:]/London Printed and Sold at the Publishing-/Office, in Bearbinder-Lane, 1707. Price 6d./Where Number I. is to be had, at the same Price./

Octavo; 1—40; A—E^4. Title-page boxed in double rule.

The second number was issued a week later. Listed in the *Term Catalogues,* July 1707. [BM; CtY]

Number III

1707—[Identical with Number I:]/London Printed and Sold at the Publishing-/Office, in Bearbinder-Lane, 1707. Price 6d./Where Number I. and II. are to be had, at the same Price./

Octavo; 1—40; A—E⁴. Title-page boxed in double rule. [BM; CtY]

Number IV

1707—[Identical with Number I to:]/London Printed, and Sold by B. Bragge, at the/Raven in Pater-Noster-Row; and S. Bunchley,/at the Publishing-Office, in Bearbinder-Lane,/1707./Where Number I. II. and III. is to be had./

Octavo; 1—40; A—E⁴. Title-page boxed in double rule.

Listed in the *Term Catalogues*, November 1707. [BM; CtY]

Number V

1708—[Identical with Number I to:]/London Printed, and Sold by B. Bragge, at the Raven in Pater-/noster-Row; where the former numbers are to be had at 6d./each. Also Hudibras Redivivus Compleat, or Single ones./ As likewise, The Diverting Muse, the Five first Numbers:/Number Six is in the Press, and will be speedily Published, 1708./

Octavo; 1—40; A—E⁴. Title-page boxed in double rule. [BM; CtY]

Number VI

1708—[Identical with Number I to:]/London Printed, and Sold by John Morphew, near Stationers-/Hall; where the former numbers are to be had at 6d. each./Also Hudibras Redivivus, Compleat, or Singles. Like-wise,/The Diverting Muse, in Six Parts; or any Single Part/thereof; every distinct Part of any of the Books aforemen-/tion'd at the Price of Six-Pence each, 1708./

Octavo; 1—32; A—D⁴. Title-page boxed in double rule. [CtY]

A collection of the six numbers of *The London Terraefilius* with cancelled title-pages together with *The Diverting Muse* make up *The Fourth Volume of the Writings* (1709).

Lord Whiglove's Elegy

1715—/[Two heavy bars across page]/The/Lord Whiglove's/Elegy:/To which is added/A Pious Epitaph upon the Late/Bishop of Addlebury./ Octavo; 1—8; A⁴. Dropped head.

Bottom of p. 8:/London,/Printed in the Year, 1715./Price Two-pence./ Included in *A Collection of Historical and State Poems* (1717).

Marriage Dialogues

1708—Marriage Dialogues; or, a Poetical Peep into the State of Matrimony; containing, A Dialogue between a pert Lady, and her Spouse, concerning superiority in Wedlock. Between a termagant Court Lady, and her 'Spouse, about settling in the Country. Between a fond Gentleman, and his coaxing Lady. Between a City-Termagant and her Mechanick 'Spouse. Between a happy Pair, concerning the Comforts of mutual Fidelity, and the innocent Pleasures of a retir'd Life. Between a young Libertine, and an old canting rich Widow, he had marry'd for her Money. With moral Reflextions on every Dialogue. To which are added, The Wars of the Elements; or, a Description of a Sea-Storm. The contemplative Angler, In Vino Veritas; or, The Tipling Philosophers. A New Riddle for the Ladies. A Natural Song after a natural folly. The taunting Reprimand of a young Wife, to an old jealous Husband. A Punch-Bowl Song. With several other diverting Poems. By the Author of the London-Spy. Sold by J. Woodward, A. Bettesworth, and J. Morphew.

Issued in September: *The History of the Works of the Learned,* September 1708. Adv.; *The Observator,* 18–22 September, 1708. This was the first edition of the *Dialogues.* The six dialogues here listed were incorporated in *Nuptial Dialogues.*

1709—[Another edition.] J. Woodward: London, 1709.
    Octavo. [BM]

1710—/Nuptial/Dialogues and Debates:/Or, an/Useful Prospect/Of The/ Felicities and Discomforts/Of A/Marry'd Life,/Incident to all Degrees, from the Throne/to the Cottage./Containing/[Description of contents]/ [—]/In Two Volumes./[—]/By the Author of the London-Spy./[—]/ [Quotation]/[—]/London Printed by A. Meere, for T. Norris at the Looking-/Glass, and A. Bettesworth at the Red-Lyon, both on/London Bridge; and Sold by J. Woodward in St. Chri-/stopher's Church-Yard, behind the Royal Exchange. 1710./(Price Bound Ten Shillings)/
    Octavo; [cut], [i—xvi], 1—396 (i.e., 400; pp. 353 to end misnumbered); A—Cc⁸. Title-page boxed in double rule. [BM; CSH; CtY; ICN; MH]

Volume II

1710—[Title-page identical with the above save for "The Second Volume."]
    Octavo; [i—iv], 1—432; A², B—Ee⁸. Title-page boxed in double rule.

    Volume II contains the following errors in pagination: 130–131 misnumbered 114–115; 134–135 misnumbered 118–119; 138–139 misnumbered 122–123; 141–142 misnumbered 127–128. See also *Female Policy Detected* (1828). [BM; CtY; ICN; CN; MH]

1711—[Another edition.]
    Listed in the *Term Catalogues,* May 1711.

Volume I

1723—/Nuptial/Dialogues and Debates:/Or, an Useful Prospect of the/ Felicities and Discomforts/Of A/Marry'd Life,/Incident to all Degrees, from the/Throne to the Cottage./Containing/[Description of contents]/ [—]/In Two Volumes./[—]/By the Author of the London-Spy/[—]/ [Six lines of verse]/[—]/London, Printed for T. Norris at the Looking-Glass on London-/Bridge: A. Bettesworth at the Red-Lyon in Pater-Noster-/Row: and F. Fayrham at the South Entrance of the Royal-/ Exchange. 1723./
    Duodecimo; [i—xx], 1—292; A¹⁰, B—N¹², O². Title-page boxed in double rule. [BM; CSH; DLC]

Volume II

1723—[Title-page identical with Volume I save for "The Second Volume."]
    Duodecimo; [i—iv], 1—296; A², B—N¹², O⁴. Title-page boxed in double rule. [BM; DLC]

Volume I

1737—[The third edition.]
    Duodecimo. [BM]

Volume II

1737—/Nuptial/Dialogues and Debates:/Or, An Useful Prospect of the/ Felicities and Discomforts/Of A/Married Life;/Incident to all Degrees, from the Throne/to the Cottage./Containing/[Description of Contents]/ [—]/The Second Volume/[—]/By Edward Ward,/Author of the London-Spy./[—]/The Third Edition, adorn'd with Cuts./[—]/[Quotation]/[—]/London: Printed for Messieurs Bettesworth and Hitch,/ Ware, and Osborn, in Pater-Noster-Row; Hodges, on/London-Bridge; Baily, in Mitre-Court, Fleetstreet; and/Cummins, at the Royal-Exchange, 1737./
    Duodecimo; [i—iv], 1—296; A², B—N¹², O⁴. Title-page boxed in double rule. [BM; DLC]

1759—/Nuptial/Dialogues and Debates:/Or, an Useful Prospect of the/Felicities and Discomforts/of a/Marryd Life,/Incident to all Degrees, from the/Throne to the Cottage./Containing/[description of contents]/[—]/ In Two Volumes:/[—]/By Edward Ward, Author of the London Spy./ [—]/The Fourth Edition, Corrected./[—]/[six lines of verse]/[—]/ London:/Printed for C. Hitch and L. Hawes, R. Baldwin,/S. Crowder and Co. J. Wren, P. Davey and B. Law,/C. Ware, and J. Hope. MDCCLIX./

Duodecimo; [i—xx], 1—292; A10, B—N12, O2. [CSH (Volume I only)]

Mars Stript of His Armour

1708—/Mars Stript of his Armour:/Or, The/Army/Display'd in all its True Colours./Containing the Characters of/[List of characters separated by rule]/[—]/By the Author of the Wooden World/Dissected./[—]/ [—]/London:/Printed for H. Serjeant, at the Black Swan, without/ Temple-Bar./Price, One Shilling, (stitch'd)./Of/Whom May be Had,/ The Wooden World Dissected: or, The Character of/a Ship of War and all its Officers, from the Captain/to the Common Sailor./Price One Shilling, (stitch'd)./

Octavo; [i—viii]; 1—72; A—K4. Title-page boxed in double rule. Issued in October: *The History of the Works of the Learned,* October 1708. Adv.: *The Observator,* 30 October to 3 November 1708. The publishers are given as J. Woodward and B. Bragge. The book was apparently issued with individual title-pages by different publishers. For ascription to Ward, see *The Wooden World Dissected* (1708). See also Chapter VIII. [DLC; NN; TxU]

1709—/Mars stript of his Armour:/Or, The/Army/Display'd in all its true Colours./Containing the characters of/[List of characters separated by rule]/[—]/By a Lover of the Mathematicks/[—]/London, Printed: And Sold by J. Woodward/in St. Christopher's Church-Yard, near the/ Royal Exchange; and B. Bragge in Pater-/Noster-Row. 1709./

Duodecimo; [i—xii]; 1—108; A—K6. Title-page boxed in double rule.

Adv.: *The Observator,* 21–25 May 1709. The publishers are given as B. Bragge, J. Woodward, and A. Bettesworth. [BM; MH]

1709—/[—]/Mars stript of his Armour: Or, the Army/Display'd in all its true Colours./Containing the characters of/[List of characters]/[—]/ By a Lover of the Mathematicks./[—]/

Octavo; 1—16; A8. Dropped head.

Bottom of p. 16: "London, Printed by J. Read, near Fleet street, 1709." [BM; TxU]

[1710]—/Mars stript of his Armour:/Or, The/Army/Display'd in all its True Colours./Containing the Characters of/[List of characters separated by rule]/[—]/The Second Edition./[—]/By a Lover of the Mathematicks./[—]/London,/Printed for J. Collyer, in Ivy-Lane, Pater-noster-Row;/F. and J. Noble, in St. Martin's Court, near Leicester-/fields; J. Wren; over against St. John's Church in Harsly-/down; and sold at the Pamphlet-Shops of London/and Westminster./(Price 1 s. stitch'd.)/

Octavo; [i—viii], 1—76; A—K4, L2. [NN]

1779—/Mars stript of his Armour:/Or, The/Army/Display'd in all its True Colours./Containing the character of/[List of characters separated by rule]/[—]/The Third Edition./[—]/By a Lover of the Mathematicks./ [—]/Edinburgh./Printed in the Year MDCCLXXIX./

Duodecimo; 1—84; [A], A—F⁶, G⁵.

See the *BMC* for another 1779 Edinburgh edition. [NN]

The Merry Travellers

Part I

1721—/The/Merry Travellers:/Or,/A Trip upon Ten-Toes,/From/Moor-/fields to Bromley./An Humorous Poem./Intended as the Wandering/Spy./[—]/Part I./[—]/By the Author of the Cavalcade./[—]/[Quota-/tion]/[—]/London:/Printed by W. Downing, and Sold by the Book-/sellers of London and Westminster. 1721./Also to be had at the Bacchus-/Tavern in Moorfields./Price One Shilling./

Octavo; [i—ii], 1—82 (i.e., 86; pp. 14, 15, 16, and 17 are inserted in duplicate); A—B⁴, C², C—K⁴, L² (E missigned F). Title-page boxed in double rule.

"By the Author of the Cavalcade" is a reference to *The Republican Procession* (1714). [TxU]

[1722]—[Another edition.] Octavo; 1—78; A²⁻⁴, B—K⁴. Title-page miss-/ing. [MH]

1723—/The/Wandering Spy:/Or, The/Merry Travellers./A/Trip upon Ten-/Toes,/From/Moorfields to Bromley./An/Humorous Poem./[—]/The/Third Edition./[—]/Part I./[—]/By the Author of the Cavalcade./[—]/[Quotation]/[—]/London: Printed for Sam. Briscoe, at the/Bell-/Savage on Ludgate hill; also at the Sun a-/gainst John's Coffee-House in/Swithen's Alley, in/Cornhill. 1723. (Price One Shilling.)/Where may be had the Second Part of the Wan-/dering Spy./

Octavo; 1—56; A—G⁴. [DLC]

Part II

1722—/The Wand'ring Spy:/Or, The/Merry Travellers./[—]/Part II./[—]/To which is added,/The Contending Candidates:/Or, The/Broom-staff/Battles, dirty Skirmishes,/and other Comical Humours of the South-/wark Election./[—]/By the Author of the Cavalcade./[—]/London/Printed: And are to be Sold by A. Bettesworth/and J. Batley in Pater-/noster-Row, J. Nook/against St. Dunstan's Church, Fleetstreet; S. Bris-/coe at the Bell-Savage Inn upon Ludgate-Hill;/M. Hotham upon Lon-/don-Bridge; and at the/Bacchus Tavern in Finsbury, against the middle/of Middle-Moorfields. Where also may be had/most of the same Author's/Writings. MDCCXXII./Price 1 s. 6 d./

Octavo; [i—ii], 1—72 (i.e., pp. 70; pp. 4 to end misnumbered); 1—40; A—I⁴, A—E⁴. Title-page boxed in double rule.

Adv.: *The Weekly Journal or Saturday Post*, 1 September 1722. [BM; CtY; MH]

1724—The Wandering Spy; or, the Merry Observator, etc. 6 pts. London, 1724.

Octavo.

This is sometimes listed as Volume VI of the *Miscellanies*. See W. T. Lowndes, *Bibliographer's Manual*. [BM]

The Metamorphos'd Beau

1700—/The/Metamorphos'd Beau:/Or, The/Intrigues/Of/Ludgate./[—]/[Ornament]/[—]/London, Printed by J. How, in the Ram-Head-Inn-/Yard in/Fanchurch-street, 1700./

Folio; 1—16; A—D². Title-page boxed in double rule.

Issued in March 1700: see the verso of the title-page, *The London*

Spy, vol. II, pts. i-v, where it is listed as one of Ward's works. [CSH; MH]

1703—[An edition.] J. How.
    Adv.: *The Observator,* 22–25 December 1703.

Miscellanies

During the years 1717–18 the earlier volumes of *The Writings* were reprinted with new title-pages by A. Bettesworth under the general title of *Miscellanies.* Compare the description of volumes below with the volumes listed under *The Writings.*

Volume I

Volume I of *The Miscellaneous Writings in Verse and Prose* was the fifth edition of *The London Spy.* See the 1718 edition of *The London Spy.*

Volume II

1717—See *The Writings,* vol. II, the fifth edition.

[1717]—/Miscellaneous Writings,/In/Verse and Prose,/Both/Serious and Comical./Containing/Twenty One excellent Poems upon/very diverting Subjects./Also/Several pleasant Letters upon various Oc-/casions, both in Town and Country./With merry Observations and Predictions upon eve-/ry Month, and every remarkable Day through-/out the Year./[—]/By Mr. Edward Ward./[—]/Vol. II./The Third Edition./[—]/London:/Printed, and Sold by A. Bettesworth and C./Hitch, at the Red Lion in Pater-Noster-Row./

Octavo; [i—viii], 1—376 (4 pp. adv.); A^4, B—Aa^8, Bb^4.

This volume is a reprint with new title-page of the 1703 edition of *The Writings,* vol. II, rather than that of the above. Its description as "The Third Edition" probably refers to the fact that it is a third issue of the *Miscellanies* series, vol. II. I have not been able to locate a corresponding "Second Edition." [DLC]

Volume III

1718—/Miscellaneous Writings,/In/Verse and Prose,/Both/Serious and Comical./Containing/Twenty-One excellent Poems upon/very diverting Subjects./Also/Several pleasant Letters upon various Oc-/casions, both in Town and Country./With Merry Observations and Predictions upon/every Month, and every Remarkable Day/throughout the Year./[—]/By Mr. Edward Ward./[—]/Vol. III./[—]/The Third Edition./[—]/London:/Printed by W. D. and Sold by A. Bettes-/worth at the Red-Lyon in Pater-noster-Row./MDCCXVIII./

Octavo; [i—xvi], 1—336; 1—40; 49—106; A—Y^8; A^4, B^4, B^8, C^4, H—O^4, P^1. Title-page boxed in double rule.

Contents of Volume III of *Miscellaneous Writings* corresponds to Volume III of *The Writings,* plus the following items: *T. B——'s Lost Letter to His Witty Companions; From a Gentleman in London to a Friend in the Country; From a Reserv'd Gentleman to His Extravagant Kinsman; The Young Libertine's Answer; From a High-Church Chapman to a Low-Church Trader; The Low-Churchman's Answer; From a Moorfield's Conjurer to a Country Astrologer; Merry Observations upon every Remarkable Day in the Year.* [CtY; DLC]

Volume IV

See *The Fourth Volume of the Writings by the author of* The London Spy (1709). There is no evidence that Volume IV was reprinted in the general series of *Miscellanies* issued in 1717–18. No copies appear in any of the libraries available to the author; Dobell lists no edition of Volume IV.

Volume V

1717—/A/Collection/Of/Historical and State Poems,/Satyrs, Songs, and Epigrams./Being the Fifth Volume of/Miscellanies./[—]/By the Author of the London-Spy./[—]/[Contents in double column separated by rule]/[—]/[Ornaments]/[—]/London printed in the Year 1717./ And Sold by A. Bettesworth at the Red-Lyon/in Paternoster-Row./Where also may be had most of this Author's Writings./

Octavo; [i—viii]; 3—43; [i—ii]; 3—36; 1—8; 3—32; 1—38 (pp. 26, 27, 30 misnumbered 50, 51, 54); [i], 1—13 (pp. in duplicate); 1—46; 3—40; 3—40; 3—40; 3—15; [i—ii], 5—24; A$^{2-4}$; A$^{2-4}$ B—E^{4}F^2; A$^{2-4}$ B—D^{4}E^2; A^4; A$^{2-4}$ B—D^4; A$^{2-4}$ B—E^4; A$^{2-4}$ B—D^4; B—F^4 G^3; A$^{2-4}$ B—E^4; A$^{2-4}$ B—E^4; A$^{2-4}$ B—E^4; A$^{2-4}$ B—E^4; A$^{2-4}$ B—E^4; A$^{2-3}$ B—C^4. Title-page boxed in double rule.

This represents a collection of remainders with cancelled title-pages. The contents include items listed below plus five numbers of *The Poetical Entertainer* (1712–13): *The Republican Procession; The Hudibrastick Brewer; The Lord Whiglove's Elegy; An Epitaph on the Late Bishop of ——; St. Paul's Church; The British Wonders; Rustica Academiae Oxoniensis; The Vanity of Upstarts; The Tory Quaker.* [BM; CtY; ICN; MH (Of the two copies at MH one is identical with the above, save that the original title-pages have not been cancelled; the other varies from the above in *The British Wonders* (1717), the edition incorporated here numbering in pages 1—62, signatures A$^{2-4}$ B—H^4); TxU]

Volume VI

See *The Merry Travellers* (1724).

Modern Religion

1699—/Modern Religion/And/Ancient Loyalty:/A/Dialogue./[—]/[Ornament]/[—]/London, Printed in the Year 1699./

Folio; 1—16; A—D^2. Title-page boxed in double rule.

Issued in March 1699: see the verso of the title-page, *The London Spy,* vol. I, pt. v. Included in *A Collection of the Writings, Hitherto Extant* (1700). Reprinted in *The Second Volume of the Writings* (1703). [BM; CSH; DLC; NNC; TxU]

The Modern World Disrob'd

1708—/The/Modern World/Disrob'd:/Or,/Both Sexes/Stript of their pretended/Vertue./[—]/In Two Parts./[—]/First, Of The Ladies./Secondly, of the Gentlemen./With/Familiar Descant upon every/Character./[—]/[Quotation]/[—]/London, Printed for G. S. and sold by/J. Woodward, in St. Christopher's Church-Yard in/Threadneedle-Street, near Stocks-Market. 1708./

Octavo; [i—xii], 1—224; A^4, a^2, B—P^8. Title-page boxed in double rule.

The Observator, 1–5 May 1708, lists this as "by the Author of the London Spy," published by J. Baker, J. Morphew, and J. Woodward. *The History of the Works of the Learned,* April 1708, lists it as a publication of that month by J. Morphew. Copies with separate title-pages were apparently issued simultaneously by different publishers. [BM; DLC; MH]

[1710]—Adam and Eve stript of their furbelows: or, the fashionable virtues and vices of both sexes expos'd to public view. . . . The second edition [of the Modern World Disrob'd]. A Bettesworth: London, [1710].

Octavo; pp. 224. [BM]

1714—[Another edition.] J. Woodward: London, 1714.

Octavo; pp. 224. [BM]

1720—Die von ihren Feigen-Blättern entblösseten Adam und Eva . . . Nach dem Englischen Exemplar. 1720.

Octavo. [BM]

The Mourning Prophet

1714—/The/Mourning Prophet:/Or,/Drooping Faction Reviv'd,/ By the Death of/Queen Anne./A/Poem./[—]/By E. W./[—]/London,/Printed for J. Woodward in Scalding-Alley,/ by Stocks-Market, 1714./(Price Three-Pence)/

Quarto; 1—16; A—D².

Adv.: *The Weekly Pacquet*, 20–27 March 1714. Price 3 d. The *BMC* lists a 1714 copy in octavo. [BM; ICN; TxU]

News from Madrid

1726—/News from Madrid./[—]/The/Spanish Beauty:/Or, The/Tragicomical Revenge./Interspers'd with the Humours of a/Merry Tinker, in conveying off the/Bodies of Three murder'd Fryars./[Band of printers' ornaments]/A Poem. By Ed. Ward./[Quotation]/[Band of printers' ornaments]/London:/Printed for the Author, and Sold by A. Bettesworth/ at the Red-Lyon in Pater-noster-Row. MDCCXXVI./Price One Shilling./

Octavo; 1—56; A—G⁴ (A² missigned B). [MH; TxU]

The Northern Cuckold

1721—/The/Northern Cuckold/Or, The/Gardenhouse/Intrigue/[—]/[Ornament]/[—]/London:/Printed in the Year MDCCXXL./

Octavo; [i—ii], 1—28 (blank leaf); A—D⁴. Title-page boxed in double rule.

See edition below. [BM; CSH; MH]

1721—[Another edition.] With an addition to the Delights of the Bottle; or, the compleat vintner . . . With the South-Sea Song . . . as likewise the Spittle-Fields Ballad on the Calicos. By the author of the Cavalcade. 3 pts. London, 1721.

Duodecimo.

Adv.: *The Weekly Journal*, 8 April 1721; the publisher is given as Sam Briscoe. Each part is separately paged; pt. II has a separate title-page. "By the author of the Cavalcade" is a reference to *The Republican Procession*. [BM]

Nuptial Dialogues and Debates

See under *Marriage Dialogues*.

Pacquet from Will's

1705—/The/Second Volume/of the/Works/of Monsieur Voiture,/Containing His Familiar/Letters/To/Gentlemen and Ladies./Made English by/[List including John Dryden, Thomas Cheek, Henry Cromwell, John Savil, John Dennis, Thomas Seymour, Mr. Atkins, Captain Barker, Thomas Brown]/To which is added,/A Pacquet from Wills: Or, a/new Collection of Original Letters on several/Subjects/[—]/The Second Edition, with Additions./[—]/London:/Printed for Sam. Briscoe, and sold by John Nutt near/Stationer's-Hall, 1705./

Octavo; i—viii, 1—134 (i.e., 144; pp. 129 to end misnumbered), 159—

234, 1—64, 224—239; A⁴, B—K⁸; M—P⁸, Q⁴, A²⁻³; Bb—Ee⁸, Ff⁴, Qq⁴. Title-page boxed in double rule.

Adv.: *Mercurious Politicus*, 22–25 September 1705. This is the earliest copy I have been able to locate of *A Pacquet from Wills*, to which Ward contributed four letters. The first edition of *The Second Volume of the Works of Monsieur Voiture* apparently appeared in 1701 (See Benjamin Boyce, *Tom Brown of Facetious Memory*, "Bibliography," p. 196) and in the earlier edition already included *A Pacquet from Wills*. The *Letters* and *Works* of Voiture were reprinted in various editions between 1699 and 1724. [MH]

1724—/Familiar Letters/Of/Love, Gallantry,/and several other/Occasions:/ By the/Wits of the last and present Age./viz./[List of writers in double column, separated by rule]/From their Originals./With their Effiges curiously Engraved by the/Best Masters./In Two Volumes./[—]/The Sixth Edition, with additions, Corrected./[—]/London:/Printed for Sam Briscoe, at the Bell-Savage on/Ludgate-Hill. 1724./

Duodecimo; [i—x], 1—256; [A], A⁴, B—L¹², M⁸. Title-page boxed in double rule. [MH]

1724—/The Second Volume/Of/Familiar Letters/Of/Love, Gallantry,/and several other/Occasions:/By The/Wits of the last and present Age./With The/Best of Voiture's Letters,/Translated by Mr. Dryden, and Mr. Tho./ Brown./[—]/London:/Printed for Sam. Briscoe, at the Bell-Sa-/vage on Ludgate-Hill, 1724./

Duodecimo; [i—xiv], 1—360; [A], A⁶, B—Q¹². Title-page boxed in double rule.

An earlier two-volume edition was advertised in *The Weekly Journal or Saturday's Post*, 10 May 1718. [MH]

The 1705 edition contains four letters acknowledged as "by Mr. Ward":

1. *A letter from Tunbridge, to a Friend in London: Being a Character of the Wells, and Company There;* 2. *A Letter of Advice from an Old Experienced City-Leacher, to his Daughter at the Boarding-School, being Rules to Raise her Fortune;* 3. *A Letter from an Enamour'd Beau, to a very Beautiful Lady, upon his Seeing her Make Exit from that Odoriferous Treasury of Human Superfluities, the House of O——;* 4. *A Comical Love-Voyage to Hampton Court, Written in a Letter to a Friend at the Bath.*

The edition of 1724 omits number four above but assigns to Ward three of the anonymous letters included in the 1705 edition, as follows:

1. *A Letter of News to Sir D. Clark; being an Account of Darien, Bear-Garden, Epsom-Wells, and Mile's Musick-House, or Sadler's Wells, at Islington;* 2. *From a Lady at the Bath, to H—— B—— Esq; in London;* 3. *A Love-Letter from a Gentleman to a Crooked Lady, etc.*

The Parish Gutt'lers

1722—/The/Parish Gutt'lers:/Or,/The Humours of a/Select Vestry./[—]/ [Quotation]/[—]/London:/Printed in the Year MDCCXXII./

Octavo; 1—64; A—H⁴. Title-page boxed in double rule.

First attributed to Ward by W. T. Lowndes, *Bibliographers' Manual*. For a discussion of the probabilities for Ward's authorship, see Chapter X of the text. [MH; TxU]

The Poetical Entertainer

Number I

1712—/The Poetical Entertainer:/Or,/Tales,/Satyrs,/Dialogues,/and/In-
trigues, etc./Serious and Comical./All digested into such Verse as most
agree-/able to the Several Subjects./[—]/To be publish'd as often as
occasion shall offer./[—]/Numb. I./[—]/London/Printed: And sold
by J. Morphew near/Stationer's-Hall. MDCCXII./Price 6d./

Octavo; [i—ii], 1—46; A, B—F⁴, G³. Title-page boxed in double rule.
Adv.: *The Spectator*, 23 July 1712. [CtY; MH]

Number II

1712—/The Poetical Entertainer:/Or,/Tales,/Satyrs,/Intrigues, etc./Contain-
ing,/[List of five titles]/[—]/To be publish'd as often as occasion shall
offer./[—]/Numb. II./[—]/London/Printed: And Sold by J. Morphew
near/Stationer's-Hall. MDCCXII./Price 6d./

Octavo; 1—40; A—E⁴. Title-page boxed in double rule. [CtY; MH
(MH copy lacks B² and B³)]

Number III

1712—[Identical with Number II to:]/Containing,/List of seven titles]/
To be publish'd as often as occasion shall offer./[—]/Numb. III./[—]/
London/Printed: and Sold by J. Woodward in Scalding-/Ally, against
Stocks-Market; and J. Morphew/near Stationer's-Hall. MDCCXII./

Octavo; 1—40; A—E⁴. Title-page boxed in double rule.
Adv.: *The Spectator*, 21 October 1712. [CtY; MH (MH copy lacks D²
and D³, E² and E⁴)]

Number IV

1712—[Identical with Number II:]/List of twelve titles]/[—]/To be publish'd as often as occasion shall offer./[—]/Numb. IV./

Octavo; 1—40; A—E⁴. Title-page boxed in double rule. [CtY; MH
(MH copy lacks B³ and E⁴)]

Number V

1712—[Identical with Number II:]/[List of twenty titles]/[—]/To be publish'd as often as occasion shall offer./[—]/Numb. V./

Octavo; 1—40; A—E⁴. Title-page boxed in double rule. [CtY]
The five numbers of *The Poetical Entertainer* are included in *A Collection of Historical and State Poems* (1717). See under *Miscellanies*,
vol. V.

The Poet's Ramble after Riches

1691—/The/Poet's Ramble/After/Riches,/Or, A/Night's Transactions/Upon
the Road/Burlesqu'd;/With Reflections on a/Dissenting Corporation:/
Together,/With the Author's Lamentation, in the/time of Adversity./
[—]/Licensed and Enter'd according to Order./[—]/London,/Printed
by J. Millet, at the Angel in Little-Brittain, MDCXCI./

Quarto; 1—24; A—C⁴.
Listed in *Stationers' Register*, 15 September 1691. See 1699 edition
below, for ascription to Ward. [BM; CtY]

1692—[Another edition.] G. Conyers: London, 1692.
Listed in the *Term Catalogues*, June 1692.

1693—A Country-scuffle over a pot of Ale; with Reflections on a Dissenting
corporation; together with Poet's Lamentation in time of Adversity:
which may serve as Second Part to The Counter-scuffle. Printed for
G. Conyers.

Listed in the *Term Catalogues,* November 1693.

1698——/The/Poet's Ramble/After/Riches./With/Reflections/Upon A/Country Corporation./Also/The Author's Lamentation in the/Time of Adversity. /[——]/By the Author of The Trip to Jamaica./[Ornament]/London, Printed for J. Nutt, near Stationers-Hall, 1698./

Folio; 1——20; A—E². Title-page boxed in double rule. [BM; CSH]

1699——/The/Poet's Ramble/After Riches./With/Reflections/Upon A/Country Corporation./Also/The Author's Lamentation in the/Time of Adversity. /[——]/The Second Edition/[——]/By the Author of The Trip to Jamaica. /[——]/[Ornament]/[——]/London, Printed and Sold by J. How, in the Ram-Head-Inn-Yard,/in Fenchurch-Street, 1699./

Folio; [1–2], 5–16 (i.e., 16; pp. 3 to end misnumbered); A—D². Title-page boxed in double rule.

J. How became Ward's publisher in May 1699. In describing the above as "The Second Edition" he obviously does not allow for any editions prior to 1698. [DLC]

1701——/The/Poet's   Ramble/After/Riches:/With/Reflections/Upon/A/Country Corporation./Also/The Author's Lamentation/in the/Time of Adversity./[——]/By the Author of the Trip to Jamaica./[——]/The Third Edition./[——]/[Ornament]/[——]/London,/Printed and Sold by J. How, in the Ram-Head-Inn-Yard, in Fanchurch-street, 1701./

Folio; 1——16; A—D². Title-page boxed in double rule.

Included in *A Collection of the Writings, Hitherto Extant* (1701). [BM; CSH; MHi; NNC]

1710——/The/Poet's Ramble/After/Riches./With/Reflections/Upon A/Country Corporation./Also/The Author's Lamentation in/the Time of Adversity. /[——]/London:/Printed and Sold by J. How, in Talbot-/Court, in Grace-Church-Street, 1710./Price Three Pence./

Octavo; 1——20; A—B⁴, C².

BMC lists an edition: London, [1710?] pp. 19. Duodecimo. [ICN; MH]

[1720]——/The/Poet's/Ramble/After/Riches/A/Poem./[——]/By the Author of the London Spy./[——]/[——]/Dublin:/ Printed, at the Rein Deer in Montrath/Street, by C. Hicks/

Octavo; 1——16; [A⁸]. [BM; CtY]

The Quack-Vintners

1712——/The/Quack-Vintners:/Or, A/Satyr/Against/Bad Wine./With/Directions where to have Good./[——]/Inscrib'd to B——ks and H——r/[Quotation]/[——]/Sold by the Booksellers of London and/Westminster. 1712./

Octavo; 1——24; A—C⁴.

According to *Brooke and Hellier, a Satyr* (London, 1712) Ward was hired to write *The Quack-Vintners* by Brooke and Hellier. [BM; CtY; MH; TxU]

The Rambling Fuddle-Caps

1706——The Rambling Fuddle-Caps: Or, a Tavern Struggle for a Kiss. Price 6 d. Sold by B. Bragge at the Black Raven in Pater-Noster-Row.

Adv.: *The Daily Courant,* 12 March 1706.

1709——/The Rambling/Fuddle-Caps:/Or, A/Tavern-Struggle/For A/Kiss./ [——]/By the Author of Hudibras Redivivus./[——]/[Ornaments]/[——]/ London./Printed and Sold by H. Hills, in Black-fryars near/the Waterside. 1709./

Octavo; 1—16; A⁸.

This was a pirated edition. The poem appears appended to the fourth edition of *Hudibras Redivivus* and is included in *A Collection of the Best English Poetry*. [BM; CtY; ICN; MH; NN; TxU]

The Rambling Rakes

1700—/The Rambling Rakes:/Or,/The London Libertines./[—]/By the Author of The Step to the Bath./[—]/[Ornament]/[—]/London,/Printed and Sold by J. How, in the Ram-Head-Inn-Yard,/in Fanchurch-street, 1700./

Folio; 1—16; A—D². Title-page boxed in double rule.

Issued in September: *The History of the Works of the Learned,* September 1700. Listed as a Ward item on the verso of the title-page, *A Step to Stir-Bitch-Fair* (1700). [BM; CSH; TxU]

O Raree-Show

1698—O Raree-Show, O Pretty-Show or the City-Feast. London.

Broadside.

Issued before December 1698: advertised on the verso of the title-page, *The London Spy,* vol. I, pt. II. Reprinted in *The Second Volume of the Writings* (1703). Reprinted in *Poems On Affairs of State, From the Year 1640 to the Year 1704,* 2nd edition (London, 1716), vol. III. [NNC]

The Reformer

1700—The Reformer. Exposing the Vices of the Age: In several Characters. viz. 1. The Vitious Courtier. 2. The Debauch'd Parson. 3. The Factious Hypocrite. 4. The Precise Quaker. 5. The Covetous Miser. 6. The Prodigal Son. 7. The City Letcher. 8. The Insatiate Wife. 9. The Amorous Maid. 10. The Beau Apprentice. 11. The City Mob. 12. The Country Squire. London, 1700.

Duodecimo.

Issued in August: *The History of the Works of the Learned,* August 1700. Adv.: *The Observator,* 29 April 1702, as sold by J. How. Listed in the *Term Catalogues,* November 1700. Listed as a Ward item on the verso of the title-page, *The Rambling Rakes* (1700); *A Step to Stir-Bitch-Fair* (1700); *The Revels of the Gods* (1701). [BM]

The Republican Procession

1714—/The/Republican/Procession;/Or, The/Tumultuous Cavalcade./A Merry/Poem./[Ornament]/Printed in the Year 1714./

Octavo; 1—44; A—E⁴, F².

Included in *A Collection of Historical and State Poems* (1717). [BM; CSH; MH]

1714—/The/Republican/Procession;/Or, The/Tumultuous Cavalcade./A Merry/Poem./[—]/The Second Impression, with Additional/Characters./ [—]/[Ornament]/[—]/Printed in the Year MDCCXIV./

Octavo; 1—44; A—E⁴, F².

The text is identical with the above. [BM; CtY; MH; NN (NN contains another copy, identical but in different type); NNC]

1727—/The/Republican Procession,/Or, The/Tumultuous Cavalcade;/An Hudibrastick Poem./To Which is added,/An Answer/By the same Author;/Being a Satyr against Himself./[—]/London:/Printed; and are to be Sold by the Booksellers/of London and Westminster. MDCCXXVII./ Price one Shilling./

Octavo; 1—48; A—F⁴. Title-page boxed in double rule. [BM ("An Answer" is missing in the BM, MH, and TxU copies); MH; TxU]

1730—Another edition.

See *The Wars of the Elements* (1730).

The Revels of the Gods

1701—/The/Revels/Of The/Gods:/Or, A/Ramble/Thro' The/Heavens./ [—]/By the Author of the Trip to Jamaica./[—]/[Ornament]/[—]/ London, Printed and Sold by J. How, in the Ram-Head-/Inn-Yard, in Fanchurch-Street, 1701./

> Folio; 1—16; A—D². Title-page boxed in double rule.

> Issued in October: *The History of the Works of the Learned,* October 1701. Included in *A Collection of the Writings, Hitherto Extant* (1702). Reprinted in *The Second Volume of the Writings,* (1703). [CSH; MH; TxU]

The Rise and Fall of Madam Coming-Sir

1703—/The/Rise and Fall/Of/Madam Coming-Sir/Or, An/Unfortunate Slip/ From the/Tavern Bar/Into the/Surgeons Powdering Tub./[—]/By the Author of the London-Spy./[—]/[Ornament]/[—]/London, Printed and Sold by J. How, at the Seven-Stars, in Talbot-/Court, in Grace-Church-Street, 1703./

> Folio; 1—16; A—D². Title-page boxed in double rule.

> Adv.: *The Observator,* 16–20 October 1703. Reprinted in *The Second Volume of the Writings* (1703). [CSH]

Rustica Academiae Oxoniensis

See *A Seasonable Sketch of an Oxford Reformation.*

St. Paul's Church

1716—/St. Paul's Church;/Or, The/Protestant Ambulators./[—]/A Burlesque Poem./[—]/[Quotation]/[Ornament]/[—]/London:/Printed for John Morphew, near/Stationers-Hall, 1716. Price 6d./

> Octavo; 1—32; A—D⁴.

> Included in *A Collection of Historical and State Poems* (1717). [CtY; MH (MH has a copy, lacking the first eighteen pages, bound with the first four numbers of *The Poetical Entertainer.*)]

A Satyr Against Wine

1705—/A/Satyr/Against/Wine./With A Poem/In Praise of/Small Beer./ [—]/Written by a Gentleman in a Fever, occasion'd/by Hard Drinking./[—]/London,/Printed: And Sold by B. Bragg in Avemary-/Lane. 1705./

> Folio; 1—16; A—D².

> Issued in November: *The History of the Works of the Learned,* November 1704. Adv.: *The Observator,* 17 February 1705. Reprinted in *The Third Volume of the Writings* (1706). [MH]

Satyrical Reflections on Clubs

See under *The History of the London Clubs.*

The Satyrical Works of Titus Petronius Arbiter

1708—/The Satyrical/Works/Of/Titus Petronius Arbiter,/In Prose and Verse./[—]/In Three Parts./[—]/Together with his/Life and Character,/Written by Mons. St. Evremont;/And/A Key to the Satyr, by a Person of Quality./[—]/Made English by/[List in two columns]/and adorn'd with Cuts./[—]/To which is added,/The Charms of Liberty; a Poem, by the late/Duke of D——/[—]/London,/Printed for Sam Briscoe, and are to be Sold/by B. Bragg, at the Raven in Pater-noster-row, 1708./

Octavo; [i—xviii], i—xvi, [i—xiv], 1—288; A⁹, a⁸ b⁷, B—T⁸. Title-page boxed in double rule.

In "The Third Part of the Satyrical Works of Petronius Arbiter, containing Epigrams, Poems, and Satyrs. By several Hands" appear four items "by the Author of the London Spy": *That the Dog of Hell Was a Lawyer; On a Wife; Concerning our Choice in Marriage; The Rope Dancer.* [MH]

1709—/The/Charms/of/Liberty:/A/Poem,/[—]/By the late Duke of D——/ [—]/To which is added,/Epigrams./Poems and Satyrs./[—]/Written by several Hands./[—]/London:/Printed in the Year, MDCCIX./

Folio; 1—16; A⁸. Title-page boxed in double rule.

According to Dr. R. H. Griffith, this was a pirated edition by H. Hills. The "Epigrams, Poems and Satyrs" represent the "Third Part of the Satyrical Works of Petronius Arbiter" as above. [BM; TxU]

A Seasonable Sketch of an Oxford Reformation

1717—/A Seasonable Sketch/Of An/Oxford Reformation./[—]/Written Originally in Latin/By John Allibond, D D/[—]/And now Reprinted, with an English Version,/that the World may see what a hopeful Re-/gulation of the Two Universities, the Re-/publican Author of the Anatomy of the State,/and his Atheistical Abettors are driving at./[—]/ [Quotation]/[—]/London/Printed: And Sold by John Morphew near/ Stationer's-Hall. 1717./ Price 6d./

Octavo; [i—iii], [iv] in duplicate, 1—13 in duplicate; A—D⁴. Title-page boxed in double rule.

Included in *A Collection of Historical and State Poems* (1717). The text is in English and Latin. [BM; CtY]

1811—Rustica Academiae Oxoniensis nuper reformatae descriptio, etc. (A Rustical Description of the University of Oxford, lately reformed . . . Translation . . . by . . . E. Ward.) 1811. [BM]

The Secret History of the Calves-Head Club

1703—/The/Secret History/Of The/Calves-Head Club:/Or, The Republican/ Unmask'd./Wherein is fully shewn/The Religion of the Calves-Head Heroes'/in their Anniversary Thanksgiving Songs on the/Thirtieth of January, by them called/Anthems;/For the Years 1693, 1694, 1695, 1696, 1697./Now Publish'd,/To demonstrate the Restless, Implacable Spirit/of a certain Party still among us, who are never to/be satisfied till the present Establishment in Church/and State is subverted./[—]/ [Quotation: Virgil]/[—]/London,/Printed, and Sold by the Booksellers of London and/Westminster, 1703./

Quarto; 1—22; [A⁴], B—C², D³ (A² missigned B²).

Issued in February: *The History of the Works of the Learned,* February 1703. Attributed to Ward by Walter Wilson, *Memoirs of the Life and Times of Daniel De Foe* (1830). See Chapter VI of the text. [BM; CSH; CtY; MH; NNC]

1703—[Identical with the above to:]/[—]/The Second Edition/[—]/[Quotation: Virgil]/[—]/London,/Printed, and Sold by the Booksellers of London and/Westminster, 1703./

Quarto; 1—22; A⁴, B—C², D³. [BM; DLC; MH]

[1703]—[The third edition.]

I have been unable to locate a copy.

1704—/The/Secret History/of the/Calves-Head Club,/or the/Republican/un-masq'd;/Wherein is fully shewn/The Religion of the Calves-Head

Heroes,/In their Anniversary Thanksgiving Songs on the/Thirtieth of January, by them called/Anthems;/For the Years 1693, 1694, 1695, 1696, 1697,/Now Published,/To demonstrate the Restless, Implacable Spirit/of a certain Party still among us, who are never to/be satisfied till the present Establishment in Church/and State is subverted./[—]/The Fourth Edition with Additions, Corrected./[—]/Dedicated to the Observator./ [—]/London, Printed; and Sold by the Booksellers of/London and Westminster, 1704./[—]/Note, Miscelaneous Works written by his Grace George late Duke of/Buckingham, containing Poems, Satyrs, Letters, and his Speeches in/Parliament; with a Collection of Speeches by several Noble Peers and/Commoners in the Three last Reigns. Price 5 s./

Quarto; [i—viii], 5–24; [A⁴], B—E².

Adv.: *The Daily Courant,* February 1704. [ICN]

1705—/The Secret/History/Of The/Calves-Head Club, Complt./Or, The/ Republican Unmask'd./Wherein is fully shewn,/The Religion of the Calves-Head Heroes,/in their Anniversary Thanksgiving-Songs on/the Thirtieth of January, by them called/Anthems; for the Years 1693, 1694,/ 1695, 1696, 1697, 1698, 1699, etc. With/Reflections thereupon. Now Publish'd to demonstrate the restless, implacable Spirit/of a certain Party still among us, who are/never to be satisfied 'till the present Esta-/ blishment in Church and State is subverted./[—]/The Fifth Edition, with large Additions, Corrected./[—]/To which is annext, A Vindication of the Royal Martyr/King Charles I./Wherein are laid open,/The Republicans Mysteries of Rebellion./[—]/Written in the Time of the Usurpation, by/the Celebrated Mr. Butler, Author of Hudibras./[—]/ With/A Character of a Presbyterian; Written/by Sir John Denham, Knight./[—]/London, Printed; and Sold by the Booksellers of London and Westminster. 1705./

Octavo; [i—iv], 1—140 (advs.: pp. 139–140); A², B—S⁴, T².

Adv.: *The Daily Courant,* 2 March 1705. [BM; CtY; DLC; MH; NN]

1706—/The Secret/History/Of The/Calves-Head Club, Complt./Or, The/ Republican Unmask'd./[Description of contents as above]/[—]/The Sixth Edition, with large Improvements; and a/description of the Calves-Head-Club, curiously engrav'd/on a Copper-Plate./[—]/To which is annex'd,/[Items as above]/And the Character of a Modern Whig; or, The Republican in Fashion./[—]/London, Printed: and Sold by B. Bragge in/Avemary-Lane, and at the Raven in Pater-Noster-Row,/against Ivy-Lane, 1706./

Octavo; [i—iv], 1—104; [i—iv], 1—36; [i—ii], 37—46; [i—ii], 49—54; A², B—O⁴; Aa—Gg⁴, Hh².

BMC lists a sixth edition printed at Dublin, 1705. [BM; MH]

1707—/The Secret/History/Of The/Calves-Head Club, Compleat:/Or, The/ Republicans Unmask'd./[Description of contents as above]/[—]/The Sixth Edition,/With large Improvements; and a/description of the Calves-Head-Club, curiously engrav'd/on a Copper plate./[—]/To which is annex'd,/[Items as above]/[—]/London, Printed; and sold by B. Bragge, at the/Raven in Pater-Noster-Row, against Ivy-Lane, 1707./

Octavo; [cut], [i—iv], 1—138 (i.e., 134. Errors in pagination: 79–80 misnumbered 73–74; 83 to end, 87 to end, 91 to end, 95 to end misnumbered); [i—ii], 49—54 (i.e., 8 pages; 51 to end misnumbered); A², B—L⁴, M², N², O—S⁴, T; H⁴. Title-page boxed in double rule.

For original sixth edition see the above (1706). There is a slight variant here in title-page and in content, i.e., *An Appendix* to the *Continuation of the Secret History.* Adv.: *The Daily Courant,* 30 January 1706. [BM; CSH; CtY; MH]

1709—/The/Secret History/Of The/Calves-Head Club:/Or, The/Republican unmask'd/With a large Continuation, and an Appendix/to the History./ Wherein is fully shewn, The Religion of the Calves-/Head Heroes, in their Anniversary Thanksgiving-/Songs on the XXXth of January, by them called/Anthems, with Reflections thereupon./[—]/The Seventh Edition, with large Improvements;/and a Description of the Calves-Head Club, and the/Effigies of Oliver Cromwel and his Cabinet Coun-/cil; curiously engrav'd on Copper Plates./[—]/To which is annexed/[Items as above]/[—]/London Printed, and Sold by B. Bragge, at the Raven/ in Pater-noster-Row. 1709./

Octavo; [cut], [i—ii], i—x, 11—104; [cut], [i—iv], 1—56; [A], B—O⁴; Aa—Gg⁴, Hh². Title-page boxed in double rule.

Adv.: *The Observator,* 22—26 January 1709. [BM; ICN; TxU]

1713—/The Whigs Unmask'd:/Being the/Secret History/Of The/Calf's-Head-Club./Shewing/The Rise and Progress of that Infamous/Society since the Grand Rebellion./Containing/All the Treasonable Songs and Ballads, sung as/Anthems by those Saints, at their/King-killing Anni-/versaries./Much enlarg'd and improv'd by a genuine Ac-/count of all the Plots and Conspiracies of the/Whiggish Faction against the Queen and/ Ministry, since the Persecution of the Church/under the Disguise of Mod-/eration./With Animadversions in Prose and Verse./[—]/Adorn'd with Cuts suitable to every particular Design./[—]/To which are added,/ Several Characters by Sir John Denham/and other valuable Authors./ Also/A Vindication of the Royal Martyr,/King Charles the First; wherein are expos'd,/the Hellish Mysteries of the old Republican Re-/bellion. By Mr. Butler, Author of Hudibras./[—]/The Eighth Edition, with large Additions./[—]/London Printed: and Sold by J. Morphew near Sta-/tioners'-Hall. MDCCXIII./

Octavo; [i—xvi], i—vi, 1—224; A⁸, a³, B—P⁸ (cuts; inserts). Title-page boxed in double rule.

Adv.: *The Evening Post,* 14-17 March 1713. [BM; CtY; DLC; ICN]

1721—[Title-page identical with 1713 edition to:]/Much enlarg'd and im-/prov'd by a genuine Ac-/count of all the Plots and Conspiracies of the/ Whiggish Faction against the late Queen/and Ministry, since the Perse-/cution of the/Church under the Disguise of Moderation./With Animad-/versions in Prose and Verse./[—]/Adorn'd with Cuts/suitable to every particular design./[—]/To which are added,/Several Characters by Sir John Denham/and other valuable Authors./Also/A Vindication of the Royal Martyr,/King Charles the First; wherein are expos'd,/the Hellish Mysteries of the old Republican Rebellion./By Mr. Butler, Author of Hudibras./[—]/The Ninth Edition with Additions./[—]/London: Printed for Samuel Briscoe, at the Bell-Savage/on Ludgate-Hill; and Sold by Tho. Bickerton, at the Crown in Pater-Noster-Row, 1721./

Octavo; [i—xvi], i—vi, 1—224; A⁸, a³, B—P⁸ (cuts inserted).

The *BMC* lists a ninth edition in octavo dated 1714. [NN]

Another edition is reprinted in *The Harleian Miscellany,* vol. VI (London, 1744).

The Secret History of Clubs
See under *The History of the London Clubs.*

Sot's Paradise

1698—/Sot's Paradise:/or,/The Humours of a/Derby-Ale-House:/with/a Satyr/Upon the/Ale./[—]/[Ornament]/London, Printed in the Year 1698./

Folio; 1—16; A—D². Title-page boxed in double rule.

Reprinted in *The Second Volume of Writings* (1703). [CSH]

1699—/Sot's Paradise:/Or,/The Humours of a/Derby-Ale-House:/With/A Satyr/Upon The/Ale./[—]/The Second Edition./[—]/[Ornament]/[—]/London, Printed in the year 1699./

Folio; 1—16; A—D². Title-page boxed in double rule. [CtY; DLC; MH]

1700—/Sot's Paradise:/Or,/The Humours of a/Derby-Ale-House:/With/A Satyr/Upon The/Ale./[—]/The Third Edition./[—]/[Ornament]/[—]/London, Printed and Sold by J. How, in the Ram-Head-/Inn-Yard, in Fanchurch-Street, 1700./

Folio; 1—16 (pp. 11 and 12 misnumbered 6 and 7); A—D². Title-page boxed in double rule.

Included in *A Collection of the Writings, Hitherto Extant* (1700). [BM; CSH; NNC]

A South-Sea Ballad

1720—A South-Sea Ballad, or, Merry Remarks Upon Exchange-Alley Bubbles. To a New Tune, call'd, The Grand Elixir, or, The Philosopher's Stone discover'd.

Appears in *Mercurious Politicus*, September 1720. Adv.: *The Weekly Pacquet*, 15–22 October 1720. For ascription to Ward, see *The Delights of the Bottle* (1720).

A Step to the Bath

1700—/A/Step/To The/Bath:/With A/Character/Of The/Place./[—]/[Ornament]/[—]/London,/Printed and Sold by J. How, in the Ram-Head-Inn-/Yard, in Fanchurch-street, 1700./

Folio; 1—16; A—D². Title-page boxed in double rule.

Listed in the *Term Catalogues*, November 1700. Included in *A Collection of the Writings, Hitherto Extant* (1701). [BM; MH; TxU]

1700—/A/Step/To The/Bath:/With A/Character/Of The/Place/[—]/The Second Edition/[—]/[Ornament]/[—]/London/Printed and Sold by J. How, in the Ram-Head-Inn-Yard,/in Fanchurch-street, 1700./

Folio; 1—16; A—D². Title-page boxed in double rule. [MHi]

A Step to Stir-Bitch-Fair

1700—/A/Step/To/Stir-Bitch-Fair:/With/Remarks/Upon The/University/of Cambridge./[—]/[Ornament]/[—]/London/Printed and Sold by J. How, in the Ram-Head-Inn-Yard,/in Fanchurch-street, 1700./

Folio; 1—16; A—D². Title-page boxed in double rule.

Listed in the *Term Catalogues*, November 1700. Included in *A Collection of the Writings, Hitherto Extant* (1701). Reprinted in *The Second Volume of the Writings* (1703). [BM; CSH; MH]

Three Nights Adventures

1701—/Three Nights/Adventures:/Or, Accidental/Intrigues./[—]/[Ornaments]/[—]/London,/Printed and Sold by J. How, in the Ram-Head-Inn-Yard in/Fanchurch-Street; and by M. Fabian, at Mercers-Chappel,/in Cheapside, 1701./

Folio; 1—14 (i.e., 16; p. 5 to end misnumbered); A—D². Title-page boxed in double rule.

Adv.: *The Post Angel*, March 1701. Listed as a Ward item on the verso of the title-page, *The Revels of the Gods* (1701). An edition was advertised in *The Observator*, 24 February 1703. [CSH; TxU]

The Tipling Philosophers

1708—[First edition.]

See *The Wars of the Elements* (1708). *The Tipling Philosophers* was apparently written first as a song of six verses on Diogenes, Heraclitus, Democritus, Copernicus, Aristotle and Plato set to music by Mr. Leveridge and sung at the theater in Lincoln's Inn Fields. CtY has an original broadside of the music and words.

1710—/The/Tipling Philosophers./A/Lyrick Poem./To which is subjoined,/ A short Abstract of their Lives and/most memorable Actions./[—]/ [Quotation]/[—]/London/Printed: And Sold by J. Woodward in/St. Christopher's Church-Yard, near the/Royal Exchange. 1710./Price Six-Pence./

Octavo; [i—vi], 1—40; A³, B—F⁴. Title-page boxed in double rule. [CtY; TxU]

1710—/Wine and Wisdom:/Or, The/Tipling Philosophers./A/Lyrick Poem./ To which are subjoined,/The Most remarkable Memoirs of the/following Ancients./[List in four columns, separated by rules]/[—]/London/ Printed: And Sold by J. Woodward in Scalding-/Ally over aginst Stocks-Market. 1710./Price Six-Pence./

Octavo; [i—viii], 1—40; A—F⁴. Title-page boxed in double rule.

This has the same impression as the above with a new title-page. [CtY; NNC; TxU]

1710—[Another copy.]

Octavo; [i—x], 1—40; [A], A—F⁴.

This copy has the title-pages of both *The Tipling Philosophers* (1710) and *Wine and Wisdom* (1710), and represents the latter text with the title-page of the former added. [MH]

1719—[Another edition.] [Identical with the one above save for date.] [CSH]

1751—/Wine and Wisdom:/Or, The/Tipling Philosophers./A/Lyrick Poem./ To which are subjoin'd,/The most remarkable Memoirs of the/following Antients./[List in four columns, separated by rule]/To which is added, a New/Litany,/Very proper to be Read by a merry Socie-/ty, over a Glass of good Liquor./[—]/Dublin:/Printed for William Williamson Bookseller at the Half-Moon in Rose-Lane, MDCCLI/

Octavo; 1—36 (blank leaf); A—D⁴, E². [MH]

To the Right Honourable Humphrey Parsons

1730—/To the Right Honourable/Humphrey Parsons/Lord Mayor of the City of London./A/Congratulary Poem/Upon/His Lordship's Accession/to the Chair./[—]/By Edward Ward./[—]/[Quotation: Latin]/[—]/London:/Printed by J. W. and Publish'd by John Wilford,/behind the Convocation-House, in St. Paul's Church-/yard, 1730./Price One Shilling./

Quarto; 1—32; A—D⁴.

Adv.: *The Monthly Chronicle*, October 1730. [TxU]

The Tory Quaker

1717—/The Tory Quaker./Or, Aminadab's/New Vision/in The/Fields,/ After/A Cup of the Creature./[—]/[Ornaments]/[—]/London/Printed and Sold by J. Morphew near/Stationers-Hall. MDCCXVII./Price Four Pence./

> Octavo; 1—24; A—C⁴. Title-page boxed in double rule.
>
> Included in *A Collection of Historical and State Poems* (1717). [CSH; ICN; MH]

A Trip to Germany

> 1705—A Trip to Germany, or the Poet turn'd Carbineer: being a Relation of several Comical Intrigues, and Diverting Adventures, with an Impartial Character of the Country. By the Author of the Step to the Bath. Printed for B. Bragge.
>
> Issued in May: *The History of the Works of the Learned*, May 1705. Adv.: *The Observator*, 19–23 May 1705. For ascription to Ward, see *A Step to the Bath* (1700). I have been unable to locate a copy.

A Trip to Jamaica

> 1698—/A/Trip/To/Jamaica:/With a True Character/Of The/People and Island./[—]/By the Author of Sot's Paradise./[—]/The First Edition./ [—]/[Ornament]/[—]/London, Printed in the Year, 1698./
>
> Folio; 1—16; A—D². Title-page boxed in double rule. [BM; CSH]

> 1698—[A second edition.]

> 1698—/A/Trip/To/Jamaica:/With a True/Character/Of The/People and Island./[—]/By the Author of Sot's Paradise./[—]/The Third Edition./ [—]/[Ornament]/[—]/London, Printed in the Year, 1698./
>
> Folio; [1—4], 5—16; A—D². Title-page boxed in double rule. [TxU]

> 1699—/A/Trip/To/Jamaica:/With a True/Character/Of The/People and Island./[—]/By the Author of Sot's Paradise./[—]/The Fourth Edition/[—]/[Ornament]/[—]/London, Printed in the Year 1699./
>
> Folio; [i—4], 1—16; A—D². Title-page boxed in double rule. [MB]

> [1699]—[The fifth edition.]
>
> I have been unable to locate a copy.

> [1699]—[The sixth edition.]
>
> I have been unable to locate a copy.

> 1700—/A/Trip/To/Jamaica:/With a True/Character/Of The/People and Island./[—]/By the Author of Sot's Paradise./[—]/The Seventh Edition./[—]/[Ornament]/[—]/London, Printed and Sold by J. How, in the Ram-Head-Inn-/Yard in Fanchurch-Street, 1700./
>
> Folio; 1—16; A—D². Title-page boxed in double rule.
>
> Included in *A Collection of the Writings, Hitherto Extant* (1700). Reprinted in *Five Travel Scripts*, Facsimile Text Society, series 1, vol. VII, 1933. [NNC]

> 1702—[The eighth edition.]
>
> Adv.: *The Observator*, 8–11 July, 1702. I have been unable to locate a copy.

A Trip to New-England

> 1699—/A/Trip/To/New-England/With A/Character/Of The/Country and People,/Both/English and Indians./[—]/[Ornaments]/[—]/London, Printed in the Year, 1699./
>
> Folio; 1—16; A—D². Title-page boxed in double rule.
>
> Issued in March: adv. on the verso of the title-page, *The London Spy*, vol. I, pt. v, March 1699. Included in *A Collection of the Writings, Hitherto Extant* (1700). Reprinted in *The Second Volume of the Writings* (1703). An edition was advertised in *The Observator*, 8–11 July 1702.

Reprinted in *Five Travel Scripts,* Facsimile Text Society, series 1, vol. VII, 1933. [CSH; CtY; DLC; ICN; NN; NNC]

1905—[Another edition.] Ed. G. P. Winship (Society for Colonial Reprints; Providence, Rhode Island, 1905).

The Tumultuous Cavalcade

See *The Republican Procession.*

The Vanity of Upstarts

[1717]—The Vanity of Upstarts. An Ode.

Apparently issued separately. Included in *A Collection of Historical and State Poems* (1717). I have been unable to locate a copy of the original edition.

Vulgus Britannicus

Part I

1710—/Vulgus Britannicus:/Or, The/British Hudibrass./[—]/Quotation: Latin]/[—]/[Ornament]/[—]/London:/Printed for James Woodward, in St. Christopher's/Church-Yard, near the Royal Exchange; and/John Morphew, near Stationer's Hall, 1710./Price One Shilling./

Octavo; [i—iv], 1—52; [A²], B—G⁴, H². Title-page boxed in double rule.

See part IV below for attribution to Ward. [TxU]

Part II

1710—/Vulgus Britannicus:/Or, The/British Hudibrass./[—]/Part the Second./[—]/[Ornament]/[—]/London:/Printed for James Woodward, in St. Christopher's/Church-Yard, near the Royal Exchange; and/John Morphew, near Stationer's-Hall, 1710./Price Six-Pence./

Octavo; [i—ii], 53—84; [A²], I—P⁴. Title-page boxed in double rule.

Parts I and II issued in April: *The History of the Works of the Learned,* April 1710. [TxU]

Part III

1710—[Title-page identical with the above save for "Part the Third."]

Octavo; [i—ii], 85—116; [A²], N—Q⁴. Title-page boxed in double rule. [TxU]

Part IV

1710—/The Fourth Part of/Vulgus Britannicus:/Or, The/British Hudibras./In Two Cantos:/[Description of contents]/[—]/Written by the Author of the/London Spy./[—]/London/Printed: and Sold by James Woodward, in/St. Christopher's Church-Yard, near the Royal Ex-/change; and John Morphew, near Stationer's/Hall. MDCCX./

Octavo; [i—ii], 117—148; [A²], R—U⁴ (U missigned T). Title-page boxed in double rule. [TxU]

Part V

1710—[Title-page identical with the above save for "The Fifth Part" and "In Three Cantos."]

Octavo; [i—ii], 149—190; [A²], X—Aa⁴. Title-page boxed in double rule. [NNC; TxU]

1710—/Vulgus Britannicus:/Or, The/British Hudibras./In Fifteen Cantos./[—]/The Five parts Compleat in one Volume./[—]/Containing the Secret History of the Late/London Mob; Their Rise, Progress,/and Suppression by the Guards./Intermix'd with the Civil-Wars betwixt/High-Church and Low-Church, down to this/time: Being a Continuation of the Late Inge-/nious Mr. Butler's Hudibras./[—]/Written by the Author of the/London Spy./[—]/The Second Edition, Adorn'd with Cuts of /Battles; Emblems, and Effigies,/Engraven on Copper-Plates./[—]/London:/Printed for Sam. Briscoe, and Sold by James/Woodward, in St. Christopher's Church-Yard,/near the Royal Exchange; and John Morphew,/near Stationer's Hall. MDCCX./

Octavo. Title-page boxed in double rule.

Pagination and signatures are the same as for the five parts above. New title-pages are either inserts for the cancelled title-pages for Parts I-III of the original issues, or exist as duplicates. Parts IV and V appear with the title-pages as above. This would suggest that the second edition of Parts I-III, four cuts inserted, were issued prior to, or simultaneously with, Parts IV and V. [BM; CtY; MH; TxU (Copies in the libraries listed are variously made up, sometimes with duplicate title-pages, again with cancelled title-pages and inserts. They defy general classification as first or second editions.)]

1711—/Vulgus Britannicus:/Or, The/British Hudibras./In Fifteen Canto's./ Containing the Secret History of the/London Mob; Their Rise, Progress,/ and Suppression./Intermix'd with the Civil-Wars betwixt/High Church and Low Church, at this time:/Being a Continuation of the Late Inge-/nious Mr. Butler's Hudibras./[—]/In Five Parts Compleat in one Volume./[—]/By the Author of the London Spy./[—]/The Third Edition, Adorn'd with Cuts,/and a Table to the Whole./[—]/London:/Printed for Sam. Briscoe, and Sold by James/Woodward, in Scaulding-Alley against Stocks-Market; and John Morphew, near Stationer's Hall. 1711./

Octavo; [i—viii], 5—180; A—H^4, K—Aa^4 (four cuts inserted). Title-page boxed in double rule. [CtY; NN; NNC]

A Walk to Islington

1699—/A/Walk/To/Islington:/With A/Description/Of/New Tunbridge-Wells,/And/Sadler's Musick-House./[—]/By the Author of the Poet's Ramble after Riches./[—]/[Ornament]/[—]/London, Printed in the year 1699./

Folio; 1—16; A—D^2. Title-page boxed in double rule.

Issued in June: advs. on the verso of the title-page include *The London Spy*, pts. I-VIII; *The London Spy*, pt. IX, June 1699, carries an adv. of the above. [BM; CSH; DLC; NNC; TxU]

1701—[The second edition. Identical with the above save for "London 1701."]

Folio; 1—16; A—D^2. Title-page boxed in double rule.

Adv.: *The Observator*, 20 May 1702, as sold by J. How. Included in *A Collection of the Writings, Hitherto Extant* (1701). [BM; CSH; MHi]

The Wand'ring Spy

See *The Merry Travellers.*

The Wars of the Elements

1708—/The/Wars of the Elements:/Or, a Description of a/Sea Storm./To which are added,/[List of items in double column, separated by rule]/ [—]/By the Author of the London-Spy./[—]/London/Printed, and Publish'd by John Morphew,/near Stationers-hall, 1708./

Octavo; [i—iv], 3—76; A^5, B—I^4, K^2 (A^2 exists in duplicate). Title-page boxed in double rule.

See *Marriage Dialogues* (1708). Note the first appearance of *The Tipling Philosophers,* here in its earlier form. The "Dedicatory Epistle" was added late as both signatures and pagination indicate. Added items are as follows: *The Contemplative Angler; A Dialogue between St. Peter and a Low-Churchman; The Honest Layman's Approbation and Dislike, etc.; The Mercenary Harlot's Reproof to an Old Miser, who Solicits her Favours; In Vino Veritas: or, The Tipling Philosophers; An Epitaph on the French Prophet, who was to make his Resurrection on the 25th of May; Another on the Same; The Frantick Lover: or, the Beau in an Extasie; A New Riddle for the Ladies; A Natural Song after a Natural Folly; Damon's Answer to Phillis; The Taunting Reprimand of a Young Wife to an Old Jealous Husband; A Punch-Bowl Song; The Lover's Detestation of Jealousie: With Advice to his Friend*. [MH]

1709—/The Wars of the Elements:/Or, A/Description of a Sea Storm./To which are added,/[List of thirteen items in double column, separated by rule]/[—]/By the Author of the London-Spy./[—]/

> Folio; 1—8; A—B². Dropped head.
>
> Bottom of p. 8: "London: Printed in the Year, 1709." [CtY]

1709—[Another edition.] London, 1709.

> Quarto.
>
> An edition for 1709, listed by P. J. Dobell, *A Catalogue of Eighteenth-Century Verse* (London, 1933), contains only *The Contemplative Angler* in addition to the title poem.

1730—/The/Wars of the Elements:/Or, A/Description/Of A/Sea Storm./To Which are added,/The Contemplative Angler,/ and/The Republican Procession, etc./[—]/All Originally Written, and now Reviv'd by/Edward Ward./[—]/London:/Printed, and are to be Sold by the Booksellers of/London and Westminster, 1730./

> Octavo; 1—32; 3—48; A—D⁴; A²⁻⁴, B—F⁴. [CtY; MH]

The Wealthy Shop-keeper

1700—/The/Wealthy Shop-keeper:/Or, The/Charitable Citizen./A/Poem./[—]/[Ornaments]/[—]/London:/Printed, And are to be Sold by the Booksellers. MCC./

> Folio; 1—16; A—D². Title-page boxed in double rule.
>
> Issued in November: *The History of the Works of the Learned*, November 1700. Reprinted in *The Third Volume of the Writings* (1706). [MH; TxU]

1702—/The/Character/Of A/Covetous Citizen,/Or, A/Ready Way to get Riches./A/Poem./[—]/London,/Printed, and are to be Sold by the Booksellers of/London and Westminster, 1702./

> Folio; 1—16; A—D². Title-page boxed in double rule.
>
> Issued in November: *The History of the Works of the Learned*, November 1701. The first forty-seven lines of the text are replaced by a new version. [MH]

The Weekly Comedy

1699—/The/Weekly Comedy,/As it is Dayly Acted at most Coffee-Houses in London;/By/[List of characters in three columns]/Note, That all These Persons will not Speak in every single Paper, but as the Author finds occasion to Introduce 'em./[—]/Wednesday May, 10, 1600./[—]/

> Broadside. Dropped head.
>
> Bottom of p. 2: "London, Printed for J. How, in the Ram-Head-Inn-Yard in Fanchurch-street." This was a weekly periodical issued each Wednesday from 10 May to 12 July, a total of ten numbers. [NNC]

[1700]—/The/Humours/Of/A Coffee-House:/A/Comedy./[—]/[Ornament]/[—]/London./Printed and Sold by J. How, . . .

Title-page defaced; this is a new title-page for the ten numbers, issued as a group. Adv.: *The Observator*, 20 May 1702. See also *The Humours of a Coffee House* (1707). [NNC]

The ten numbers were reorganized as a three-act play with all traces of periodical printing removed and were reprinted in *The Second Volume of the Writings* (1703) as "The Humours of a Coffee-House, a Comedy. As it is daily Acted at most Coffee-Houses in London."

The Whigs Unmask'd

See under *The Secret History of the Calves-Head Club* (1713).

Wine and Wisdom

See *The Tipling Philosophers*.

The Wooden World Dissected

1706—The Wooden World Dissected. By a Lover of the Mathematics. B. Bragge. Price 1 Shilling.

Adv. as "in the Press": *The Observator*, 25–26 December 1706, and as "now publish'd" in *The Observator*, 29 January—1 February 1707. An edition "Printed by H. Meere for the Author" is advertised in *The Observator*, 15–18 January 1707. For attribution to Ward, see the 1708 edition below. See also the edition for 1744. Geoffrey Callender, *The Wooden World* (The Society for Nautical Research, Occasional Publications, no. XI; London, 1929) gives the first edition as a duodecimo and states that it is now practically unknown.

1708—/The/Wooden World/Dissected/In The/Characters/Of/[List of characters in double column, separated by rule]/[—]/By a Lover of the Mathematicks./[—]/The Second Edition, Corrected and/Amended by the Author./[—]/London, Printed by H. Meere in Black-/Fryars; and Sold by J. Woodward in Thread-/needle-Street near the Royal Exchange, and/B. Bragge at the Raven in Pater-Noster-/Row. 1708./

Duodecimo; [i—xii], 1—108; A—E^{12}. Title-page boxed in double rule.

Adv.: *The Observator*, 21–25 February 1709. A second edition by B. Bragge had, however, been advertised in *The Observator* as early as 20 July—2 August 1707. Advertised as "by the same Author" in this edition are *Mars Stript of his Armour* (1708) and *The Modern World Disrob'd* (1708), the latter clearly one of Ward's items. This edition carries the following adv.: "N. B. The Bill lately brought into the House of Commons, for securing Property in Printed Books, not having pass'd, has encourag'd the Pyrates to proceed in their wicked Practices, of making a Profit at the Expense of other Men; the Reader is desir'd to take Notice, That if this Book, call'd, the Wooden World dissected, etc. should appear without an Advertisement in this Character, it is done Clandestinely, and in Prejudice of the Proprietors." [CtY; DLC; MH (MH contains a second copy, title-page missing, with a reconstructed title-page dated 1706. This is almost certainly an error, since the above advertisement appears.)]

1709—[Another edition.]

Adv.: *The Observator*, 9–12 April 1709.

1711—[Another edition.] London, 1711. Printed for T. Norris at the Looking Glass on London Bridge.

Listed in the *Term Catalogues*, May 1711.

1744—/The/Wooden World/Dissected,/In The/Character/Of A/Ship of War; /As Also/The Characters of all the Officers, from/the Captain to the Common Sailor; viz./[List in double column, separated by rule]/[—]/ By the Author of the London-Spy./[—]/The Third Edition./[—]/London:/Printed for M. Cooper at the Globe, in Pater-noster-row;/and Sold at the Pamphlet-Shops of London and Westminster,/<Price One Shilling>MDCCXLIV./

Octavo; [i—viii], 1—78 (blank leaf); A—K⁴, L³. [CtY; NN]

1749—[The fourth edition.] Robinson and Fuller: London, 1749.

Octavo. [BM; ICN]

1756—/The/Wooden World/Dissected:/in The/Character/of A/Ship of War: /As also, The/Characters of all The Officers,/From the/Captain to the Common Sailor;/Viz./[List in double column separated by rule]/[—]/ By the Author of the London Spy./[—]/The Fifth Edition./[—]/ London./Printed for J. Wren, in Salisbury-Court, Fleet-street;/and sold at all the Booksellers and Pamphlet-/shops, in London and Westminster. 1756./(Price One Shilling.)/

Octavo; [i—viii], 1—76; A—K⁴, L².

Geoffrey Callender in *The Wooden World* (The Society for Nautical Research, Occasional Publications, no. XI; London, 1929) cites a fifth edition in 1751. [MBB; MH]

—[The sixth edition.]

1760—/The/Wooden World/Dissected:/In The/Character/Of A/Ship of War:/As Also, The/Characters of all the Officers,/From the/Captain to the Common Sailor./Viz./[List separated by rule]/To which is added,/ The better to illustrate the character of a Sailor, two very/interesting and entertaining Stories never yet printed in/any of the former Editions; and containing more in/Quantity than any ever yet publish'd./By the Author of the London-Spy./The Seventh Edition./London:/Printed for and Sold By the Booksellers of London and/Westminster. 1760./(Price One Shilling.)/

Octavo; i—viii, 1—72; A—K⁴. [NN]

1801—/The/Wooden World dissected:/In The/Character/Of/A Ship of War. /As Also, The/Characters of All The Officers/From the Captain to the common Sailor./Viz./[List separated by rule]/[Title-page defaced]/ London:/Printed by J. Skirven, Ratcliff-Highway;/For Alexander Clough, 14, Ratcliff-highway./1801./

Octavo; 1—80; A—K⁴. [NN]

The World Bewitch'd

1699—/The/World Bewitch'd./[—]/A/Dialogue/Between Two/Astrologers /And the/Author./With/Infallible Predictions of what will/happen in this Present Year, 1699. From/the Vices and Villanies Practic'd in Court, City, and Country./[—]/London, Printed in the year 1699./

Quarto; 1—32 (p. 32 misnumbered 30); A—D⁴. Title-page boxed in double rule.

Issued in February: *The Flying Post*, 11–14 February 1699. The second part, i.e., *The Infallible Predictions*, was reprinted in *The Second Volume of the Writings* (1703) with the first three paragraphs of "To the Reader" under the title of "The Infallible Predictor." [BM; MH]

The Writings

Volume I

See *The London Spy* (1703). See also *The London Spy* (1704).

Volume II

1703—/The Second Volume/Of The/Writings/Of the Author of the/London-Spy./[Contents in double column, separated by rule]/[—]/London, Printed and Sold by J. How, at the Seven-Stars in/Talbot-Court, in Grace-Church-Street, 1703./

Octavo; [i—iv], 1—372; A⁴, B—Aa⁸. Title-page boxed in double rule. The first edition: *The Observator*, 9–13 October 1703. [BM; TxU]

1704—[Identical with the above, save for:]/[—]/The Second Edition/[—]/London, Printed and Sold by J. How, at the Seven-Stars in/Talbot-Court, in Grace-Church-Street, 1704./

Octavo;[i—viii],1—402 (i.e. 400; pp. 233 to end misnumbered; 8 pp. advertising); A—Cc⁸ (A⁸ missigned B⁴). Title-page boxed in double rule.

Adv.: *The Observator*, 16–20 June 1705. [BM; DLC]

1706—[Identical with the above, save for "The Third Edition" and "1706."]

Octavo; [i—viii], 1—402 (i.e., 400; pp. 233 to end misnumbered; 6 pp. advertising); A—Bb⁸, Cc⁷. Title-page boxed in double rule. [ICN; MBA]

1709—[Identical with the above, save for "The Fourth Edition" and "1709."]

Octavo; [i—viii], 1—402 (i.e., 400; pp. 233 to end misnumbered); A—Bb⁸, Cc⁴. Title-page boxed in double rule. [BM; DLC; ICN]

1717—/A/Collection/Of The/Writings/of/Mr. Edward Ward./Viz./[Contents in double column, separated by rule]/[—]/Vol. II./[—]/The Fifth Edition/[—]/London, Printed for A. Bettesworth, at the Red-/Lion in Pater-Noster-Row, 1717./

Octavo; [i—viii], 1—402 (i.e., 400; pp. 233 to end misnumbered); A—Bb⁸, Cc⁴ (A⁴ missigned D⁴). Title-page boxed in double rule.

This represents the first edition of Volume II of the miscellaneous writings. See *Miscellanies*. [MH]

The contents of *The Second Volume* are as follows: *Bookseller to the Reader; Postscript to the Second Edition* (not included in the 1703 edition); *The Poet's Ramble after Riches; Sot's Paradise; Ecclesia et Factio; Modern Religion and Ancient Loyalty; A Walk to Islington; The Insinuating Bawd; The Revels of the Gods; Battle without Bloodshed; O Raree-Show, O Pretty Show; The Cock-Pit Combat; A Hue and A Cry after a Man-Midwife; The Dutch Guards Farewel; A Trip to Jamaica; A Trip to New-England; A Frolick to Horn-Fair; The Dancing-School; A Step to Stir-Bitch Fair; The Humours of a Coffee-House; The Infallible Predictor; The Rise and Fall of Madam Coming-Sir; An Elegy on White Hall* (not included in the 1704 and 1717 editions).

Volume III

1706—/The/Third Volume,/Consisting Of/Poems/On/Divers Subjects:/[Contents in double column, separated by rule]/[—]/By the Author of the/London-Spy./[—]/[Quotation: Latin]/[—]/London:/Printed, and Sold by B. Bragg at the Raven in/Pater-noster-Row. 1706./

Octavo; [i—xvi], 1—384; A—Bb⁸. Title-page boxed in double rule. The first edition: *The Daily Courant*, 19 April 1706. [BM; ICN; MH; TxU]

The contents of *The Third Volume* are as follows: *Epistle Dedicatory; Preface; Author to the Reader; A Journey to Hell; The Wealthy Shop-Keeper; All Men Mad; Helter Skelter; Honesty in Distress; A Satyr against Wine;*

A Poem in Praise of Small-Beer; On the Success of the Duke of Marlborough; Fortune's Bounty; A Protestant Scourge; A Musical Entertainment; Bribery and Simony; A Dialogue between Britannia and Prudence; Pinkeman—Prologue and Epilogue; A Song; A Song; The Libertine's Choice; The Religious Turncoat; Upon the Alteration of Coin; The Mad-Song.

Volume IV

1709—/The/Fourth Volume/Of The/Writings/Of the Author of the/London-Spy./[—]/Prose and Verse/[—]/London:/Printed for George Sawbridge at the/Three Flower de Luces in Little Bri-/tain, 1709./

Octavo; [i—xiv]; 3—32; 3—40; 3—40; 3—40; 3—40; 3—32; 1—32; 41—78; 91—128; 131—168; 171—208; 211—248; [A⁷], A—D⁴; A—E⁴; A—E⁴; A—E⁴; A—E⁴; A—D⁴; A—B⁸; F²⁻⁴, G—K⁴; L²⁻⁴, M—P⁴; Q²⁻⁴, R—U⁴; X²⁻⁴, Y—Bb⁴; Cc²⁻⁴, Dd—Gg⁴. Title-page boxed in double rule.

Issued in September: *The Post-Man*, 9 September 1709, carried an advertisement "On Thursday will be publish'd, etc." It had, however, been contemplated as early as July 1708. See *The Observator*, 21–24 July. This volume is made up of remainders with cancelled title-pages, the new title-page, and preface, i—xiv being added. The volume includes the six numbers of *The London Terraefilius* (1707–08) and the six numbers of *The Diverting Muse* (1707). [BM; DLC]

1709—[Another copy. Title-page missing but reconstructed as:] "Writings of the Author of the London-Spy. Prose and Verse. Vol. I. Printed for George Sawbridge at the Three Flower de Luces in Little Britain, 1709."

Octavo; [i—xiv]; 3—32; 3—40; 3—40; 3—40; 3—40; 3—32; 3—40; 41—78; 91—128; 131—168; 171—208; 211—248; A⁷, A—D⁴; A—E⁴; A—E⁴; A—E⁴; A—E⁴; A—D⁴; A—E⁴; F²⁻⁴, G—K⁴; L²⁻⁴, M—P⁴; Q²⁻⁴, R—U⁴; X²⁻⁴, Y—Bb⁴; Cc²⁻⁴, Dd—Gg⁴.

The reconstructed title-page is an error. This is really *The Fourth Volume of the Writings*. [CtY]

Volume V

See *The History of the London Clubs* (1710).

Appendix B

Doubtful Attributions

Among the doubtful attributions it has seemed desirable to include all items not appearing in the preceding list which have been assigned to Ward in printed bibliographies or in articles. This includes all items assigned to Ward by Theophilus Cibber, *The Lives of the Poets*, IV, 293–294; W. T. Lowndes, *Bibliographers' Manual*, V, 2835–37; Baker, Reed, and James, *Biographia Dramatica*, I, 736; George Aitken in his article on Ward in *DNB;* the printed catalogue of the Wrenn Library at the University of Texas. In so far as possible it also includes any questionable items assigned to Ward in articles in the learned journals. It does not include, however, items listed under Ward in unprinted library catalogues.

The basis for including the item among the doubtful attributions is presented in each case in a note, followed by a brief discussion of its validity or by a reference to the text where the question has already been taken into consideration.

The Ambitious Father

[1730]—/The/Ambitious Father:/Or, The/Politician's Advice/To His/Son. /[Band of printers' ornaments]/[Ornament]/[Band of printers' ornaments]/London:/Printed by E. Shaw for the Author./

Octavo; [i—ii], 1—70; A—I⁴.

Theophilus Cibber lists this as the last work Ward left finished. This seems to me an extremely doubtful attribution on the basis of internal evidence. The verse is too regular for Ward, the satire and irony too sustained, and the style is totally unlike that in any of his known works. [VaU]

Bacchanalia

1698—Bacchanalia; or a Description of a Drunken Club. London, 1698. Folio.

Assigned to Ward by W. T. Lowndes. The poem is not included in any of the collected writings and appears in no advertisement of Ward's works. MH contains a poem with the same title by Charles Darby, dated 1680. I have not been able to locate a copy.

The Ball

1723—/The/Ball;/Or,/Un Passo Tempo:/A/Poem./Displaying/The Vices, Follies, Extravagancies, A-/mours, and Intrigues of our Modern/Gentry to Pass away their Time./Particularly the Ridotto-Ladies, at the Opera-Theatre./[—]/[Quotation]/[—]/London,/Printed for A. Dodd, at the Peacock without Temple-Bar./MDCCXXIII./(Price Four-Pence.)/

Folio; 1—8; A—B².

Assigned to Ward by *WLC*. The subject matter, language, and style are characteristic of Ward. I have, however, been unable to find any evidence directly pointing to Ward's authorship.

Basia Joannis Secundi Nicolai

1731—/Basia/Joannis Secundi Nicolai/Hagensis:/Or The Kisses/of Joannes Secundus Nicolaius/Of The/Hague./In Latin and English Verse./[—]/ With the Life of Secundus,/and a Critic upon his Basia./[—]/Adorn'd with a Cut of the Author,/and another of his Mistress Julia,/engrav'd by the famous Bernard Picart/the Roman./[—]/London,/Printed for Henry Lintot, at the Cross-Keys./between the Temple Gates, Fleetstreet./ MDCCXXXI./

Duodecimo; [i—ii], i—xxxvi, 1—98; [A], a—c⁶, B—I⁶, K.

Assigned to Ward by Aitken. It is not Edward Ward, however, who is the joint author with Fenton, but one Jones Ward, who was later appointed to an Irish Deanery, according to the account on pages 73–98, under the title, "To Sir Richard Meade, Bart. A Dissertation. In which is contain'd, A Critic upon the Basia of Secundus." Other works of Jones Ward mentioned in the account are *Phoenix-Park, The Foot-Race at Fingles,* and *The Grotto.* [BM; NN]

The Character of a Sneaker

1705—/The/Character/Of   A/Sneaker./[—]/[Ornament]/[—]/London, Printed in the Year MDCCV./Price One Penny./

Quarto; [i—ii], 1—6; [A⁴].

Assigned to Ward, *WLC.* The assignment remains a doubtful one, however, in this case, as it does in a number of other minor political pieces dating 1702–05 mentioned below, since Ward did not include them in any of his collected writings, and that at a moment when obviously more offensive pieces were included. [TxU]

The City Madam and The Country Maid

1702—/The City Madam,/And The/Country Maid:/Or, Opposite Characters /Of a Virtuous Housewifely/Damsel,/And a Mechanick's/Town-Bred Daughter./[—]/By the Author of the Pleasures of a/Single Life. etc./ [—]/London:/Printed for John Nutt near Stationers-Hall. 1702./

Quarto; [i—iv], 1—12; A—D⁴. Title-page boxed in double rule.

Assigned to Ward by W. T. Lowndes. *The Pleasures of a Single Life, or the Miseries of Matrimony* was a poem published by J. Nutt in 1701. I can find no basis for assigning either of these items to Ward. The fact that they were never included in any of the collected writings warrants their rejection. [MH; TxU]

A Dialogue Between Claret and Darby-Ale

1692—/A/Dialogue/Between/Claret and Darby-Ale,/A/Poem./Considered in an accidental Conversa-/tion between two Gentlemen./[—]/London:/ Printed for E. Richardson, 1692./

Quarto; [i—ii], 1—10; A—C². Title-page boxed in double rule.

Assigned to Ward by Aitken. The poem is not Ward's, however, but may with certainty be assigned to Richard Ames. See note 20, Chapter I. [BM; MH; TxU]

Fair Shell, but a Rotten Kernel

1705—Fair Shell, but a Rotten Kernel; Or, a Bitter Nut for a Facetious Monkey. London, 1705.

Adv.: *The Daily Courant,* 25 October 1705. Assigned to Ward by Aitken. I have been unable to locate a copy.

The Fidler's Fling at Roguery

1730—The Fidler's Fling at Roguery. A Poem, in several Cantos. London, J. Jackson, J. Hooke, C. Rivington. Price 1s.

Adv.: *The Monthly Chronicle*, May 1730. Assigned to Ward by W. T. Lowndes, who gives the date as 1734. I have been unable to locate a copy.

Four Hudibrastick Cantos

1715—/Four/Hudibrastick/Canto's,/Being/Poems on Four the greatest He-roes/That liv'd in any Age since Nero's,/Don Juan Howlet, Hudibras, /Dicko-ba-nes and Bonniface./[—]/London,/Printed for J. Roberts in Warwick-lane./1715. Price 6d./

Octavo; 1—36; A—D⁴, E².

Assigned to Ward by *WLC*. I have been unable to find any basis for its ascription to Ward. It is unlike any of his known writings both in style and spirit. [TxU]

The Long Vacation

1708—/The/Long Vacation/[—]/A Satyr:/Addres'd to all/Disconsolate Traders./[—]/London:/Printed and Sold by H. Hills, in Black-Fryars,/ near the Water-side. 1708. Price 1d./

Octavo; 1—16; A⁸.

A pirated edition. The first edition was apparently published by J. Morphew. See *The Postman*, 22 June 1708. See also *The Observator*, 12–16 June 1708. Assigned to Ward by *WLC*. The ascription remains doubtful since the poem is not included in any of the collected writings. [TxUG]

1709—/The/Long Vacation:/A/Satyr/Address'd to all/Disconsolate Traders./ [—]/[Ornaments]/[—]/London:/Printed and Sold by H. Hills, in Black-fryars,/near the Water-side. 1709./

Octavo; 1—16; A⁸.

This was likewise a pirated edition. [TxUG]

The Miracles Performed by Money

1692—/The/Miracles/Perform'd by/Money;/A Poem./[—]/By the Author of the Humours of a Coffee-House./[—]/[Quotation]/[—]/London:/ Printed, and are to be sold by the Book-/sellers of London and West-minster: 1692./

Quarto; [i—iv], 1—20; A—F². Title-page boxed in double rule.

Assigned to Ward by W. T. Lowndes. The attribution, however, re-mains doubtful. See note 20, Chapter I. "The Humours of a Coffee-House" is a reference to a poem entitled *The School of Politics, or the Humours of a Coffee-House* listed in the *Term Catalogues* for June 1690.

The Prisoners' Opera

1730—/The/Prisoners Opera./To which is added,/Several other Entertain-ments,/Interchangably perform'd at/Sadler's Wells,/During the Summer Season./Where also the best of Wines, excellent/Ale, brew'd of the Well-Water, and/all other Liquors may be had in per-/fection./[—]/[Orna-ment]/[—]/London Printed:/And Published at the Wells. 1730./

Quarto; [i—ii], 1—20; [A³], B—C⁴.

Assigned to Ward by Aitken. There is no external evidence to support the assignment; neither is the work itself particularly characteristic of Ward either in manner or in design. [CSH]

Protestant Divisions

1702—/Protestant Divisions;/Or,/Party against Party./With/A View of the Old Buildings/At/Westminster./[—]/[Printers' Ornaments]/[—]/Lon-don,/Printed in the Year, 1702./

Folio; [i—ii], 1—26; A—G². Title-page boxed in double rule.

Assigned to Ward by *WLC*. See note to *The Character of A Sneaker* above. [TxU]

A Step to the Lobby
1704—/A/Step/To The/Lobby./[—]/[Quotation]/[—]/[Ornaments]/[—]/ London: Printed in the Year MDCCIV./

Quarto; 1—32; A—B⁴, C—D², E³. Title-page boxed in double rule.

Adv.: *The Review*, 4 April 1704. Assigned to Ward by *WLC*. See note to *The Character of a Sneaker* above. [TxU]

A Trip to Holland
1699—/A/Trip to Holland,/Being A/Description/Of The/Country, People and Manners:/As also some Select/Observations/On/Amsterdam./[—]/ [Quotation]/[—]/Printed in the Year, 1699./

Folio; [i—iv], 1—12; A—D². Title-page boxed in double rule.

See "Bibliographical Note," *Five Travel Scripts* (Facsimile Text Society, series 1, vol. VII; New York, 1932). See also Chapter II. [NNC; TxU]

A Trip to Ireland
1699—/A/Trip to Ireland,/Being A/Description/Of The/Country, People and Manners:/As also some Select/Observations/On/Dublin./[—]/[Ornaments]/[—]/Printed in the Year, 1699./

Folio; [i—iv], 1—12; A—D². Title-page boxed in double rule.

Assigned to Ward by W. T. Lowndes. See Chapter II, also note 12, Chapter II. [CSH; NNC]

A Trip to North-Wales
1701—/A/Trip/to/North-Wales:/Being/a Description of that/Country/and/ People./[—]/[Quotations: Latin]/[—]/London:/Printed in the year, 1701./

Folio; [i—iv], 1—12; A—D².

Issued in March: *The History of the Works of the Learned*, March 1701. See "Bibliographical Note," *Five Travel Scripts*. See also Chapter II. [MH]

A Trip to Nottingham
1705—/A/Trip/To/Nottingham./With A/Character/Of/Mareschel Tallard/And The/French-Generals./[—]/London:/Printed, in the Year MDCCV./

Folio; 1—14 (i.e., 16; pp. 5 to end misnumbered); A—D². Title-page boxed in double rule.

There is no external basis for its ascription to Ward. Its similarity in subject and treatment to *A Step to Stir-Bitch-Fair* and *A Step to the Bath*, though no proof of Ward's authorship, warrants including it among the doubtful items. [TxU]

A Vade-Mecum for Malt Worms
1720—A Vade-Mecum for Malt Worms; or a Guide to Good Fellows. London, 1720. In two parts.

Adv.: *The Weekly Pacquet*, 11–18 June 1720. Part II adv.: 17–24 September. Assigned to Ward by Aitken, who gives the date as 1715. The ascription probably grew out of the confusion of this item with *The Quack Vintners* (1712). But there is little resemblance and no reason for assigning it to Ward. The second part was "done by several hands." Neither of the two taverns with which Ward was connected receive mention in the poem. A reprint of the original, dated 1866, exists at DLC; MH; and CSH. [BM]

The Wandering Spy

> 1705—/The/Wandering Spy:/Or, The Way of the World inquired into;/ With Reflections on the Humours of/the Town./[—]/Deliver'd by Way of Fable./[—]/[Description of contents]/[—]/From Saturday, June 30th to Saturday, July the 7th./[—]/
>
> Quarto; 17—114 (i.e., 88; pp. 81 to end misnumbered); E—Cc². Dropped head.
>
> The title-page represents Number V, Volume I of the periodical. In the Trent Collection, MB, the first four numbers are missing. The periodical ran from June to September 1705, a total of twenty-seven numbers. Pagination and signatures are continuous, as indicated. No Number XXI appears in the above collection, though pagination and signatures are uninterrupted. The publisher for Numbers I–XV was Mrs. Maltus; for Numbers XIX–XXVII, B. Bragge. Assigned to Ward by T. F. M. Newton, William Pittis and Queen Anne Journalism, *MP*, XXXIII (1936), 169–186; 279–302. See note 11, Chapter XI. [MB]

A Whip for the Whiggs

> 1705—A Whip for the Whiggs.
>
> Quarto; 1—4; A⁴. Dropped head.
>
> Bottom of page 4: "Buckinghamshire. Printed at the Catherine-Wheel, for the Right Worshipful the Mayor of Chipping Wiccomb, 1705."
>
> Assigned to Ward by *WLC*. Never reprinted in any of Ward's collected writings; moreover the text contains autobiographical references inapplicable to Ward.

Index